DISARM AND VERIFY

DISARM
AND VERIFY

*An Explanation of
the Central Difficulties and
of National Policies*

By
SIR MICHAEL WRIGHT

FREDERICK A. PRAEGER

Publisher

NEW YORK

BOOKS THAT MATTER

Published in the United States of America in 1964
by Frederick A. Praeger, Inc., Publisher
64 University Place, New York 3, N.Y.

Printed in Great Britain

This book is dedicated to the memory of the late T. G. Narayanan of India, for three years the representative of the Secretary General of the United Nations at the Nuclear Test Ban Conference at Geneva. His life was a proof that a man can be a devoted son of his own country, and at the same time a loyal and impartial international servant.

Contents

Introduction   ix

PART ONE

1 The Course of Post-War Disarmament Negotiations   17
2 The Basic Need   26

PART TWO

3 Verification: Tasks and Staff   45
4 Verification Organizations   56
5 Keeping the Balance   67
6 Adequate and Bearable?   75
7 Peace-keeping Machinery and an International Force   86
8 Partial and Collateral Measures   93

PART THREE

9 The Soviet Approach   107
10 The American Approach   118
11 The British Approach   130
12 The Role of the Scientist   142
13 Choice of Risks   150
Bibliography   163

APPENDICES

I Conclusions from the Report of the Conference of Experts, Geneva, 1st July to 21st August 1958   165

II Joint Statement by the United States and the U.S.S.R. of Agreed Principles for Disarmament Negotiations, 20th September 1961   171

III Letters between Mr. John J. McCloy and Mr. V. Zorin, 20th September 1961   174

IV Revised Soviet Draft Treaty on General and Complete Disarmament under strict international Control, 24th September 1962   176

V United States' Outline of Basic Provisions of a Treaty on General and Complete Disarmament in a peaceful World, 18th April 1962   203

VI United Kingdom Paper on the technical possibility of international control of fissile material production, 31st August 1962   234

VII Treaty banning Nuclear Tests in the Atmosphere, Outer Space and Under Water, 25th July 1963   253

Introduction

MANKIND is living under the threat of increasingly horrible arms of mass killing and increasingly effective means of delivering them to their target. The genie of nuclear destruction has been let out of the bottle; scientists and governments push on with the hunt for the ultimate weapon, not to master the microbe or tame the lightnings, but to give man the power of exterminating himself. Like Captain Ahab, we pursue what will destroy us. To be able to wipe out human life in whole countries with a few bombs in a few hours is not thought enough. Governments tell their scientists to seek something still more devastating to which there can be no defence or reply, and in back rooms and laboratories the search is continuing now. Stifling their own feelings and in spite of the revulsion of ordinary men and women the experts talk coldly of overkill and megadeaths. To make these weapons powerful states risk bankruptcy; yet to use them may end human life.

If then by general consent the need for a reversal of the arms race is urgent, why has no comprehensive international arms agreement yet been reached? Are there in fact no forms of accord which are realistically possible? If the genie cannot be put back into the bottle, can it not at least be brought under fully international and effective control?

In the search for such agreement there have been sustained negotiations since 1958 between Communist and Western countries both for a nuclear tests ban and for a partial or total disarmament treaty. For over five years the problems have been explored in depth at the 3-Nation Nuclear Test Conference, at the 10-Nation Disarmament Conference, at the 18-Nation Disarmament Conference, and in the United Nations. By the summer of 1963 the only constructive result of any substance was the agreement in July by the United States, the Soviet Union and the United Kingdom on a partial test ban Treaty. This covers nuclear weapon tests in the atmosphere, in space and under water, relies for verification on national detection systems, and leaves the problem of underground tests for future negotiation. The scope of the ban is less than had been hoped, since underground tests are left out and the question of international verification does not arise. It is a step in the right direction, to be welcomed as such and as a modest initial success opening a door to further progress. It is on concluding more far-reaching agreements of greater depth and scope that effort must now be concentrated. This book is an attempt by a participant in the negotiations to make a critical assessment of the obstacles which have emerged during five years of negotiation and which remain to be resolutely tackled and overcome.

Disarmament problems have grown more difficult and complex since World War II than they were before 1939 or 1914. The new weapons of mass destruction are small and portable, are easy to conceal, yet can be delivered from great distances and achieve decisive results quickly. And a vast closed state has emerged as one of the two strongest military powers. Solutions which might have safeguarded peace had they been adopted fifty or thirty years ago cannot be tailored to meet the needs of the nuclear and space age.

— Three points stand out today above all others. First, major states will not disarm and remain disarmed without adequate verification that other states are doing the same. Any government therefore which is sincere in seeking an honest and lasting agreement on disarmament will accept as well as require adequate international verification that obligations are being loyally observed. Since this cannot be one-sided, willingness to accept adequate international verification is the real test of the sincerity of any government about disarmament.

— The second point is that if there is to be general and complete disarmament, as both the Western and the Communist sides are urging, adequate arrangements must be made for strengthening international peace-keeping machinery, and these must include some form of international peace-keeping force. Such a force must be so organized that its existence can serve to deter a possible violation of a disarmament agreement; and for this end it must possess both an effective command structure and sufficiently powerful weapons to deal with a state which concealed nuclear arms and threatened totally disarmed neighbours. This is the more necessary since even with the most rigorous verification there will always remain a marginal possibility of concealment of nuclear weapons. Without an effective international peace-keeping force, general and complete disarmament even with the maximum of verification will not create a secure world.

Third, there is the need to ensure that during years when disarmament is proceeding all the agreed measures are balanced so that at no stage of the implementation of a treaty could any state or group of states gain military advantage.

The possibility must of course be faced, and it is a matter constantly in the minds of unaligned states, eight of which have participated in the 18-Power Conference at Geneva, that either or both of the two allied and heavily armed sides, and in particular the United States and the Soviet Union, are not sincere in professing to want a full test ban or a disarmament agreement. In that case all negotiations become either on one or both sides nothing but an exercise in propaganda and in trying to pin upon the other side the blame for failure.

But if the approach is in good faith, then that good faith must be shown in willingness to reach a fair and reasonable compromise on the three key issues, namely adequate and bearable verification, improved peace-keeping machinery, and a balance of military security during the years of the disarmament process. In seeking such a compromise it must be recognized that free and open societies such as Western democracies are more ready to accept verification than the closed societies of Communist countries. To bridge this gap is the main task which negotiators and political leaders have to face. In so doing they are frequently confronted with conflicting advice from scientists and strategists, both professional and amateur, and hampered by political allies as well as political opponents.

The role of the scientist is one of special importance but also of special difficulty. It is the scientist who during the last twenty years has shown how mankind can create weapons of mass destruction; it is the scientist alone who can indicate how far bans on the testing or making of these weapons can be rendered effective and with what ease they could be evaded. These problems cannot be solved without the help and advice of scientists familiar with the technical problems which, in the nuclear and space age, lie at the heart of all disarmament issues. If this help and advice is to be objective, it must be based strictly upon the scientific data available. Moreover, in an era of intensive research new data constantly emerge, so that the sum of scientific knowledge changes and the scientific advice, if it is to remain objective, must change with it. If the scientist allows any subjective considerations whether emotional or political to colour his advice, he ceases to that extent to be speaking as a scientist.

It would be easier for political leaders to feel sure they were taking the right decisions on national defence policy if the scientific advice were either consistent or unanimous. But since it must necessarily be based on constantly changing data, it is likely to be changeable if it is to be honest. Nor at any given moment is it always unanimous; and when eminent scientists disagree they cannot all be right. The fact is that scientific, like military or political advice, is fallible.

Both scientists and military experts can always make out a strong case for the need for more knowledge and more arms. It can always be argued persuasively that without this new piece of knowledge and without those new arms national security is insufficiently safeguarded. These arguments can and are used with equal cogency by leaders of the free world and of Communist states alike. They remain a major stumbling block in bringing about an atmosphere in which general and complete disarmament can be achieved.

Yet however disturbing the prospect of a continuing arms race may be, the risk is great that agreement on total or even far-reaching disarmament may prove too difficult to secure until the international atmosphere is improved by the settlement of major political issues, such as Berlin, and perhaps not even then. But there is no security reason, very much the contrary, why partial measures of disarmament requiring a minimum of international verification should not be agreed upon without delay as steps towards total disarmament. There is equally no reason why partial measures of disarmament involving some limitation or actual destruction of weapons should not be accompanied by collateral measures, such as agreements to prevent the spread of nuclear weapons or to take precautions to prevent surprise attack. Not only would such steps have value in themselves, but the confidence they would create would be an important contribution to lowering international tension as a whole, and could pave the way to more comprehensive agreements.

There is of course also the possibility of voluntary undertakings to refrain from testing, or to limit or reduce armaments, without these being embodied in a treaty, and consequently without any sanction being provided for in the event of their being repudiated. Unilateral declarations in varying terms not to resume testing were in fact made by the United States, the Soviet Union and the United Kingdom during the test ban negotiations from 1958–61. But in August 1961 the Soviet government repudiated its declaration; and it became evident how little security such declarations can afford, and indeed how dangerous they may prove for countries which observe their pledged self-restraint while the other side is able to make nuclear or military preparations in secret. It is a further weakness of self-imposed restraints of this kind that they can be repudiated without breaking a treaty obligation. And since they involve no international verification they afford no guarantee of observance by others.

The volume of conference documentation on all these questions is already formidable. In addition there have been many independent contributions on both sides of the Atlantic to constructive thinking about the problems associated with arms control. But scientific research and discovery are outstripping documentation and comment. Weapons both of attack and defence are changing rapidly and the problems of disarmament and verification are changing with them. The last five years have brought new data, new dilemmas and new light on the needful and the possible. Further, since March 1962 eight unaligned countries, Brazil, Burma, Ethiopia, India, Mexico, Nigeria, Sweden and the United Arab Republic, have taken part in the 18-Nation Disarmament Conference and have given a new impetus to the search for agreement. This wealth of new material and new initiative justifies and indeed calls for fresh examination of the issues. That is the purpose of this book.[1]

Anyone who wishes to understand what is really involved in a complete test ban and disarmament must first grasp the basic and underlying dilemmas. The points at issue are often intricate; the considerations and the supporting data are complicated and hard to compress. Chapters 3–7 deal with technical aspects of the requirements and available means of verification, the possible structure of a verification organization, and the need for improved peace-keeping machinery including an international peace-keeping force. It requires an effort to master and digest even the bare facts of these as of other problems. Unless this

---

[1] The author must make it clear that the views expressed in this book are his own and not necessarily those of the British government

effort is made no expression of view can have more than limited value; yet much is constantly written and said without even the most elementary acquaintance with the essentials. Sometimes this is merely the outcome of emotion or of a desire to strike a moral or political attitude. Often it is based on the assumptions that even without international verification and effective peace-keeping machinery disarmament will bring lasting security and peace, or alternatively that a full and verified test ban and disarmament agreement are unattainable. Neither of these assumptions is necessarily or even probably true.

What is undeniable is that the world is faced by a balance of risks. In the one scale must be placed the risk of the arms race, including the testing of more and more deadly nuclear weapons and the spread of nuclear weapons to more and more countries. In the other scale must be set the risks that disarmament agreements may be secretly evaded, or that verification may endanger national security through espionage. There are risks either way. Let us hold up the scales, but in awareness and not in ignorance of the nature and degree of the respective risks.

PART ONE

1

The Course of Post-War Disarmament Negotiations[1]

THE PHASE OF U.S. MONOPOLY OVER
ATOMIC WEAPONS 1945–1949

THE atomic age opened in August 1945 with the American bombing of Hiroshima and Nagasaki. Amid the relief at the unexpected curtailment of Japanese resistance there was widespread concern at the new power of destruction seen to exist. The need for disarmament and for the strengthening of international institutions was generally and rightly felt to merit more positive attention than it had received immediately after World War I.

The principal international institution, the United Nations, established at San Francisco in June 1945, was in some ways an improvement on the defunct League of Nations, especially in that it originally included all the great powers. One notable feature was the provision in the Charter whereby each of the five great powers were given a right of veto on any action proposed at the Security Council. Yet whatever its shortcomings the U.N. did at least come into existence; whereas any rapid measures of agreed disarmament proved to be wholly beyond reach.

Hopes for disarmament were at first high. One great power, the United States, had a complete monopoly of nuclear weapons —a unique global advantage without parallel in history. But this power, with unexampled generosity, offered to surrender that advantage provided only that a system of strict international control of all atomic energy was instituted. The cause of the failure of the world to obtain a nuclear arms ban in 1946 was the unexpected attitude of the Soviet Union which refused to accept the American offer. Had the plan been generally adopted there would have been no nuclear arms race and no fall-out.

[1] The author is indebted to Mr. David Carlton, Research Student in Disarmament at King's College, London, for most of the work in compiling Chapter One, and for assistance in documentation throughout

The sequence of events was as follows. In November 1945 President Truman, Prime Minister Attlee and the Canadian Premier MacKenzie King issued a declaration offering to share nuclear secrets for peaceful purposes and to institute through U.N.O. an effective control system for the abolition of nuclear weapons. Largely as a result of this initiative the U.N. General Assembly in January 1946 set up the (U.N.) Atomic Energy Commission for this purpose. It consisted of the permanent members of the Security Council with the addition of Canada.

As the United States was then the only nation in possession of nuclear arms it was appropriate that she should be the first to present an outline proposal for their control and elimination. This took the form of the Baruch Plan of June 1946, named after Bernard Baruch, the United States representative on the (U.N.) A.E.C. The plan was in fact closely modelled on the Acheson-Lilienthal Report issued in Washington earlier in the year, and this had been largely the brain-child of Robert J. Oppenheimer. The essence of these proposals was that the United States offered to relinquish possession of nuclear weapons and the national control of all fissionable material even for peaceful purposes. There were, however, two main conditions. First, all other countries would have to agree to a scheme for international ownership and control of all nuclear developments, including those for peaceful purposes. Second, a satisfactory veto-free control body, the projected International Atomic Development Authority (I.A.D.A.) would have to be functioning before the United States would agree to relinquish its stockpile of atomic weapons.

Certain criticisms have been levelled at the nature of the conditions laid down by the United States. For example, it has been alleged that international ownership and control of all peaceful nuclear expansion might have had the result of keeping less advanced nuclear states (including, of course, at that time, the Soviet Union) in a condition of permanent inferiority. Neither the discussions in the United Nations in 1946 nor the temper of American opinion at the time support a suggestion of this kind. The people who were generous enough to propose relinquishing all national control of nuclear development when their country was alone in the field were not likely to seek to pack a jury; nor could any such manoeuvre have succeeded.

Other criticisms of the Baruch plan were even more far-fetched. For example, it was sometimes suggested that the

United States would in the end find some excuse for refusing to relinquish her stockpile, having meantime gained valuable military information about the Soviet Union. The answer to this kind of innuendo is surely to be found in the conduct and record of the United States in the international field in the immediate post-war years. Far from using overwhelming military superiority for the purpose of aggression or domination, as anti-American propagandists would lead others to expect, her conduct was more passive and pacific than that of the weaker Soviet Union. Even American man-power was reduced at a rapid rate which was far from being matched on the Russian side.[1]

What in fact was the Soviet reaction to the Baruch Plan? With remarkable candour they rejected it summarily and made it clear that they did not want a ban on nuclear weapons except on terms that would have given no semblance of satisfactory verification arrangements. They showed their hand on this occasion with the same indifference to world opinion, and the same lack of any attempt to put a gloss on their actions, which they displayed in 1961 when they resumed testing unilaterally and proceeded to explode a 60-megaton bomb which they claimed could be adapted to give a 100-megaton explosion, in defiance of an appeal from the United Nations. It has fairly been said that the Baruch Plan could have controlled the nuclear threat in its infancy, and that it is one of the tragedies of history that the Soviet Union chose to reject it and to adopt instead a policy that led to the thermo-nuclear arms race.

The Soviet counter-proposals presented to the (U.N.) A.E.C. in June 1946 amounted to a demand for unilateral nuclear disarmament by the United States with only the promise of discussions on control aspects to follow. There was no guarantee that such discussions would ever prove fruitful; on the contrary there were many indications that the U.S.S.R. would allow only minimum inspection facilities and would definitely insist on great power unanimity for international action against a violator.

Here then was already an impasse on nuclear arms. In 1948 after tedious and seemingly interminable wrangles the (U.N.) A.E.C. adjourned and reported back to the U.N. General Assembly on its failure to reach agreement. The Baruch Plan was then overwhelmingly endorsed by the Assembly but, as the

[1] For an account of American policy at this time see Walter Millis (ed.), *The Forrestal Diaries* (Viking Press, New York, 1951)

Soviet bloc voted against it, inevitably became a dead letter.

Meanwhile in the sphere of conventional armaments no greater success had been achieved. In February 1947 a U.N. Commission for Conventional Armaments was set up with the same members as the (U.N.) A.E.C. The Soviet Union called for a straight one-third cut in all the armed forces of the great powers; and sought to link the question of conventional arms with that of nuclear weapons. The United States, for some reason never made clear, seemed to be reluctant to contemplate disarmament in the conventional sphere until the Baruch Plan had been settled—in spite of their considerable disadvantage vis-à-vis Moscow in respect of conventional forces. The result was total deadlock.

STALEMATE, 1950–1953

The first successful Soviet atomic test took place in 1949—somewhat earlier than had been expected in the West. Having put an end to the American monopoly, the Russians perhaps no longer felt the same need to play for time. Be that as it may, early in 1950 they withdrew from both the Atomic Energy and Conventional Armaments Commissions of the U.N. These events together with the worsening international situation made prospects of disarmament seem even more remote. The Soviet attitude showed no signs of changing; while that of the United States hardened, especially as hope faded of ever being able to discover all the stocks of fissionable material by then in existence.

In January 1952 the U.N. General Assembly recommended that the U.N. Atomic Energy Commission and the Conventional Armaments Commission should be united in order to bring back the Soviet Union to the conference table. All the powers involved agreed on this step at least, and the U.N. Disarmament Commission was accordingly established. It was, however, no more successful than its predecessors in bridging the gap between East and West. The Soviet Union still asked for a 'Ban the Bomb' treaty as a first step, without offering any adequate verification provisions. On the conventional side she continued to call for a one-third cut without being prepared to reveal her actual manpower level until this principle had been unconditionally accepted. The West countered with a specific proposal of 1·5 million men for the U.S.S.R., the U.S.A., and Communist China,

800,000 for Great Britain, and 700,000 for France.[1] These proposals were rejected by the Soviet Union. The impasse consequently remained unchanged as both sides concentrated on developing the more advanced thermo-nuclear weapons (i.e. hydrogen bombs).

RENEWED EFFORTS: THE DISARMAMENT SUB-COMMITTEE 1954–1957

Meanwhile in 1953 an event of far-reaching importance had occurred in the Kremlin: the death of Stalin. This, in conjunction with relief at the ending of the Korean War, opened the way for a lessening of tension between East and West. The results included the signing of the Austrian State Treaty, the Geneva Summit Meeting of 1955, and some resumption of activity in the field of disarmament.

The first sign of a possible new Soviet approach to the disarmament question came early in 1954 when Moscow fell in with Western proposals for the creation of a five-man sub-committee of the Disarmament Commission consisting of the three fully-fledged nuclear powers together with France and Canada. A smaller negotiating body certainly improved the chance of progress, but at first none ensued. In June 1954 France and Great Britain in an attempt to meet the Soviet position presented their three-stage plan for a comprehensive and balanced disarmament convention. In the first stage there was to be a simple freeze of conventional forces. This was to be followed in the second stage by 50 per cent of the projected conventional cut, accompanied by a 'cut-off' in the production of fissile material for use in nuclear weapons. Not until the third stage were nuclear stockpiles to be destroyed and then only after the remaining 50 per cent of the conventional cut had been effected. Control measures were to be developed progressively at each stage.

The Russians began by rejecting the Anglo-French proposals out of hand, and called instead for an immediate ban on nuclear arms and the familiar one-third all-round reduction in conventional forces. Later in 1954 they agreed to take the Anglo-French proposals as a basis for discussion and thereby kept the sub-committee in being. In March 1955, the Western powers,

[1] At this juncture the West still believed itself to hold a commanding lead in the nuclear weapons field

in a move which proved to have been too hastily improvised, offered to destroy all nuclear weapons halfway through stage III in their plan (i.e. after 75 per cent of the conventional forces had been disbanded). Then with a surprising lack of military fore-sight, they offered new force levels. The U.S.A., the U.S.S.R., and Communist China were to have $1\frac{1}{2}$ million men, Great Britain and France 650,000 each; West Germany was not speci-fically mentioned but was presumably to remain an insignificant military power. Perhaps this additional incentive was a deciding factor in leading the Soviet Union to perform the turn round that followed. At all events on 10th May 1955 Mr. Malik accepted the proposals in two important respects. First, he dropped the one-third reduction demand and fell in with the West's projected force levels. Second, he accepted the West's stage-by-stage plan, abandoning the former Soviet insistence on an immediate ban on nuclear arms. This has been characterized by Mr. Noel-Baker as 'The Moment of Hope'[1]—and so in some senses it was. On the other hand, the Soviet proposals were vague and pessi-mistic on the problems associated with control, and were complicated by an attempt to link control with political problems and with the existence of foreign bases. But the West failed to concentrate on these aspects of the Russian proposals. Instead, the United States made it apparent that she had changed her mind on the proposals offered only three months earlier. After a Western-inspired adjournment, Mr. Harold Stassen, President Eisenhower's Special Assistant on Disarmament, told the sub-committee that the United States placed a reservation on all its previous offers. Her allies with some reluctance took much the same line. The impression was thereby given that because of Pentagon pressure the West was unwilling to take yes for an answer.

Subsequent efforts of the Eisenhower administration to per-suade the Soviet Union to accept alternative proposals met with little favour in Moscow. The President's own Open Skies pro-posal (advanced at the Geneva Summit in July 1955) was dismissed as 'inspection without disarmament'. Equally un-acceptable to the Russians was the revised Anglo-French plan of March 1956 which made no specific suggestions for force levels and did not provide for the destruction of nuclear weapons even at the end of the disarmament process, ostensibly because

[1] P. Noel-Baker *The Arms Race* (Stevens, London, 1958) p. 12

of the Soviet Union's own admission on 10th May 1955 that even the most determined international control authority could probably never be certain that all fissionable material had been discovered.

In the latter half of 1956 and during 1957 the disarmament sub-committee turned to the consideration of possible partial measures, particularly in the conventional field. Perhaps as a result of her increasing nuclear strength, the U.S.S.R. consented for the first time to discuss force levels in isolation. But agreement proved impossible, the Russians objecting that the Americans were asking for higher force levels at the end of the partial plan than previously. The United States specified $2\frac{1}{2}$ million for herself, the U.S.S.R. and China; 700,000 each for France and Great Britain; and up to 500,000 for others (including presumably West Germany). The Soviet Union, after making the most of this increase in Western demands, indicated a willingness to accept the new levels only on the obviously unacceptable condition that they were accompanied not merely by a removal of all foreign bases but also by an undertaking by all powers to destroy nuclear stocks within two years.

Subsequent proposals and counter-proposals were all in the form of package deals rejected by one side or the other. Arguments on a separate test ban also ran into difficulties; the U.S.S.R. wanted a self-policing ban, while Great Britain at one stage expressed opposition to a test ban not linked to a cut-off in production of nuclear weapons. In September 1957 these tedious negotiations were brought to an end when the sub-committee adjourned. Subsequently at the U.N. Assembly the Soviet Union called for a completely new arrangement, rejected the offer of a 25-man commission, and suggested instead an all-nation disarmament commission (eighty-two in all). As 1957 drew to a close deadlock was therefore once again practically total.

THE LATEST PHASE 1958–1963

But in 1958 events took a new and more encouraging turn. In March the Soviet Union, after completing a long series of tests which caused a great deal of fall-out, announced that she was suspending nuclear weapon tests unilaterally. This led to fresh efforts to arrive at an East-West test ban agreement.

In July and August 1958 an experts' conference[1] on nuclear

[1] For the conclusions of this Conference see Appendix I

test control problems, attended by representatives from the Soviet Union, the United States, Great Britain, France, and four other countries, reached the hopeful conclusion that given an adequate international control system, which they outlined, with fixed control posts, over-flights, and on-site inspection, all tests could be adequately monitored as regards the atmosphere, underwater, and underground, leaving the monitoring of tests in space to be further considered. The report was endorsed and accepted by Moscow, Washington, and London. Accordingly, in October 1958 a 3-Power test ban conference opened at Geneva to draw up an appropriate treaty between the only three nuclear powers at that time: the Soviet Union, the United States, and Great Britain. The negotiations lasted, with some interruption in 1961–2, until they came under the umbrella of the 18-nation Disarmament Conference at Geneva which opened in March 1962. In August 1963 the partial test ban treaty was signed in Moscow by the Soviet Union, the United States, and Great Britain. Most other nations adhered, with the exception of France, Communist China, and Albania.

From October to December 1958 a Surprise Attack Conference was held in Geneva which failed to reach any agreement. The Soviet Union showed no inclination to offer or accept any useful measures unless they were linked to the liquidation of all foreign bases and measures of disarmament.

In August 1959 the foreign ministers of the four major powers met in Geneva and decided to make a new effort on general disarmament. Accordingly the U.N. General Assembly in September 1959 established a 10-nation Disarmament Conference which opened in March 1960. It was composed of equal numbers of N.A.T.O. and Warsaw Pact states. Rival plans for general and complete disarmament had been put forward originally by Mr. Selwyn Lloyd and Mr. Khrushchev at the U.N. General Assembly in September 1959—and both were advanced again at the 10-nation conference in somewhat modified form. The two sides were far apart on problems of timing, control measures, and the means of achieving balance throughout the various projected stages of disarmament. After the failure of the Summit Meeting in May 1960 the Soviet bloc representatives walked out of the 10-nation conference in June.

The next significant development came in June 1961 when bilateral Soviet-American talks took place on the general

problems of disarmament. By September Mr. Zorin and Mr.
McCloy were able to publish a joint statement of agreed principles. In December 1961 the General Assembly endorsed the
principles and set up an 18-nation Disarmament Conference
(including eight non-aligned states) to consider the problems
in further detail. When this met in March 1962 both the Soviet
Union and the United States tabled more thorough and detailed
plans for general and complete disarmament than hitherto.

In general, then, the negotiations during the years 1958 to
1963 led to exploration of the problems of a nuclear test ban and
of disarmament in greater depth and detail than had ever been
undertaken before. Discussion round the conference table between Communist and Western countries, much of it with the
participation of representatives of unaligned countries, has
thrown new light on the factors involved. In the following
chapters an attempt is made to give an account of the principal
elements which have emerged.

2

The Basic Need

SOVIET rejection in 1946 of the American proposal contained in the Baruch plan, that all nuclear development whether of weapons or otherwise should be taken for ever out of national hands and placed under an international agency, was a turning point. It marked the failure to extend into the peace years the wartime co-operation between the Soviet Union and her former Western allies. In place of a relationship of at least reasonable confidence and forbearance, there grew up a deepening political distrust of the intentions and good faith of the other side. This distrust soon extended to doubting the value of the other side's signature to a treaty unless its loyal execution could be impartially verified. Since this distrust, if genuinely held, is the principal barrier to the conclusion of a complete test ban or of a treaty for partial or total disarmament, it is desirable to have a close look at the reasons advanced by the two sides.

Distrust of Communist policy by the West rests partly on Communist doctrine and partly on Communist actions. Since Franklin Roosevelt recognized the Soviet Union in 1933 the pragmatic leaders of the Western democracies have been apt to pay less attention to doctrine than to actions, a course of doubtful wisdom in that Communist actions can often be predicted and usually explained at least partly in terms of doctrine. In any case Western leaders have avoided treating the Soviet Union as impossible to negotiate with, even though her policies are avowedly designed to promote the disruption of the social systems of the Western countries, and although she rejects the codes of international conduct normally accepted by the non-Communist world (except where she judges such rejection to be tactically and temporarily injudicious). When the Soviet Union shows signs of observing normal international rules the West usually prefers to welcome and even to encourage the development by turning a blind eye to the ideological basis of the Soviet State. For a time, of course, this attitude of the West found a natural justification in a sense of wartime comradeship. But even if it is wise at least up to a point to judge the Soviet Union by

26

actions and to overlook doctrine, it cannot be said that Communist actions have been such as to inspire confidence; and while the Soviet interpretation of the doctrine of the inevitability of war has changed, Soviet dedication to world revolution has not. It is noteworthy that in the 18-Power negotiations at Geneva in 1962 and 1963 the Soviet Government steadfastly refused to admit that the goal of general and complete disarmament is a 'disarmed and peaceful world'; 'disarmed' yes, but 'disarmed and peaceful' Moscow has rejected even though the word 'peaceful' has appeared earlier in the preamble to the agreed disarmament principles of 20th September 1961.

In fact, the Communists continue to preach the inevitability of the victory of Communism over capitalism and of the establishment of the socialist system on a world scale. As Mr. Khrushchev put it in April 1962:

'Sooner or later Communism will win everywhere in the world and consequently Communism will "bury" capitalism.'

The Communists are committed to pursuing policies designed to accelerate this 'inevitable' process. The policy of peaceful co-existence was originally conceived by the Soviet leadership as a means of providing a breathing space in which to increase their forces before the inevitable conflict with world capitalism. As Stalin said in 1927:

'We cannot forget Lenin's statement that as regards our work of construction very much depends on whether we succeed in postponing war with the capitalist world, which is inevitable. . . . Therefore the maintenance of peaceful relations with the capitalist countries is an obligatory task for us. The basis of our relations with capitalist countries consists in admitting the existence of the two opposed systems.'

But the advent of weapons of mass destruction has caused Soviet (although not yet Chinese) leaders to re-think the doctrine of the inevitability of war, which they now state to be no longer valid. Moscow's new concept, which Mr. Khrushchev defined at the 22nd Party Congress, is called 'peaceful co-existence'. It connotes the victory of world Communism without war through the superiority of the Communist economic system, a victory which must of course be pursued by all means short of war and remains inevitable.

But whether the new Moscow concept of peaceful co-existence involves the abandonment of other Communist dogma is a different question. The classic Communist view is that compromises in negotiation are merely tactical measures in the struggle with the capitalist system. Lenin wrote in 1920:

'The strictest loyalty to the ideas of Communism must be combined with the ability to make all the necessary practical compromises, to "tack", to make agreements, zigzags, retreats and so on, in order to accelerate the coming into power . . . and subsequent loss of power of . . . the representatives of petty bourgeois democracy.'

In the light of these statements the Soviet claim that it has 'no desire to interfere in the internal affairs of other countries because their way of life is an inalienable right of every nation' (Khrushchev, October 1960) is scarcely convincing.

Nor does the Soviet record inspire confidence. Soviet annexations in 1940 of the Baltic States of Latvia, Estonia and Lithuania are classic illustrations. The Baltic States were allocated as a Soviet sphere of influence by the Nazi-Soviet agreement of September 1939. By the summer of 1940, Soviet troops had entered these territories under various pretexts, elections had been held from which all non-union independent candidates were barred as 'public enemies', and Communist governments set up. The states were then declared to be Soviet republics and incorporated in the Soviet Union.

In a different category but even more disturbing as a warning of future possibilities was the establishment of Communist dictatorships over the countries of Eastern Europe during the years 1945–8. Ex-enemy states (Hungary, Rumania and Bulgaria) were taken over by minority Communist parties protected by Soviet occupation forces, in breach of specific provisions in the Peace Treaties of February 1947 to the effect that they were to be given democratic political systems. In Poland, the Moscow-orientated 'Lublin Government' established itself in power having arrived in the baggage of the Red Army; it made the merest pretence of compromising with the Polish Government-in-Exile before driving the latter's representatives out of the uneasy coalition. Many of the anti-Nazi underground leaders of the traditional Polish political parties had already been lured to Moscow for 'negotiations' and sentenced to long terms of imprisonment for allegedly impeding the Red Army.[1]

---

[1] For details of the developments in Poland see E. J. Rozek, *Allied Wartime Diplomacy: A Pattern in Poland* (Willey, New York, 1958)

But the climax came with the Communist *coup d'état* in Czechoslovakia in February 1948. Here, with no Soviet forces in the country and elections imminent, the minority Communist leaders in the coalition government provoked a political crisis through arbitrary action by their Minister of the Interior against non-Communist police officials. When twelve non-Communist ministers resigned from the government in protest, the Communists under Gottwald consolidated their authority by force.[1] Two of the leading Czech democratic politicians who chose to continue at their posts, President Benes and Foreign Minister Jan Masaryk, died shortly afterwards, the latter from unnatural causes. The brutality of this *coup* in what had been held to be the stronghold of East European democracy demonstrated Communist intentions beyond any possible further doubt, and helped to speed the negotiations which led to the formation of N.A.T.O. in 1949. Ironically enough the *coup* has been upheld by the Soviet government since 1956 as a model for future 'peaceful parliamentary transition to socialism' (notably by Mikoyan at the 20th Party Congress).

Parallel to their expansion in Eastern Europe, the Soviet Union consistently refused to implement the four-power machinery agreed upon in 1945 for the control of Germany. Soviet obstruction culminated in the Soviet withdrawal from the Allied Control Council in March 1948 and from the Berlin Kommandatura in July the same year. This was immediately followed by the imposition of a complete blockade of Berlin in an attempt to force the Western powers out of the city, an attempt which was only defeated by the allied airlift.[2] In the autumn of 1948 the Soviet authorities began their re-arming of the Soviet Zone of Germany by the creation of para-military police units in violation of the four-power agreements for the disarmament and de-militarization of Germany. These units were subsequently built up into a strong military force which by the spring of 1950 numbered nearly 50,000 men. By January 1956, when the East German Constitution was amended to authorize the creation of a 'National People's Army', East Germany already had a fully trained and well equipped force of some 130,000–140,000 men.

[1] For an account of the fall of Czechoslovakia see J. Korbel, *The Communist Subversion of Czechoslovakia 1938-48* (Princeton University Press, 1959)

[2] See W. P. Davison, *The Berlin Blockade: A Study in Cold War Politics* (Princeton University Press, 1958)

In contrast the German Federal Republic by that date was holding its first parade of 1,600 raw recruits for the newly established *Bundeswehr*.

In the Far East the attack on South Korea by the Communist North in the summer of 1950 leading to the prolonged hostilities in that country finally dispelled any lingering illusions there may have been in the West about Communist intentions. It led directly to the massive Western re-armament programmes designed to offset the long lead which the Communist Bloc had gained in all but nuclear weapons as a result of the Soviet refusal to disarm after 1945 and of the Soviet re-equipment programmes introduced since the War.

To these reasons for Western distrust of Communists can be added many others, among them the repression in Hungary in 1956; the abrupt walkout of the Communist delegates from the 10-power Disarmament Conference at Geneva in June 1960; the resumption of nuclear testing in September 1961 by the Soviet Union after nearly three years abstention by both sides while negotiations were still continuing; the repudiation by the Soviet Union in November 1961 of everything they had agreed upon during three years of negotiation for a nuclear test ban; and Soviet and Chinese actions in Cuba and India respectively. The list is illustrative rather than exhaustive. Whether these statements and actions on the Communist side justify the deep-seated distrust they have aroused in the West may by some be regarded as a matter for debate. But the distrust created, whether justified or not, is a political fact to be reckoned with in the field of disarmament. Above all it means that the West does not trust the Soviet Union to observe a comprehensive nuclear test ban or a disarmament agreement without adequate and impartial international verification.

It is not so easy for any Westerner to attempt to define the reasons for the distrust of the Western powers expressed by the Soviet Union; but whatever the true causes the Communist countries profess on their side a profound lack of confidence in Western intentions towards the Communist world. This is clearly illustrated by the incessant Communist propaganda against the policies of containment, and of negotiation from a position of strength, associated with the late John Foster Dulles. Soviet fears may also have been genuinely heightened by the success of Western re-armament programmes, by the American

lead in nuclear weapons, and above all by the re-emergence of
West Germany as a major force in Europe. This professed
Soviet distrust can be illustrated by almost daily quotations from
Pravda and other Soviet newspapers. For example, a *Pravda*
editorial stated in 1963:

> 'The bellicose circles of the imperialist powers, above all the
> United States and Western Germany, have not renounced their
> mad plans for "rolling back" Communism, even by military means.'

More specifically they claim that the West is preparing for War.
West German re-armament and N.A.T.O. bulk large in these
expressions of fear. L. I. Brezhnev, the Soviet President, said on
2nd October 1962:

> 'There still exist in the world forces of imperialism which are
> trying to kindle the flames of a new world war. The imperialists of
> the United States of America now head these forces. With their
> support the West German militarists are again raising their heads.
> The strategists of N.A.T.O., like poisonous spiders, are weaving a
> black web of conspiracies against peace.'

In the Communist vocabulary N.A.T.O. is always the
aggressive N.A.T.O. bloc. A particular target for invective as
supposed evidence of hostile intentions towards the Soviet Union
is the stationing of American forces outside their countries in
places where they could help to defend small and frightened
neighbours of the Soviet Union against surprise attack. These are
represented as 'daggers pointed at the heart of the Soviet
Union'.

In further justification of their claims the Communists have
elevated 'anti-Communism' into a distinct policy of the West.
'Not to see the grievous consequences of the policy of anti-
Communism', wrote *Pravda* on 23rd February 1963, 'means
either to be politically blind or to be an open accomplice of
imperialism.' In addition the Communists seize on statements
by Western personalities of small or no responsibility, often
retired officials or members of the Armed Services, as proof of
their charges against Western policies. They quote at length from
newspapers of any shade of independent opinion and imply that
they have the same authority as an article in *Pravda* or a statement put out by the Tass Agency. They also make use of inter-
party debates in free democratic countries. If, for example, the
Leader of the Opposition in Great Britain makes an election
speech with perhaps a slightly exaggerated criticism of, say, the

slum clearance policy of the government, he may for domestic purposes paint as black a picture as possible; the Soviet propaganda machine will use this to claim that the condition of the masses under capitalism is intolerable. Similarly, if an American Senator in opposition makes a tough speech on foreign policy, his words are misinterpreted as indicating that the United States is contemplating hostile action against the Soviet Union. It may be argued that Communist fears of the Western powers, while ill-founded and based on faulty ideological theories, are nevertheless sincere. Alternatively it may be the case that the misrepresentation is deliberate and calculated on the part of the foremost Soviet leaders. But however that may be, and from whatever causes it may spring, the ostensible distrust of the West professed by Communist leaders is a factor which must be reckoned with. Certainly, if these alleged suspicions of the West have the force of political dogma, or if the Soviet leaders—or any significant section of them—have come to believe their own propaganda, then this is a fact that profoundly affects the chances of definitive disarmament and verification agreements being reached.

Since it is relevant to the problem of disarmament, it should further be borne in mind that lack of confidence is not confined to relationships between the Great Powers, or between Western and Communist countries. Many other countries, large and small, aligned and unaligned, distrust each other, especially in many cases their immediate neighbours. The relations of fear and suspicion between Israel and the United Arab Republic, and between India and Pakistan, are cases in point; in differing degrees there are parallels in Africa, in Latin America and indeed throughout the world. These fears and suspicions lead the countries harbouring them to acquire more and more arms for their defence; and if partly the effect they are also largely the cause of the arms race.

If, then, there exists in the world such deep suspicion, it is fair to ask whether re-establishment of trust in the observance of agreements by others can ever precede the re-establishment of general political confidence. Another way to put it is to ask whether a full nuclear test ban or a disarmament agreement can ever precede a settlement of those political questions which at any given moment are the principal causes of international tension. It may in fact prove to be the case that a full test ban and disarmament can only follow and reflect rather than precede and create a political *détente*. Certainly if a political *détente* came first the attitude of the two sides could be expected to become more reasonable and practical, and disarmament agreements less difficult to negotiate. But to argue from this that attempts to ban all nuclear weapon tests, or to disarm, should be laid aside until the political outlook is fairer is to ignore the horrible compulsion of the development of nuclear weapons and the risk of their spread to more and more countries. It is this which is the driving force, and rightly so, in the minds of those most closely concerned with the problem. To wait may be a counsel of despair or folly. *Rusticus expectat dum defluat amnis*—the rustic waits for the river to run dry before trying to cross it.

If this view is accepted and if attempts to call a halt are to be pursued without waiting for the political climate to improve first, then any full test ban or far-reaching disarmament agreement must be effectively and internationally verified. The fact must be faced that in the prevailing atmosphere of international suspicion nations, at any rate Western nations, will not incur the risk to their national security inherent in these steps without what they judge to be adequate verification of observance by others. This can and does hold true of small countries as well as of powerful states. It is a central fact in the disarmament nexus.

The necessity of international verification both for a test ban and disarmament has been repeatedly endorsed by the U.N. Assembly and by unaligned countries. For example, General Assembly Resolution 1649 of 8th November 1961 urged states to renew their efforts to conclude a treaty which 'should have as its objective the cessation of all nuclear weapons tests in all environments under inspection and control machinery adequate to ensure compliance with its terms'. The resolution was approved by a vote of seventy-one in favour, fifteen abstentions and only the Soviet bloc and Cuba voting against. On disarmament Western countries and particularly the United States and the United Kingdom have been categoric on the need for verification. The United States' disarmament plan provides for thorough international verification when general and complete disarmament is achieved, and for adequate verification during the three intervening stages. The Soviet Government has made its own statements on this matter. Briefly, they endorse the principle but deny the practice. No. 6 of the statement of principles agreed between Mr. Zorin and Mr. McCloy on 20th September 1961

on behalf of the Soviet Union and the United States, and
endorsed by the United Nations Assembly, reads as follows:

'6. All disarmament measures should be implemented from
beginning to end under such strict and effective international
control as would provide firm assurance that all parties are
honouring their obligations. During and after the implementation of general and complete disarmament, the most thorough
control should be exercised, the nature and extent of such
control depending on the requirements for verification of the
disarmament measures being carried out in each stage. To
implement control over and inspection of disarmament, an international disarmament organization including all parties to the
agreement should be created within the framework of the
United Nations. This international disarmament organization
and its inspectors should be assured unrestricted access without
veto to all places as necessary for the purpose of effective
verification.'[1]

On the surface that sounds like full acceptance of the principle
of adequate international verification. But in fact it is something
quite different. When Mr. Zorin and Mr. McCloy were negotiating the statement of agreed principles the United States government wished to include the following clause in paragraph 6:

'Such verification should ensure that not only agreed limits and
reductions take place, but also that retained armed forces and
armaments do not exceed agreed levels at any stage.'

This was rejected by Mr. Zorin in his famous letter of 20th
September 1961, which contains the following sentences:

'While strongly advocating effective control over disarmament and
wishing to facilitate as much as possible the achievement of agreement on this control, the Soviet Union is at the same time resolutely
opposed to the establishment of control over armaments. It appears
from your letter that the United States is trying to establish control
over the armed forces and armaments retained by states at any
given stage of disarmament. However, such control, which in fact
means control over armaments, would turn into an international
system of legalized espionage, which would naturally be unacceptable to any state concerned for its security and the interests of
preserving peace throughout the world.'[2]

In other words the Russian agreement was limited to verification
of arms destroyed. It would be difficult to gather this from the
statement by the Soviet Foreign Minister, Mr. Gromyko, at the

[1] See Appendix II
[2] See Appendix III

opening meeting of the 18-nation Disarmament Conference at Geneva on 15th March 1962 at which he said:

'The Soviet Union wishes to have the necessary guarantees that the disarmament obligations that have been agreed upon will be strictly carried out and that there are no loopholes which will permit the clandestine production of aggressive armaments once the process of general and complete disarmament has begun. Our country does not intend to take anyone at his word, least of all states which have established close military alignments, are pursuing a policy of building up armaments and have placed their military bases as close as possible to the Soviet Union. Nor do we expect others to take us at our word. The Soviet Union is a firm advocate of strict control over disarmament.'

It would also be difficult to appreciate the truth about the Soviet attitude from a first perusal of Article 2 of the Soviet disarmament plan submitted on the same day.[1] The relevant clauses in Article 2 read:

'1. The states parties to the treaty solemnly undertake to carry out all disarmament measures, from beginning to end, under strict international control, and to ensure the implementation in their territories of all control measures set forth in parts II, III, and IV, of the present treaty.

2. Each disarmament measure shall be accompanied by such control measures as are necessary for verification of that measure.

3. To implement control over disarmament, an international disarmament organization including all states parties to the treaty shall be established within the framework of the United Nations. It shall begin operating as soon as disarmament measures are initiated. The structure and functions of the international disarmament organization and its bodies are laid down in Part V of the present treaty.

4. In all countries parties to the treaty the international disarmament organization shall have its own staff, recruited internationally and in such a way as to ensure the adequate representation on it of all three existing groups of states.

This staff shall exercise control, on a temporary or permanent basis, depending on the nature of the measure being carried out, over the compliance by states with their obligations to reduce or eliminate armaments and their production and to reduce or disband their armed forces.'

This also does not turn out to mean what it seems to say. As will be shown further below, this article is explained by the Soviet

[1] See Appendix IV. (A later version but in this respect unchanged)

government as intended to cover only arms destroyed, and not arms retained.

In fact, of course, the need to be satisfied that other signatory states are observing their obligations not merely to destroy, but not to replace or conceal, is inherent in any form of disarmament agreement, since successful and secret evasion of an agreement may place the security of innocent powers at the mercy of the successful violator. But the risks involved and the need to be satisfied of observance by others have been made more compelling by the development of modern arms. Before the advent of nuclear weapons, wars were fought with what have now come to be called conventional weapons; disarmament was a matter of being satisfied that conventional weapons were not being illicitly or secretly produced or concealed. When only conventional weapons were in question no country or group of countries could acquire in secret and within a short period striking power capable of inflicting decisive and almost instantaneous damage upon an enemy. There had to be production on a large scale of powerful warships, heavy artillery, tanks, bomber aircraft and so forth. Numbers of men had to be trained to use them, and their maintenance under arms or their call up from civilian occupations could not be concealed. None of these preparations could easily by kept secret; almost inevitably they had to be spread over a number of years and became known to other countries. The re-armament of Germany after the First World War contrary to treaty agreements was known to other countries; they did not lack the knowledge of the build-up, but the will to stop it.

In the inter-war years disarmament negotiations were concerned not at all with the problem of verification. Nor did the issue of surprise attack cause any difficulties. The only disarmament conventions which were signed and ratified were the Naval Agreements of 1922 (Washington) and 1930 (London); these contained no paragraphs referring to verification, or for that matter to sanctions in the event of a breach. In fact all the parties prior to the rise of Hitler had at least a residue of trust in one another. The trouble arose rather out of their inability in most cases (especially in regard to land armaments) to reach agreement on yardsticks whereby differing military strengths were to be evaluated. Given that, because of geographic differences, nations had differing requirements, how was a fair ratio to be arrived at? The French argued against power parity with the Germans, since they claimed that Germany's '*potentiel de guerre*' was greater in terms of population, economic resources, and so forth.

On the surface the chances of disarmament were indeed much greater between 1919 and 1932 than they were in 1963. There was not the same basic suspicion on a global scale; the dominating distrust was between Germany and France, and this in the Briand-Stresemann era seemed to be of diminishing significance. Furthermore, the acute need for balance in the disarmament process did not exist in its present form, since no power could hope in the pre-nuclear age to gain an advantage by sleight of hand that would allow it to hold up the world to ransom.

The picture has now changed. Diversion of fissile material for nuclear warheads could easily be concealed without a system of international verification. Secret laboratory work on nuclear weapons could be followed by tests carried out at very short notice, or without any advance notice at all, and if detected might in some circumstances be identifiable only by on-site inspection.

These considerations add up to the fact that, in a disarmed world, attack in overwhelming strength by modern weapons could be prepared in secret and launched with the prospect of decisive success unless an adequate system of international verification exists. When account is taken of this situation against the background of the deep and widespread distrust in the political field, it becomes more and more inescapable that adequate international verification is the key to disarmament. It is futile to talk about any far-reaching disarmament as if it were a possibility in itself; disarmament and verification must at least in the present state of the world go hand in hand. The compulsion is not simply to disarm but to disarm and verify.

But in fact and in practice the issue of verification presents itself differently to the Western world and the Communist world. The United States, the United Kingdom and most of their friends and partners are states which are open societies. Except in times of war or acute emergency there is freedom of the press, freedom of speech and no censorship or control of news. Parliamentary representatives have various privileges and immunities in making information public. Secrecy is difficult to preserve, and there is an instinctive dislike of secrecy rather than of verification. In spite, therefore of the fact that the Soviet Union has admitted that concealment of nuclear weapons and fissile material is hard to guard against, and in spite of their statement that they will not take the word of the West over disarmament, they may calculate that in open societies a degree of self-verification operates automatically.

But in a closed Communist society the position is widely different. The controls and powers of the state are such that large-scale evasions of disarmament obligations could be concealed without undue difficulty except from strict international verification. Western countries accordingly require such verification if their basic requirement is to be met, namely that of being satisfied that an agreement is kept by others; and although they may dislike it, they accept strict international verification themselves. Communist countries look at it otherwise. Any form of international verification, the presence on Soviet soil of any foreign observers or inspectors even from neutral countries, is extremely distasteful to the Soviet Union. Secrecy was a characteristic of life in Russia under the Czars; it is still more so in Communist Russia. The reason adduced by the Soviet government is fear of espionage by Western countries who may be meditating an attack on the Soviet Union. Even a neutral inspector, it appears, even a Dag Hammarskjold or a U Thant, might turn out to be James Bond in disguise.

This Soviet attitude has been carried to the point that Soviet agreement on international verification during all the stages before total disarmament is specifically stipulated by Moscow to be limited to three fields:

   (i) verification of arms destroyed

  (ii) verification at any factories where the Soviet Government declares that arms production has ceased

 (iii) verification at any missile sites declared by the Soviet Government to be the only missile sites remaining, including verification of missiles upon them.

In other words the Soviet Union does not agree that there should be international verification of replacement, of production, of remainders, or of non-concealment of weapons.

Probing of the meaning of article 2 of the Soviet disarmament plan, quoted above, has revealed that it has been intentionally drafted to contain these reservations. To put it shortly, the Soviet government agrees that if it undertakes to destroy 1,000 bombers, their destruction may be witnessed by international observers; but refuses to allow verification that the 1,000 bombers are not replaced by other bombers or that weapons are not being concealed. How this can be reconciled with Mr. Gromyko's statement at Geneva that 'the Soviet Union wishes to have the necessary guarantees that the disarmament obligations which have been agreed upon would be strictly carried out and that there are no loopholes which would permit the clandestine production of aggressive armaments once the progress of general and complete disarmament has begun' has never been explained.

The truth about this professed Soviet dislike of international verification is hard to judge. Is it fear, and if so, of what? Of identification of missile sites or of possible targets for hostile missiles? Fear of the exposure of weakness? Of aggressive preparations being found out? Of opportunities for the spread of non-Communist ideas? Or is it simply an excuse for scuttling any disarmament measures? Whatever the reason, the attitude appears strangely antiquated in a twentieth century world; yet whether pretended or real it is a state of mind to be reckoned with. The political fact that the West has no such Victorian inhibitions does not alter the political fact that the Communist world has them or affects to have them.

But there is a second difference in the approach to verification on the part of Western countries and Communist countries which has proved troublesome. This is the refusal of the Soviet government to admit the concept of an international civil servant, or to agree that even a neutral can act or verify impartially. Article 100 of the Charter of the United Nations lays down that:

'1. In the performance of their duties the Secretary General and the staff shall not seek to receive instructions from any government or from any other authority external to the Organization. They shall refrain from any action which might reflect on their position as international officials responsible only to the Organization.

2. Each Member of the United Nations undertakes to respect the exclusively international character of the responsibilities of the Secretary General and the staff and not to seek to influence them in the discharge of their responsibilities.'

The concept of an international civil servant, either seconded from the service of his own country or volunteering to serve an

international organization, was developed under the League of
Nations. There grew up a body of men and a code of behaviour
and loyalty which was one of the more valuable legacies of the
League. But although embodied in the Charter, the concept has
increasingly been called in question by the Soviet government.

The truth is of course that the Russians are not 'bourgeois
internationalists' and there can be no real compromise, as
distinct from temporary and tactical accommodation, for men
with a global objective of world revolution. They can hardly
endorse the traditional principle of non-interventionism except
as a temporary expedient; nor can they fundamentally accept the
idea that other nations are entitled to solve their internal
problems in any way they choose. Hence when they pay lip
service to normal diplomatic practice in international organizations, and in particular to Article 100 of the U.N. Charter, it is
important to grasp that it is in reality only lip service and
nothing more.

The fact is that it is difficult for a Communist to act even for a
time as a loyal international civil servant, subordinating loyalty
to Communist interests in a given situation to over-riding
loyalty to the international organization he is serving; and
Communist governments may find it distasteful to admit that
nationals of non-Communist countries can practice loyalty to an
international organization whereas a Communist cannot. However that may be, the Soviet government since 1961 has professed
to believe that experience of the working of the United Nations
has shown that there is no such thing as a reliable international
civil servant. No individual, even a national of a neutral state, so
the Soviet government has recently maintained, can be trusted
to act impartially, to adopt norms of thought and behaviour
which are not either Communist or anti-Communist. There is no
such thing, Mr. Khrushchev has said, as a neutral man. Therefore, the new Soviet doctrine runs, the U.N. Secretariat itself
should be organized strictly on a troika basis, namely equal
thirds from Communist, Western and unaligned states; there
should be three Secretaries General instead of one; and decisions
must be taken unanimously by the three, that is to say each of
the three should have a veto. The Soviet government claimed in
1961 that the same doctrine should apply to a control organization for a nuclear test ban. No single individual, the Russian
argument ran, even from an unaligned country, could be trusted

to act impartially as chief Executive Officer; there must be three co-equal administrative heads, acting by agreement in every case. Subordinate echelons down the line should be organized in the same way. This involves the concept of an international verification organization in which the individual members would to a greater or lesser degree be representing their national interests instead of being loyal to the organization and to nothing or no one else. This is entirely contrary to the concept of an international civil servant enshrined in the Charter. Moreover a system in which at any or all executive levels there must be the unanimous consent of three co-equals before an order is carried out can only lead to administrative paralysis.

When Dag Hammarskjold died on 18th September 1961 and the question arose of his replacement as Secretary General of the United Nations, Moscow did not press its demand for a troika, and while reserving its position agreed to the appointment of U Thant. Whether this was in fact only a temporary and tactical retreat from the demand for a troika remains to be seen. What is significant in the context of disarmament is that the Soviet draft treaty imples, although without posing it specifically, a demand for a troika in a control commission; and when it comes to the command of a peace-keeping force, the Russians are definite that there must be a troika.

The position, therefore, is that Western countries offer strict international verification in their own territories at all stages of a comprehensive nuclear test ban or of a disarmament agreement; they offer to satisfy the other side by any requisite form of impartial and international verification that they are observing their treaty obligations; and they require equal satisfaction from the other side in return. They are also prepared to trust an internationally staffed control organization to carry out impartially and loyally the tasks laid down for it; what they require is that it should be administered effectively and be able to work without a veto by anyone on its operation. By contrast the Soviet Union does not offer strict international verification before there is total disarmament, nor any verification that arms are not being concealed, nor will it apparently trust an international verification organization unless it works on a troika basis.

There are many other difficult issues in the field of disarmament which remain unresolved. Many of these centre round the practical application to be given to No. 5 of the agreed principles, namely that 'all measures of general and complete disarmament should be balanced so that at no stage of the implementation of the treaty should any state or group of states gain military advantage and that security is ensured equally for all'. The application of this principle, to which both sides subscribe and which they constantly invoke, raises formidable problems especially in respect of the timing of the destruction of nuclear weapons and delivery vehicles. Nonetheless it is the question of verification and verification machinery which is the most refractory. Here is the main gap separating the two sides, whether over a full test ban or over disarmament. In trying to determine whether and how the gap can be bridged it may be useful to examine more precisely what it is that needs to be verified, and what means of verification exist.

PART TWO

3

Verification: Tasks and Staff

DISARMAMENT

THE agreed principles to govern disarmament negotiated between Mr. McCloy for the United States and Mr. Zorin for the Soviet Union on 20th September 1961, and endorsed by the U.N. General Assembly,[1] contain the following clause:

'4. The disarmament programme should be implemented in an agreed sequence, by stages until it is completed, with each measure and stage carried out within specified time-limits. Transition to a subsequent stage in the process of disarmament should take place upon a review of the implementation of measures included in the preceding stage and upon a decision that all such measures have been implemented and verified and that any additional verification arrangements required for measures in the next stage are, when appropriate, ready to operate.'

The text of Clause 6 of the agreed principles, dealing with verification, has been given in chapter 2, together with the statement on verification made by the Soviet Foreign Minister, Mr. Gromyko,[2] on 16th March 1962 at Geneva. These three texts, together with the letters exchanged by Mr. McCloy and Mr. Zorin on 20th September 1961,[3] are key documents.

TASKS

It is necessary to look closely at the measures of verification required to ensure the practical implementation of these principles. For a nuclear test ban, excepting underground tests, reliance must and can be placed largely upon recordings by distant scientific instruments; but for disarmament, reliance upon scientific instruments has not yet been proposed and does not enter into the picture, except for the possible use of air photography or visual air reconnaissance. The requirement is for observers stationed in or visiting the territories of signatory states.

[1] See Appendix II
[2] See *Documents on Disarmament 1961* (United States Arms Control and Disarmament Agency), pp. 442–3
[3] See Appendix III

What these observers need to verify falls into four categories which are more or less distinct.

The first requirement is to verify the actual destruction of any quantities of arms which it is agreed should be scrapped. Signatory states may insist upon being satisfied that destruction is taking place simultaneously, and if so simultaneous destruction in different countries must be verified. No great difficulties need attend verification of such destruction of weapons, which is often termed verification of bonfires. The weapons can be assembled at one or more designated places and destruction can be visibly carried out by or in the presence of international observers. Neither Western governments nor the Soviet government foresee any drawbacks or complications. Both the American and the Soviet disarmament plans provide for it at all stages.

The second requirement is to verify that, if states have undertaken to reduce their national forces by say 1,000 bombers, and in fact carry out this destruction in the presence of international observers, they do not replace these by other bombers, perhaps more up-to-date, rolling off the production line. This is usually referred to as verification of non-replacement or non-production. It is obviously a complicated matter. To make certain that illicit replacement is not taking place international inspectors or observers would have to maintain continuous checks upon all possible production and assembly sites, and perhaps upon points of entry by land, sea and air.

The United States and Great Britain are willing to accept such verification in their territories. But however inconsistent with their other utterances this may seem, the Soviet government has refused to do so until total disarmament has been completed, with two exceptions only by the end of 1963:

(a) that there may be a continuous check on factories or production plants where they have declared production to have ceased;

(b) that there may be a continuous check upon those missile launching sites declared by the Soviet government to be the only missile sites remaining in Soviet territory, together with a check upon missiles on these sites.

The Russians refuse to admit verification that no other production plants, missile sites or missiles exist beyond those declared. In short, they refuse during the whole disarmament process to accept adequate verification of non-replacement or non-production. They maintain that such verification (see Mr.

Zorin's letter of 20th September 1961 in Appendix III) would be verification of armaments and not of disarmament and would involve an unbearable risk of leakage of Soviet secret defence information through espionage.

The third requirement is to verify that if the obligation is not (or not merely) to destroy a given number of weapons, say 1,000 bombers, but to reduce national forces down to a level of say 500 bombers, this level is not exceeded by the retention of a larger number. This requirement, known as verification of remainders, the Western countries also accept and the Soviet government refuses until total disarmament has been completed, basing its refusal on the same grounds as its refusal of verification of non-replacement or non-production.

The fourth requirement, which may overlap the second and third requirements in some circumstances, is to verify that arms are not illicitly concealed. This is often termed the problem of 'arms hidden under the jacket'. The United States and Great Britain accept such verification in their territories at all stages of disarmament. If such words mean anything, Mr. Gromyko's statement of 16th March 1962 that 'there must be no loopholes which will permit the clandestine production of aggressive armaments once the process of general and complete disarmament has begun' would seem to be a clear indication that the Soviet government would both require and agree to this. But no. The Soviet government in fact refuses it until total disarmament has been completed, just as it refuses adequate verification of non-replacement and verification of remainders.

Yet it is clear that all these four requirements must be met if there is to be an acceptable degree of assurance that a disarmament treaty is being observed by all parties. There can be no international confidence, no assurance of safety, without them. Since here lies the key to disarmament, let us take a close look at what would be involved.

POWERS OF VERIFICATION STAFF

Owing to the negative Soviet attitude to three out of these four necessary forms of verification, there has been less study and discussion, either between the two sides or otherwise, of the numbers of international staff needed, and the powers they would have to possess. But it is evident that to carry out these four forms of verification extensive rights of access and interrogation would have to be vested in the international verification organization, and that signatory states would have to bind themselves to grant these rights. While the matter has never been hammered out in debate, these rights might have to include:

(a) unrestricted freedom of movement and communication within the area to be inspected

(b) right of access without prior notice to all government establishments, industrial plants and factories within the area to be inspected.

(c) right to search, take samples where appropriate, and examine all records and documents in government and industrial installations to which there is right of access

(d) right to interrogate (in so far as items for verification are concerned) military commanders, members of the armed forces, managers of government and industrial establishments, their staff and workers

(e) right to check movement by land, sea and air across boundaries, with rights of search.

In addition there might be requirements for verification of internal movements of forces or weapons by land, sea and air, and continuous checks on army, navy and air headquarters. It would be desirable to make use of visual air reconnaissance and, in areas where communications are bad or which are not thoroughly charted, there might be need for air photography on a considerable scale.

NUMBERS OF STAFF

The verifying staff would have to check production by declared plants and factories, watch for diversion of production to illicit use, and assure themselves that clandestine plant was not being concealed in any suitable building. A rough estimate for an area of about 5,000 square miles in the United Kingdom, containing two or three million inhabitants, suggests that there might be a verification requirement of a few hundred officers to verify declared inventories, with similar numbers to verify declared output, to check for clandestine production, and to verify movements across boundaries. There would be additional staff requirements for air photography, visual reconnaissance and headquarters control. In all, this suggests a minimum total of about 1,000 inspecting officers for such an area, exclusive of administrative, clerical and transport supporting staff.

A detailed British study of the technical possibility of international control of fissile material production[1] reached the conclusion that for the United Kingdom alone the staff needed to verify that fissile material was not being and had not been concealed would be in the neighbourhood of 160 scientists, and a total, with supporting staff, of 730. A rough estimate for world-wide verification of the non-concealment of fissile material was about 1,500 scientists and a total, with supporting staff, of about 10,000 of all grades including technicians, administrative staff and guards.

A further United Kingdom study of the problems connected with the elimination of rockets as nuclear delivery vehicles reached the conclusion that the number of inspectors required world-wide for the control or supervision by the International Disarmament Organization of production of rockets would be in the neighbourhood of several thousand.

It is extremely difficult to apply these rough figures to an estimate of the total number of international staff which would be required to verify total disarmament on a world-wide basis. If, for an industrialized area in the United Kingdom containing 3 million inhabitants, about 1,000 officers would be required, it may be supposed that for the United Kingdom as a whole, with a population of over 40 million, the requirement would not be less than 5,000, after allowing for agricultural areas and so forth. If so, it must be supposed that at least four times as many would be required for the United States, a highly industrialized country with a population of about 180 million, that is to say 20,000 with additional supporting staff; and a similar figure for the Soviet Union. Without counting the rest of the world the figure already totals up to about 45,000 officers with supporting staff, and a total world figure would inevitably be much higher. For a world-wide organization communications and transport would involve considerable additional commitments.

It is worth mentioning in this context that the American plan (Section G, paragraph 3) proposes a system of verification by progressive zonal sampling to try and alleviate the incidence of verification during the three stages of disarmament. The Russians have declined to accept it; but were it adopted the requirements of staff for verification during the three stages of disarmament would be lessened.

[1] See Appendix VI

D.V.–D

COST

Whether or not these figures are even approximately indicative of what the total requirement might be (and they are only put forward as illustrative and as liable to be very wide of the mark, perhaps in either direction), it is undeniable that the requirements for full verification of general and complete disarmament would be considerable and costly. It is often assumed that disarmament would automatically result in massive economies releasing large sums of money for other purposes. The volume on the Economic Consequences of Disarmament produced by the Economic Intelligence Unit sponsored by the United World Trust contains some interesting statistics. These indicate that while a saving on salaries and manpower occasioned by disarmament may not prove to be very striking, a considerable factor is introduced by the saving on military equipment and on research and development costs. An expectation which constantly arouses interest is that sufficient savings might result from disarmament to enable substantial sums to be released to help under-developed countries. This is certainly conceivable, but an offsetting factor might be the degree of adjustment of national economies required by disarmament, particularly in the early stages and if disarmament were rapid. On balance, the savings from disarmament are unlikely to be as dramatic to begin with as is sometimes hoped, particularly when the cost of effective verification is taken into account. The initial expenditure on setting up a verification organization might be a particularly large item, and might fall to be met while national economies were in a difficult period of adjustment to the other strains imposed by disarmament. It should not be overlooked that a tentative estimate for installing a control system for a full test ban recommended by the experts in 1958 was in the neighbourhood of 2–3 billion dollars (say £700,000,000–£1,000,000,000), and for running it some 500 million dollars (say £178,000,000) a year. A proportion of this expenditure would have fallen on the United Kingdom. The cost of a world-wide international disarmament organization might or might not be of this or of a comparable order of magnitude. But it could hardly be small.

The point to be made here is a double one. On the one hand staff requirements for effective verification of total disarmament would be considerable and costly. On the other hand the cost of effective verification ought to be very much less than the amount at present allocated to defence in national budgets, and should represent a burden which would beyond question be financially bearable. How the cost would be divided would be a matter for negotiation, but the proportionate allocation country by country of the cost of maintaining the United Nations might afford some guide.

NUCLEAR TEST BAN

We have had a look at what is needed to verify observance of a disarmament agreement. The requirements for a partial or full nuclear test ban are quite different, consisting in the main of scientific instruments accurate at a distance instead of large numbers of foreign observers on the home ground.

A nuclear weapons test can be conducted either in the atmosphere, in space, underwater or underground; these are known as the four possible environments. If an illicit test in any one of these environments is not to pass unnoticed it must be recorded by scientific instruments appropriate for the environment, i.e. by one or more types of instruments if the test were carried out above ground, and by seismographs if carried out below ground or underwater. In the latter case hydroacoustic instruments would also apply. But all the instruments used record phenomena which may be generated by natural causes, as well as by nuclear explosions, and this unfortunate complication gives rise to a need for identifying the cause of the recorded event; it is not enough merely to obtain a record that may be characteristic of either a natural or man-made event. An underground event as recorded by a seismograph may be either an earthquake, or a nuclear or a chemical explosion. A nuclear explosion, a meteor, or a lightning storm may produce similar records on instrumentation used for recording nuclear explosions above ground. Hence the importance of being able to identify the cause of all recorded events. Clearly a mistaken identification could have very serious consequences, as for example when obligations under a test ban treaty may be involved. Yet, without very great care in identification, such mistakes can be made, as was shown by the French and the Swedes as recently as the Autumn of 1961. Mr. Khrushchev had at that time said the Soviet Union would shortly explode a 60-megaton bomb; and when, soon afterwards, the Swedish and French recording systems detected an earthquake and a small test at the same time, they prematurely and erroneously claimed to have recorded and identified the 60-megaton explosion. They were proved to be in error, and the 60-megaton explosion did not, in fact, take place until some time later.

Before 1958 nobody knew whether a system to verify a test ban could be devised at all. But the Experts' Conference at Geneva in that year agreed that it was possible, and specified an actual form of system.[1] They unanimously recommended an international control system operating:

(a) a world-wide network of about 170 land control posts separated by 1,000 kilometres in seismic areas and 1,700 kilometres in aseismic areas; these permanent control posts, each manned by about thirty technicians, would contain the most up-to-date scientific instruments and would report to Control Headquarters in a neutral country

(b) special aircraft sampling flights over the territory of any country in whose airspace it was suspected that a nuclear weapons test had taken place

(c) on-site inspection of all those events which could be detected by the network of fixed control posts but which could not positively be identified without on-site inspection as being either an earthquake or a man-made nuclear explosion.

The Experts estimated that while such a system could positively identify about 90 per cent a year of continental earthquakes above a significant size (5 kilotons) there might be from 20–100 seismic events of this size each year in any continental area which while detected could not be identified without on-site inspection by an International Control Commission. To detect and identify tests under the oceans instruments could be used which would monitor hydroacoustic waves, and ten internationally manned control ships would be needed. They agreed that the question of monitoring explosions in outer space required further study. It should be noted that in the case of the most difficult environment, namely underground, the Experts thought that recording instruments reasonably close to the epicentre of the event would provide the most reliable findings, and that for this reason the world-wide network of fixed internationally manned posts, supplemented when necessary by visits of inspection teams, would be necessary.

[1] See Appendix I

The report was accepted by the governments of the three nuclear powers at that time—the Soviet Union, the United States and the United Kingdom. The control system, accepted in principle by the Soviet Union, involved on-site inspection and air sampling flights over Soviet territory, in addition to fixed control posts in Soviet territory. It would have been costly and cumbersome, but the new and welcome fact was that a test ban could, it had now been agreed, be adequately verified.

In November 1958 negotiations opened at Geneva between the three nuclear governments to draft a treaty on the basis of the agreed technical report. In the course of the talks the question of the monitoring of high altitude tests was dealt with by a Technical Working Party of Experts from the United States, the United Kingdom and the Soviet Union which met in Geneva and reported to the 3-Power Conference on 10th July 1959. They made the following agreed recommendations on ways of detecting high altitude tests:

(1) a system of five to six earth satellites in orbits at altitudes of more than 30,000 kilometres (18,641 miles), equipped for the detection of gamma rays, neutrons, and soft X-rays;

(2) a satellite appropriately placed in relation to the earth's magnetic field, equipped with a simple electron counter to detect trapped electrons;

(3) a system of four satellites in appropriate solar orbits; and

(4) additional equipment at the ground control posts to aid in detection of space tests.

The assessments underlying some of these recommendations, namely those dealing with explosions behind the sun and the moon and the placing of satellites in orbit beyond the sun and the moon, were in part based on theoretical considerations in the light of the scientific knowledge then available.

An excellent and factual account of the negotiations up to September 1962 is contained in two volumes entitled 'Geneva Conference on the Discontinuance of Nuclear Weapon Tests—History and Analysis of Negotiations' and 'International Negotiations on Ending Nuclear Weapon Tests—September 1961–1962', issued as Department of State Publication 7258 Disarmament Series 4 of October 1961 and United States Arms Control and Disarmament Agency Publication 9, of October 1962. A further volume follows. It would be out of place here to try and give even a brief review of the course of the negotiations, but short accounts of the Soviet, American and British attitudes are contained in chapters 9, 10 and 11 of this book. It is sufficient to note the following salient points.

First, the Russians for three years admitted the principle of international verification. They accepted fifteen permanent control posts on Soviet territory, involving the permanent presence of some 200 foreign observers on Soviet territory, and a small quota of veto-free inspections (three a year). But from the outset they tried either to make verification unworkable or to reduce it below the minimum level at which it could be effective. Thus they attempted to obtain a veto on any inspection on Soviet territory, and agreements that heads of control posts in Russian territory should be Russians and the leaders and half the members of an inspection team should be Russians. In November 1961 the Soviet Union repudiated altogether their acceptance of control posts and on-site inspection in the Soviet Union, together with the whole of the 1958 Experts' Report. The United States and the United Kingdom, on the other hand, were prepared throughout to admit any degree of effective verification on their territory in order to make a total ban possible, and they remain so.

Second, while the political negotiations were continuing on the basis of the 1958 Experts Report, research was undertaken to try and improve the range and accuracy of scientific instruments particularly in the field of seismology. The Americans launched the Vela research programme, backed with ample funds but begun rather late. The British embarked on a parellel programme at the Atomic Weapons Research Establishment at Blackness which was somewhat starved for funds, but made some notable contributions. Both the Americans and the British repeatedly invited the Russians to co-operate in joint research, but without avail.

The result of this research was that by 1962 the problem of verification had become greatly simplified, and Washington and London felt justified in offering that, under any treaty, tests in the atmosphere, space and underwater might be monitored by national systems alone. But many Western scientists considered that after using all known methods for distinguishing earthquakes from explosions there would still be about thirty events a year due to shallow earthquakes of magnitude 4 or greater in the Soviet Union which could not be distinguished from nuclear explosions. Other Western scientists contended that the number must be doubled, while Soviet estimates of the number of doubtful events were lower.[1] By the end of 1962, the United States and the United Kingdom were asking for seven or perhaps fewer annual on-site inspections provided they could be effectively conducted, while the Soviet Union were speaking of only two or three, combined with three unmanned stations in Soviet territory, sometimes referred to as Black Boxes. The need for internationally manned control posts or air sampling flights by international aircraft, as well as control ships and an international satellite system, was no longer maintained.

The gap between Soviet and Western views on verification for tests in the atmosphere, in space and underwater had in fact been reduced to nil, and agreement on this was embodied in the Partial Test Ban Treaty of August 1963. The gap over verification of underground tests had been reduced to small proportions, but remained unbridged. By comparison with the requirements for verification of disarmament what is needed for a full test ban has become very small indeed. Soviet refusal to accept even this minimum, which is so much less than what they had been willing to accept for three years from 1958, is hard to comprehend and harder to justify.

[1] See an article by Sir John Cockcroft in *The Times*, 3rd September 1963

4

Verification Organizations

INTRODUCTION

THERE are a number of precedents between the two World Wars for disarmament negotiations; but the issue of verification organizations is new and there is little previous experience on which to build. Moreover the fact that verification organizations must be largely concerned with the possible concealment of nuclear tests, nuclear weapons, and fissile material means that entirely fresh ground must be broken.

It is clear that if governments are not prepared to accept the word of other governments as adequate satisfaction of observance of a treaty, there must be verification of some kind either by other countries acting nationally, or by an international organization. In the case of two countries, or two groups of countries, it is possible to conceive verification taking the form of national inspection visits by one side to the other. In 1959 in the early stages of the nuclear test ban negotiations such a system was apparently in the minds of the Russians. The Soviet delegate said on a number of occasions 'We will inspect you and you will inspect us'. There is no reason why such bilateral arrangements should in all circumstances be ruled out; but there are obvious objections. In the first place they would be hard to apply to multi-national agreements, indeed to any agreements which were not limited to two countries or two sides; and disarmament agreements must be multi-national. Second, bilateral verification systems would run into the difficulty that there would be no check upon the accuracy of the findings of the inspecting side. Hence the inspecting side could claim to have discovered an infraction and might proceed to denounce the agreement on the basis of this unsupported unilateral assertion. In the case of a test ban, to take one example, the consequences might be extremely serious for third countries who would have had no chance of satisfying themselves of the truth of accusations by one side or of denials by the other. Satisfaction on this point could only be obtained by some impartial international investigation.

Thus in the end there would be need for impartial international verification after all, and this would of course constitute a more reliable and effective system from the outset. Indeed in the case of suspicion of an illicit nuclear weapons test it may only be possible to establish the truth within a very short time after the event; that is to say, before radio-activity disperses, if the event occurred above ground, or before external and visible signs were eliminated, if the event had been carried out underground. If there is to be effective checking, it must in some cases be swift.

Study and discussion during the last few years have led to a general consensus that verification of a disarmament agreement must certainly be of an international character, and verification of a full test ban probably so in some degree.

Between 1958 and November 1961, when the Soviet Union repudiated it, there was in fact a wide measure of agreement between the two nuclear sides on the structure of an international verification system to monitor a full test ban. About two-thirds of the treaty had been drawn up in the form of seventeen agreed articles out of about twenty-four and two agreed annexes out of three.[1] Progress had also been made towards agreement on the remainder of the treaty. The shape and composition of the international control organization for a nuclear test ban which was so nearly hammered out then between the two sides forms to a large extent the basis of the proposals in both the Soviet and the American plans for an international verification organization for general and complete disarmament. It is worth examining more closely the points of agreement and disagreement which emerged.

ORGANIZATION FOR A NUCLEAR TEST BAN

The structure of an international verification organization for a nuclear test ban which began to take shape in the negotiations between the United States, the United Kingdom, and the Soviet Union from 1958 to 1962 was approximately as shown in the diagram on page 58.

As will be seen from the diagram, the verification organization was to consist of a control commission (perhaps with eleven members) and a chief executive officer or administrator, who would be the servant of the commission and would under their

[1] For the text of these see *Geneva Conference on the Discontinuance of Nuclear Weapons Tests: History and Analysis of Negotiations*, U.S. Department of State Publication 7258, Disarmament Series 4, October 1961, p. 437

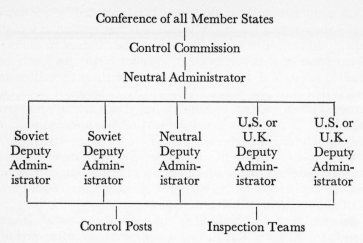

orders and directives administrate the headquarters, fixed control posts, inspection teams, and any other elements of the organization. He would have a balanced team of deputies. Over all these there would be a conference of parties of which all signatory states would be members.

This structure would in some respects resemble that of the United Nations, with the conference having a role somewhat analogous to that of the General Assembly, the control commission fulfilling some of the functions of the Security Council, and the administrator some of those of the Secretary General. But the resemblance is only partial since the control commission, unlike the Security Council, would have wide executive duties and would have a different voting procedure; while the administrator as distinct from the U.N. Secretary General, upon whom the Charter has conferred certain independent functions, would be in all respects the servant of the control commission.

If such a control system is to function with adequate effectiveness it is essential first, that no state or individual should be able to veto an inspection visit or the findings of an inspection team; second, that all states should give freedom of access to elements of the control organization in carrying out the duties entrusted to them (but no others); and third, that the administrator should be able to carry out the duties laid upon him and the directives given him (but no others) without any state or individual being able to veto or obstruct either him or his subordinates.

On each of these essential points difficulties arose which were only partially resolved before the Soviet Union repudiated in November 1961 all that had been settled. The Soviet government stood out at first for the power to veto any inspection on its territory, but eventually agreed to a quota of veto-free inspections and offered an annual figure of three; freedom of access within strict limits was agreed for a veto-free inspection, but the area round the epicentre of an event to be inspected was never fully settled, the West asking for an area of up to 500 square kilometres and the Soviet government seeking to limit it to an area of 200 square kilometres.[1] The issue whether either nuclear side would possess a built-in veto by being able to count on a blocking number of votes must obviously depend upon the composition of the commission. A composition of four from each nuclear side and three neutrals, and a voting system of a simple majority, would not confer a built-in veto on either side since neither could ever block a vote without carrying two of the neutral members with them. This principle, and indeed the actual composition of 4–4–3, was eventually agreed between the two sides.[2] The main point is that no individual member, and neither nuclear side, should possess either an open or a built-in veto; although there may, of course, be special agreement for a power of veto on a particular subject such as the budget or revision of the treaty.

The third requirement, namely that the administrator should be able to carry out the duties laid upon him without obstruction, gave rise to differences between the two nuclear sides that were never solved. The Soviet Union from the outset showed concern over the nationality, powers and reliability of a single administrator, but were content for over two years with the position that he should be entirely under the orders of the commission, and should be a neutral. Mr. Tsarapkin, the Soviet delegate, stated in January 1960: 'Out of the three thousand million human beings on earth we shall always be able to find someone on whom you and we can agree'.[3] On the 3rd February 1960 he said: 'We still consider, however, that in neutral countries it will always be possible to find a person, a really neutral person, who can be used for the job of carrying out the duties of adminis-

[1] *Ibid.*, p. 107
[2] *Ibid.*, p. 196
[3] 3-Power Test Ban Conference, 153rd session, p. 15

trator'.[1] On 21st June he repeated that 'It will always be possible to discover in the world a person acceptable to both sides for nomination for the post as administrator'.[2] But on 21st March 1961 the Russians' attitude changed; they said that the actions of the Secretary General of the United Nations, Dag Hammarskjold, over the Congo had not been impartial and that the system of a single administrator for a control organization for a nuclear test ban was no longer acceptable to them. Instead there must be a troika or triumvirate of three administrators, one from each nuclear side and one neutral. The three must act unanimously. In other words any of the three could veto the execution by the control staff of any action whatsoever. To meet Soviet fears that a single administrator might in fact exceed his powers or prove partial to one side or the other the United States and the United Kingdom proposed that the administrator could be removed from office by a veto-free vote of seven members of the commission, which would mean that neither nuclear side could veto his removal either directly or indirectly; on a commission of four members from each nuclear side and three neutrals, the neutrals would have the deciding vote if the nuclear sides were split.

These points have a relevance beyond their immediate context since in one form or another they may arise in the case of an international disarmament organization for general and complete disarmament. We shall revert to them later.

Meanwhile, the United States and the United Kingdom's new alternative proposal of 27th August 1962, for a treaty banning nuclear tests in all environments, embodied the principle that national means of detection could be relied upon sufficiently for detecting and identifying tests in the atmosphere, space, and under the oceans, and in some but not all cases underground. It proposed a simplified control organization to carry out the more limited verification duties inherent in this approach to a comprehensive test ban. (The alternative proposal for a partial ban made by the United States and the United Kingdom on the same day, and accepted by the Soviet Union in substance a year later, required no international verification system. Reliance for the partial ban is on national detection systems alone.)

Under these simplified proposals there would be a verification

[1] Ibid., 165th session, pp. 11–12
[2] Ibid., 216th session, p. 47

system with an international staff headed by an international scientific commission of fifteen members, four from or chosen by each nuclear side and seven nominated jointly, and a conference of parties. The duties of the verification system would be to co-ordinate reports from national detection stations and to organize on-site inspection on the comparatively few occasions required. The commission would supervise the maintenance by national detection stations of the necessary scientific standards. These stations would be pledged to maintain continuous operation of equipment as the commission deems desirable at each station including apparatus for the collection of radio-active debris, for the recording of fluorescence of the upper atmosphere, visible light, cosmic noise absorption, telluric currents, resonance scattering of sunlight, acoustic waves, seismic waves, and electro-magnetic signals.

The international scientific commission would vote by a simple majority unless otherwise provided, and on this basis the composition of 4–4–7 would ensure that neither nuclear side possesses a built-in veto.

ORGANIZATION FOR A TREATY FOR GENERAL AND COMPLETE DISARMAMENT

The main features of an international verification organization which had begun to take shape between the two nuclear sides in the test ban negotiations are embodied in the proposals for an international disarmament organization contained in both the Soviet and the American plans.[1] Both sets of proposals provide for a conference of parties, a control council, and staff recruited on an international basis. The vexed question of what the organization will be empowered to verify is outside the scope of this chapter, and is discussed elsewhere. Leaving this aside, two of the main issues which caused so much difficulty in the test ban negotiations for a verification organization remain a shaded area—namely the composition of and voting system in the control council, and whether there is to be a single administrator whose work as a servant of the control council cannot be obstructed.

The Soviet plan provides for a council consisting of the five states which are permanent members of the U.N. Security Council and an unspecified number of other states elected by

[1] See part 1, Article 2 (3) and part 5, Articles 40–42 of the Soviet Plan and Section G of Stage I of the American plan in Appendices IV and V

the conference for a period of two years. The composition of the
council must ensure proper representation of the three principal
groups of states existing in the world. Voting on procedural
matters is to be taken by a simple majority, and on other matters
by a two-thirds majority. Thus the exact composition of the
council, which is important in connection with the existence or
not of a built-in veto, is left open for negotiation; but it may be
inferred from the wording of Article 42 of the Soviet plan that
no built-in veto is contemplated. Article 42(d) provides that
among the duties of the council will be to

> 'review the results of the implementation of the measures included
> in each stage of general and complete disarmament with a view to
> reporting on them to the states parties to the treaty, and to the
> Security Council and the General Assembly of the United Nations.'

The Soviet plan skates over the question whether there is to be
a single administrator or a troika, but Article 2 (4) provides that

> 'in all countries parties to the treaty the international disarmament
> organization shall have its own staff recruited internationally and
> in such a way as to ensure the adequate representation on it of all
> three existing groups of states.'

It appears from these provisions that it will be the function of
the control council and not of the administrator or administrators to report to states parties to the treaty and to the Security
Council, and perhaps also to the General Assembly, any breach
or non-fulfilment of obligations. Such a decision would presumably not be considered procedural and therefore would require
a two-thirds majority on the control council, who would by their
vote be placing on record their own view whether a breach or
failure to observe obligations had taken place.

The Soviet plan also provides in Article 1 (3) that the states
parties to the treaty should undertake

> 'to carry out general and complete disarmament simultaneously, in
> three consecutive stages, as is set forth in Parts II, III & IV, of the
> present treaty. Transition to a subsequent stage of disarmament shall
> take place after adoption by the international disarmament organiza-
> tion of a decision confirming that all disarmament measures of the
> preceding stage have been carried out and verified, and that any add-
> itional verification measures recognized to be necessary for the next
> stage have been prepared and can, when appropriate, be put into
> operation.'

As we have seen above, Article 42 2(d) lays this task on the control council. If the control council were unable to find that all disarmament measures of the preceding stage had been carried out and verified, the question would presumably be referred to the U.N. Security Council in accordance with the provision in Article 40 that

'all questions for the safeguarding of international peace and security which may arise in the course of the implementation of the present treaty, including preventive and enforcement measures, shall be decided by the Security Council in conformity with its powers in the United Nations Charter.'

On the Security Council the five permanent members have a veto.

The United States proposals are somewhat different. They will be found in section G of stage I of the American plan. This provides for a single administrator acting under the direction of the control council (G 4 (3)). Among his functions would be (G 7 (b):

'making available to the parties to the treaty data produced by the verification arrangements'

and (G 7 (d)):

'making reports to the control council on the progress of disarmament measures and of their verification and on the installation and operation of the verification arrangements.'

Under G 6 (e) the control council would consider reports of the administrator on the progress of disarmament measures and on their verification, and on the installation and operation of the verification arrangements. The parties would therefore receive direct from the administrator reports on possible breaches in parallel with consideration of such reports by the control council. Finally, section I provides that if one or more of the permanent members of the control council is not satisfied that all undertakings in each stage had been carried out in that stage, the question would go to the Security Council. In practice, therefore, under both plans permanent members of the control council would have a veto in the question of a breach or non-fulfilment of the treaty, since they could ask that the matter be considered by the Security Council where they, as permanent members, possess veto powers; but the American plan provides for discussion of other possibilities (Stage I, H, Stage II G and Stage III G and H):

The American proposals differ from the Soviet proposals in giving (in G 3) specific functions and powers to the international disarmament organization to verify not only destruction of weapons but non-replacement, production, levels of remainders and non-concealment.

The American plan leaves open for negotiation the composition of and voting system in the control commission.

ACTION IN THE EVENT OF A BREACH

An essential issue in considering a verification organization, whether for a test ban or for general and complete disarmament, is the action to be taken in the event of accusation of a breach by one party against another, or of a finding of a breach by the verification organization. It is obviously desirable that there should be machinery of some kind to consider an accusation by one party against another party, and provision for some form of impartial international investigation and judgement on who is in the right and who is in the wrong. Both investigation and an expression of view can in the first instance be made the responsibility of the administrator and staff of the verification organization, acting under the instructions of the commission; and indeed this is their *raison d'être*. Under the Western proposals the administrator would report both to the control council and to all member states simultaneously; under the Soviet proposal reports from the staff would apparently go first to the council alone. If the matter were pushed still further there could under either plan be a discussion by a conference of parties, and if necessary by the U.N. Security Council, and perhaps by the General Assembly. The same procedure could and would no doubt be followed if the accusation or finding of a breach originated from the organization's own staff. In either event the ultimate question is what action should be taken if a breach has been established. Efforts would no doubt first be concentrated upon restoring the situation. But if these failed there would in the last resort be two main alternative courses. The first would be that other members would exercise the natural right, probably written into the treaty, to withdraw from their obligations and to resume their freedom of action, whether to test or to rearm. The treaty would thus lapse, but no direct action or sanction would be taken against the violator. The second alternative is that all the resources of the Charter, or of other arrangements agreed upon in a treaty, should become operative up to and including the use of international force against a violator.

NUCLEAR TEST BAN

The sanction of the right of withdrawal by other parties was the course contemplated during the three-power negotiations for a nuclear test ban from 1958–61. It was embodied in an agreed article which read as follows:

> 'This treaty shall remain in force indefinitely subject to the inherent right of a party to withdraw and be relieved of obligations hereunder if the provisions of the treaty and its annexes, including those providing for the timely installation and effective operation of the control system are not being fulfilled and observed.'

Who would be the judge whether the provisions of the treaty and its annexes were not being fulfilled and observed was not laid down. The Russians showed at one time a disposition to demand a vote in the control commission, and beyond that in the Security Council, where they would have a veto. The West were not prepared to agree that the party guilty of a breach should be able to veto the finding of a breach. They were agreeable to discussion in the control commission, but wanted to be sure that findings about a breach would be communicated to the parties direct by the administrator. The next step or steps would be up to the parties concerned. Neither side considered that a breach of a test ban should be dealt with by the use of armed force. The principal and perhaps only sanction foreseen was that embodied in the agreed duration article, namely that other countries would be free to resume testing themselves.

In the Western draft treaty of 27th August 1962 for a ban on all nuclear tests in all environments (E.N.D.C./58), under simplified verification procedures, there were different withdrawal provisions. These were, briefly, that in the event of a breach any party to the treaty might ask for a conference of all parties which would examine the facts and assess the significance of the situation. After the conclusion of the conference or at the end of sixty days any party could give notice of withdrawal from the treaty. The partial Test Ban Treaty signed on 5th August 1963 contains a still more simple withdrawal clause. Article 4 reads:

> 'This treaty shall be of unlimited duration. Each party shall, in exercising its national sovereignty, have the right to withdraw from the treaty, if it decides that extraordinary events, related to the subject matter of this treaty, have jeopardised the supreme interests of its country.

D.V.–E

It shall give notice of such withdrawal to all other parties to the treaty three months in advance.'

GENERAL AND COMPLETE DISARMAMENT

The action to be taken in the event of a breach of a treaty for general and complete disarmament might be very different. We have already seen that both sides agree that an accusation or finding of a breach should be considered by the U.N. Security Council (under the American plan, different arrangements might be worked out), and Article 40 of the Soviet plan makes it clear that the Soviet government have in mind Chapter 7 of the Charter, dealing with threats to international peace and security, under which the five permanent members have a veto. This would of course mean that no action could ever be taken by the Security Council over a breach or alleged breach of a disarmament agreement against the wishes or interests of any of the five permanent members. Such a provision might be considered unsatisfactory by smaller states, and perhaps by some of the permanent members.

The gravity of the situation created by a breach or an alleged breach would depend partly on whether it occurred in stage I, II or III of the disarmament process, or after disarmament was completed. If it took place at an early stage every effort would no doubt be made to settle the matter otherwise than by termination of the treaty or by force, and to restore progress towards disarmament. If the breach were at a late stage in the disarmament process, or after supposed completion, grave action might no doubt be contemplated. Should these efforts fail, the ultimate sanction might be armed action against the violator by a U.N. peace-keeping force; but if the threat of escalation to this degree of action is to be credible, there must be no right of veto on the use of the force.

These matters require further consideration in chapter 7 dealing with peace-keeping machinery. Meanwhile, it may be desirable to look next at the question of balance throughout the disarmament process, since it has given rise to much argument and difficulty.

5

Keeping the Balance

NO. 5 of the American-Soviet agreed principles of 20th September 1961 reads as follows:

'All measures of general and complete disarmament should be balanced so that at no stage of the implementation of the treaty could any state or group of states gain military advantage and that security is ensured equally for all.'

This principle is specifically written into both the Soviet and the American disarmament plans (Article 1 (4) of the Soviet plan and B (2) of the American plan).

Neither plan proposes to alter the existing levels, and therefore the existing balance, of manpower and armaments, before the process of disarmament begins. On the contrary, both plans involve starting from the balance of manpower and armaments which would exist at the date of the signature of the treaty, and maintaining that balance throughout the process of disarmament until the end. Both plans provide for the process of disarmament to be carried out in three consecutive stages; the Soviet plan would spread these stages over about four years, with perhaps eighteen months for the first stage, and the American plan over about nine years, that is to say three years or so for each stage, provided there are no delays between stages.

In both plans there would thus be a common starting point, namely existing levels of manpower and of both nuclear and conventional weapons, and a common finishing point, namely total disarmament apart from small militia forces. The issue of maintaining balance arises during the four or nine years, or whatever other period may be agreed upon, during which disarmament is taking place, and balance must be observed throughout.

How far does each of the two plans in fact preserve the principle of balance? Let us look at the American plan first. This seeks to maintain balance throughout the whole process of disarmament by reduction of manpower to progressively lower but equal levels, and roughly speaking by equal percentage cuts stage by stage both for nuclear and conventional armaments; and above all by phasing the elimination of nuclear weapons and nuclear delivery vehicles to run parallel with the building up of improved peacekeeping machinery and an effective peace-keeping force. The exact means proposed for achieving this objective are summarized in introductory sections A and B of the American plan. Finally, by providing for all the four necessary forms of verification—destruction, non-replacement, remainders and concealment—it affords means of assurance for all states that the balance is not being clandestinely upset. It is interesting to note that the Russians have not alleged that the American plan would create imbalance at any stage, and indeed any such criticism would be hard to substantiate. The Soviet attack on the plan has been based on the allegations that it demands too much verification too soon, and that it does not go far enough fast enough.

The Soviet plan is conceived on entirely different lines and heavily loads stage I which is to be completed within about two years or less. It provides that in stage I all foreign bases shall be eliminated and all troops withdrawn from foreign countries. This would of course mean that in stage I all American and Canadian forces overseas would be withdrawn to North America and all British forces to the United Kingdom, and that the entire military apparatus of N.A.T.O. would be dismantled. The process would be world-wide and would cover the with-drawal of Soviet forces from the satellite countries, and all American forces from the Far East and South East Asia as well as from western and southern Europe. In addition, the Soviet plan first proposed the destruction in stage I of all nuclear delivery vehicles, which were defined as including all rockets, military aircraft, surface warships, submarines and artillery systems capable of delivering nuclear weapons, together with their depots and production centres. Actual nuclear weapons would be retained until stage II. The Soviet government amended this proposal in 1962 to provide for the retention until the end of stage II of a strictly limited number of intercontinental missiles, anti-missile missiles and anti-aircraft missiles by the Americans and themselves exclusively in their own territory; and amended it again in 1963 to extend this provision into stage III. In spite of persistent and friendly questioning at Geneva, the Russians declined to specify a number; but it has been guessed that they had a maximum of some 50 or so inter-continental ballistic missiles in mind. A summary of the Soviet proposals for stage I and for the other two stages will be found in article 1 of the Soviet plan.

Whether stage I of the Soviet plan, unless amended, would leave an approximately equal balance of manpower and conventional weapons between the N.A.T.O. and the Warsaw Pact countries at once gave rise to protracted argument. The Soviet government claim that N.A.T.O. resources in manpower and conventional weapons are equal if not superior to those of the Warsaw Pact powers. The West maintain that it is doubtful whether this is true of readily available manpower if reserves are counted, and that it is certainly not true of tanks and a number of other important weapons; but that in any case the geographic position of the Soviet Union would enable her to concentrate forces at any point of her choice and strike effectively at countries in northern, central and southern Europe before American, Canadian and British help could be brought back across the seas. They argue that in fact Soviet forces could reach the Bay of Biscay before adequate American forces could be in position to help effectively to stop them; and that *a fortiori* military objectives such as Berlin, Norway, West Germany or Greece could beyond doubt be overrun by a determined Soviet thrust.

The Western view was put with force and clarity by the American representative at Geneva, Mr. Arthur Dean, at the 92nd plenary meeting on 14th December 1962, in these words:

'United States officials will not be impressed by exhortations, such as those from the Soviet bloc delegations here, that the highest norm or standard for disarmament negotiations must be the elimination of the risk of nuclear war in the first stage. Eliminate it we intend to do in our overall disarmament programme, in our three stages, in harmony with the objectives set forth in the Joint Statement of Agreed Principles, but of this you may be sure: we shall not be led into palpably one sided moves at the beginning of the disarmament process which would clearly favour the Soviet bloc and jeopardise the security of the free world.

The first stage is not our ultimate goal: our goal is rather a complete programme of total and complete disarmament in a peaceful world. There is nothing sacrosanct about either the measures of the first stage or its duration. That is a portion of a total programme, to be executed in a time period subject to negotiation, and proposals regarding its length have already been subject to change in some instances as a result of our deliberations in this 18-Nation Committee.'

Mr. Dean went on to state that disarmament schemes which would radically alter the world balance of power during the process of disarmament were not acceptable, nor would the United States consent to any plan which would mean her leaving her Western allies in the lurch. He said:

> 'It should by now be clear to one and all that no amount of debate and casuistry will be able to convince the United States to abandon its allies in the West and elsewhere to the mercies of the Soviet military machine. Let me be very clear: we will not allow N.A.T.O. to be fragmented, as would be the case under the Soviet proposals, into fifteen isolated military compartments, forbidden from joint activity and co-operation and separated into split North American and European districts. We shall not permit that situation to arise while the mighty Soviet military machine remains essentially intact in its own part of Eastern Europe under a single and unified command. That is especially true when, whatever may be the approximate nominal equality in manpower when totals are cumulated in Eastern and Western Europe, the clear superiority of the Soviet Union alone in tanks, artillery, and other armoured vehicles over combined N.A.T.O. forces is quite substantial—I repeat, quite substantial . . . Without such bases, the Soviet superiority in conventional strength would become overwhelmingly great . . .'

To sum up, there are two major objections to the Soviet plan on the score that it fails to preserve balance. First, the proposals in stage I would result in a radical change in favour of the Soviet Union, both of the military and political balance. If the process of disarmament were to be halted at the end of Soviet stage I even without hostilities breaking out, the Soviet government would have altered the whole world picture to their advantage. It must be recognized that there is an inevitable risk that the process of disarmament may not be continuous, and may be halted temporarily or permanently before it is completed. This would happen, for example, if there were disagreement at the end of stage I or stage II that the measures provided for in that stage had not been carried out by some or all states. Moreover, bad faith or a worsening of the international situation might interrupt the process at any time. This makes it the more necessary that there should be no moment of imbalance when it might suit one or more states to contract out on some pretext or other, and so perpetuate the advantage thus gained. For example, it might benefit the Soviet Union to contract out as soon as all American forces are withdrawn from overseas, and all foreign bases closed down, unless a stable balance were assured at that point by some other means such as an effective peace-keeping force which would compensate for the vacuum created. Under the Soviet plan this moment would be reached by the end of stage I, that is to say, within about two years or less.

The second major objection is that the Soviet plan does not, as it stands, admit during any of the three stages verification of non-concealment, or adequate verification of non-replacement or remainders. Yet if no adequate verification is permitted on these points, no state could feel certain at any time that balance was being maintained; even the reviews at the end of stages I and II provided for in the Soviet as well as in the American plan could not possibly be meaningful. This point is obviously crucial. Verification is clearly the key to balance, as to so much else.

Some of the grounds of objection to the Soviet plan in respect of balance could perhaps be removed by compromises which ought not to be too difficult to work out. There ought, for instance, to be room for negotiating a different allocation or spread of measures—measure X in stage II instead of stage I; measure Y spread over the three stages, and so on. If both sides negotiated in good faith, adjustments of this kind ought to be possible. But in making them, account must be taken of the fact that a number of the measures involved can never be as cut-and-dried as might appear superficially. For example, it is impossible to make a satisfactory definition of a nuclear delivery vehicle (were the Paris taxis that took Gallieni's troops to the battle of the Marne civil or military vehicles?). A nuclear weapon can be delivered by civil aircraft and not only by military aircraft; some forms of artillery can fire both conventional and nuclear shells, and so forth. These considerations reinforce the argument for reductions of all weapons right across the board in successive stages rather than for attempts, so likely to fail, to abolish whole categories of weapons at one particular stage.

But however far it may be possible, as well as so clearly desirable, to adjust other differences between the two plans in respect of balance, there is one point, apart from verification, which is basic. Unless and until it is resolved, other issues are relatively minor. This point is, whether countries will ever give up nuclear weapons and means of delivering them, when it is their possession by both sides that serves to keep the peace today, except when they are assured that other and reliable forms of keeping the balance of peace have been set up.

The hard fact must surely be recognized that peace is at

present kept, certainly in western Europe and wherever the essential interests of the two nuclear sides are at stake, by the threat that any military action is likely to escalate into an all-out nuclear exchange. It is sometimes assumed that this need not and will not be the case, and that even war in which the two nuclear sides were involved might be decided by conventional weapons alone, without the use of nuclear weapons any more than of poison gas or germ warfare. But this is not the view expressed by the Soviet leaders, who have twice gone on record to the contrary. The Moscow statement of 30th August 1961 on the Soviet decision to resume nuclear tests at that time contained the following passage:

'The experience of history teaches that it has never been possible to keep the fire of war within predetermined limits. Wars have in-exorable severe laws of their own. An aggressor starts a war to bring his victim to its knees and to impose his will on it. But even the aggressor is aware that in the case of defeat the fate that he was preparing for his victim will befall him. Therefore each state that takes part in the war, regardless of the fact whether it attacks or defends, will stop at nothing for attaining victory and will not accept defeat without having used and spent all means in its possession of waging war. Under these conditions any armed conflict, even insignificant at first, would inevitably grow into a universal rocket and nuclear war should the nuclear powers have been drawn into it.'[1]

On 5th September 1961 Mr. Khrushchev in an interview with Cyrus Sulzberger of the *New York Times* said:

'We shall never be the first to start a war against any country. We want to live in peace with all nations and do not want to attack anyone . . . But I must say that it would be untimely at present to say that in the event of war, atomic weapons would not be em-ployed. Anyone who made such a statement would turn out to be untruthful, even though when making such a pledge he is sincere and does not lie. Let us assume both sides were to promise not to employ nuclear weapons, but retained their stockpiles. What would happen if the imperialists unleashed war? In such a war if any side should feel it was losing, would it not use nuclear weapons to avoid defeat? It would undoubtedly use its nuclear bombs.

Furthermore, let me refer to this example; at the close of World War II the United States was considerably stronger than Japan and was waging successful offensive action against it. Yet, to bring victory closer, the United States dropped atomic bombs on

[1] Press Release 190 of Soviet Embassy in Washington, 1961

Japanese cities. All this goes to show that if atomic weapons are preserved and if war is unleashed it will be a thermonuclear war.'

Unless we are to disregard the Soviet view—and it is a view which commands considerable support in the West also—it follows that whatever else we might do in making adjustments in the levels of conventional forces, we must not heedlessly tamper with the mechanism which convinces us that a minor military action could escalate into all-out nuclear war; a manifest mechanism of escalation is at present an essential ingredient in national security and, indeed, in the maintenance of world peace. This situation is often called 'the balance of terror'; it might be better termed 'the balance of prudence'. If it is to be replaced, it should be by something more stable and not less stable.

In Europe, at any rate, the presence of conventional forces (including American and British contingents) ensures that all countries in both the N.A.T.O. and Warsaw Pact alliances realize that an attack on any N.A.T.O. country would necessarily involve the N.A.T.O. alliance as a whole. The conventional forces are or ought to be at sufficient strength to make it possible for N.A.T.O. to identify an aggression and resist it to the degree necessary to pose the aggressor with the choice either of persisting in his aggression and risking escalation to all-out nuclear warfare, or of giving up his designs. Thus, an important part of the escalation mechanism is played by the presence of tactical nuclear weapons on the ground in areas which might be attacked.

But if nuclear weapons were given up the situation would change. Once tactical nuclear weapons were withdrawn, once the use of long range nuclear weapons in sufficient quantities to inflict unacceptable damage were ruled out by the progress of disarmament, the essential ingredient in the existing balance of prudence would be removed. If because of geography and logistics, and the possibility of concealing nuclear weapons, a balance of conventional weapons cannot by itself be made stable, the only new ingredient in the mix which could remedy the imbalance created by the elimination of nuclear weapons and means of delivery would be improved peace-keeping machinery and an effective international peace-keeping force. Unless and until such a force can begin to take practical and reliable shape, sufficient nuclear weapons and nuclear delivery vehicles to inflict unacceptable damage can only be eliminated at the cost of upsetting the balance that keeps the peace. Either, therefore, there must be general and complete disarmament with adequate verification and an effective peace-keeping force, or the process of disarmament cannot safely be pushed beyond a certain point. For a gap in time between the elimination of sufficient nuclear weapons and means of delivery, and the creation of effective peace-keeping machinery, would be too dangerous to peace.

6

Adequate and Bearable?

NO nation enjoys the prospect of international observers
stationed in or visiting its territory. But in politics if you
will the end you must will the means. To secure a reliable and
complete test ban and a reliable treaty for partial or total disarmament, the United States and the United Kingdom are
willing to pay the price of accepting on their territories international verification which will be sufficiently rigorous to afford
reasonable certainty that they are observing their obligations.
They require this of others and they accept it themselves.

The Soviet Union accepts the principle of international verification for disarmament; but alleges that it can be misused for
espionage purposes, and is concerned to reduce its incidence in
practice to the minimum it considers to be bearable. For a nuclear
test ban the Soviet government accepted the principle of international verification in 1958; repudiated it in 1961 on the ground
that national means of verification had become scientifically
adequate; and early in 1963 half-heartedly offered again to
accept a minimum, which it withdrew before long. By the
summer of 1963 the Soviet Union, the United States and Great
Britain agreed to a partial test ban without international verification, omitting tests underground. The distinction was that
while other sorts of tests could by that date be adequately identified by national as contrasted with international means, this was
not yet true of underground tests which could not always be
identified without some international on-site inspections which
Moscow was no longer prepared to accept as bearable.

The final judgement of what is 'adequate' and what is 'bearable' can only be subjective. These concepts are not absolute and
cannot be defined in terms of science or measured exactly by any
practical yardstick. What can be said is that the judgement of
what is adequate is broadly speaking a matter for the states
which demand that there must be reliable international verification; and that 'adequate verification' can be interpreted either
in terms of degree of certainty afforded—whether 100 per cent,
80 per cent, or some other degree—or alternatively in terms of

deterrent effect on a potential violator. The judgement of what is bearable is of special concern to the states which dislike international verification, either on grounds of interference with national sovereignty or of risk of espionage. The general pattern of negotiation between 1958 onwards proved to be that what the West considered adequate the Communist countries rejected as unbearable; what the Communist countries considered bearable the West rejected as inadequate. The task of negotiation has been and must remain to try and hammer out arrangements which both sides will end by accepting as being bearable as well as adequate. In this task unaligned countries who are interested in both sides of the coin can be of material assistance; and the eight uncommitted states represented at the 18-power Disarmament Conference at Geneva have played a useful role. They have provided a background of representative unaligned opinion against which the views of the committed and more heavily armed powers could be developed and weighed; they have also thus been given and have used the opportunity to make contributions and proposals of their own.

Since the assessment of what is adequate and bearable cannot be absolute but only subjective, the judgement either for a test ban or disarmament must be a political and not a scientific or military one. It is the duty of scientists and military experts to advise their governments on what is practicable and what degree of risk of evasion is involved, but at that point their duty ceases. It is for governments to weigh these risks in the light of scientific and military advice, and having done so to take the political decision of what they accept or reject. The decision ought to be taken against the scientific and technical background and thus be based upon it; but the decision itself must be a political act.

NUCLEAR TEST BAN

As has been seen, the United States and the United Kingdom by 1962 had accepted that national means of detection and identification for tests in the atmosphere, in space and under the oceans were adequate; in August 1962 they offered to conclude a treaty covering these three environments with no on-site inspection or over-flight, and in July 1963 concluded a test ban on this basis. For the underground environment the United States and the United Kingdom had already accepted that a small annual deterrent quota of international on-site inspection would be adequate. By the end of 1962 they were proposing a quota of seven or less, involving visits of small numbers of international staff for short periods. Since the number of detected but unidentified underground events in each country varies from year to year it is impossible to express as a fixed annual percentage what proportion of unidentified events would be inspected by a deterrent quota of say seven, but the percentage might work out in any given year as somewhere between 1 in 4 and 1 in 10. Because, however, a violator would probably wish to conduct a series of tests and not a single test, his chances of being detected would be correspondingly higher.

If scientific instruments can be developed which will identify as well as detect all underground events, no on-site inspections would ever be necessary. The Soviet government claims to possess such instruments, but refuses to demonstrate them to others. If in fact such instruments become known to the West, the problem of on-site inspection for a ban on underground tests would cease to exist, assuming they could distinguish not only between earthquakes and explosions but also between nuclear and chemical explosions. But on present scientific evidence it may be doubted whether complete certainty of identification in all cases by distant instruments alone is likely, since as instruments become more sensitive they detect smaller and smaller events and more and more of them, still without being able to identify all of the increased numbers they detect. It may therefore prove that there will always remain some detected but unidentified underground events although of smaller and smaller size. If so, this is perhaps an argument for grasping the nettle now.

However that may be, the requirements of the United States and the United Kingdom for adequate international verification for a comprehensive nuclear test ban had by 1963 become minimal. But experience had shown only too clearly that the Soviet government constantly dismissed any fresh compromise offer as being inadequate and continued to raise objection to every scaling down of verification requirements as still being too onerous. In the attempt to work out arrangements which both sides could accept as being at once adequate and bearable the United States and the United Kingdom made the following additional proposals to meet any legitimate fears on the part of the Soviet government that international verification could constitute an espionage risk. First, it had been agreed from the outset that visiting on-site inspection teams could only visit areas indicated by scientific instruments as the site of a detected but unidentified event, and the West offered to limit the area to a maximum of 500 square kilometres. Next, they offered to agree that international inspection teams could be transported to the areas blindfolded in a Soviet aircraft flown by a Soviet pilot. They further suggested that since 85 per cent of the area of the Soviet Union is free from earthquakes and only 15 per cent is seismic, the small annual quota might be mainly concentrated in the seismic areas, leaving 85 per cent of the Soviet Union almost free from on-site inspection. They also expressed their willingness to embody in a verification system unmanned detection stations, containing recording instruments but no resident staff. Such unmanned stations could not be a direct substitute for on-site inspection. But if situated in the right areas their recordings could provide a valuable check on the accuracy of reports from manned national stations. Thus if there were to be six or eight unmanned stations in the Soviet Union, or even only three as the Soviet government offered, their recordings could be flown to an international control centre outside the Soviet Union and used to check the accuracy of the Soviet national reporting system as well as perhaps helping to identify comparatively local seismic events; the increased reliability thus given for a verification system might enable fewer on-site inspections to be considered as adequate. Members of the staff of the international verification organization would of course have to pay occasional visits to the stations to collect the records, and to service them. On top of all this the United States and the United Kingdom had from the outset agreed that the host state could attach any number of its own observers to international inspection teams to ensure that they do not indulge in espionage.

A small annual quota of inspection visits with the above safeguards against misuse for espionage obviously constitutes an extremely modest assessment of what is adequate. It involves no inspection of factories, no control of airfields, no checking of frontiers, no inspectors at liberty to travel around the country. It must be borne in mind that Western public opinion, and not least the United States Congress, was justifiably outraged at the bad faith of the Soviet government in resuming nuclear weapon testing unilaterally in September 1961 after a suspension of nearly three years by both negotiating sides, and while talks for a ban were continuing. The lengthy series of massive tests which the Soviet Union proceeded to conduct must have taken a year or perhaps more to prepare. During that period the two Western countries were negotiating in good faith with the Soviet Union and refraining from testing themselves. They suddenly found themselves confronted with a situation in which the Soviet government by deception had gained experience which they themselves could only match through an emergency test programme in the following year. This drove home the lesson that voluntary declarations of abstention from nuclear weapon testing without any formal treaty obligation and without any international verification confer little or no security against sudden resumption of testing. President Kennedy summed up American feeling by saying, 'If the other man fools you once it is his fault; if you allow him to fool you twice it is your own fault'. A full nuclear test ban without adequate safeguards could never be expected to pass the American Senate; nor, if it did so, to outlast the first suspicion of a breach by the other side.

It must also be remembered that from the end of 1958 until November 1961 the Soviet Government had publicly committed themselves to the position that a degree of control for a nuclear test ban much more rigorous than the above was bearable and fully compatible with Soviet security. They had themselves formally proposed the principle of a small quota of on-site inspections, and had offered fifteen control posts in the Soviet Union largely manned by foreign nationals. On this basis two-thirds of a treaty had been agreed. It is difficult to understand why, when for three years more rigorous international verification involving several times as many foreigners on Soviet soil was bearable, less stringent verification should be unbearable and unthinkable in 1963. The Soviet contention is that any on-site inspection had been rendered unnecessary by the development of more accurate scientific instruments. But since they decline to say what these instruments were, and since the West does not possess such instruments, this contention does not advance matters. Nor in view of the safeguards described above is it easy to take the pretension of espionage seriously. The risk is clearly very small if it exists at all. For three years from 1958–61 the Soviet Union stated that they were prepared to accept the principle of on-site inspection together with any risk involved; the West are prepared to do so now. It is hard to see how a government could be considered sincere in arguing that a full test ban is of importance for the peace and safety of mankind if they were not prepared in 1963 to accept a lesser risk of espionage than they had been willing to accept for three years previously.

GENERAL AND COMPLETE DISARMAMENT

The difficulties inherent in making international verification of general and complete disarmament both adequate and bearable are vastly greater than for a comprehensive nuclear test ban. To be adequate, verification must, in the view of the West, provide reliable evidence that all countries are observing their obligations to destroy weapons, not to replace them or produce them, not to exceed agreed limits of remainders, and not to conceal arms. Both sides provide in their draft treaties for disarmament in three stages; stage I to be completed before stage II is begun, and stage II to be completed before stage III is begun. Unless verification covers adequately these four aspects of disarmament, no state can be certain that other states have completed any of the three stages. Verification of destruction only, or of declared factories or missile sites, cannot possibly give this assurance.

Now it may be confidently assumed that if the staff of an international verification organization are sufficiently numerous and if they possess freedom of movement and adequate powers of checking, inspecting and interrogating, satisfaction of full or nearly full observance of disarmament obligations can be obtained in respect of most categories of weapons, especially heavy weapons. The powers required for the verification staff might of course be considered burdensome by the inspected country, but the degree of certainty could probably be made adequate or nearly so.

But this does not hold equally good for the most dangerous weapons, namely nuclear weapons and the fissile material which goes into them. The Soviet government made on 10th May 1955 an important statement to the Disarmament Sub-Committee at the United Nations of their view on this point, namely that complete certainty regarding the concealment of stocks of fissile material would never be possible. The Soviet document in question presented by Mr. Malik deserves study from several points of view. In this particular context the relevant passages are as follows:

'... peace-loving peoples are most apprehensive with regard to the existence of atomic and hydrogen weapons, in respect of which the institution of international control is particularly difficult. This danger is inherent in the very nature of atomic production. It is well known that the production of atomic energy for peaceful purposes can be used for the accumulation of stocks of explosive atomic materials, and moreover, in even greater quantities. This means that states having establishments for the production of atomic energy can accumulate, in violation of the relevant agreements, large quantities of explosive materials for the production of atomic weapons. The danger of this state of affairs becomes still more apparent if account is taken of the fact that, where the corresponding quantities of explosive atomic materials exist, production of actual atomic and hydrogen bombs is technically fully feasible and can be effected on a large scale.

Thus, there are possibilities beyond the reach of international control for evading this control and for organizing the clandestine manufacture of atomic and hydrogen weapons, even if there is a formal agreement on international control. In such a situation the security of the states parties to the international convention (treaty) cannot be guaranteed, since the possibility would be open to a potential aggressor to accumulate stocks of atomic and hydrogen weapons for a surprise attack on peace-loving states.

Until an atmosphere of trust has been created in the relations between states, any agreement on the institution of international control can only serve to lull the vigilance of the peoples. It will create a false sense of security, while, in reality, there will be a danger of the production of atomic and hydrogen weapons and, hence, the threat of surprise attack and the unleashing of an atomic war with all its appalling consequences for the peoples.'

The importance of this question for the future of any plans for disarmament and verification was recognized in London and the government set on foot an experimental exercise to test the ease or difficulty of concealment of fissile material. The exercise, to which reference has already been made in chapter 3, was carried out in British fissile material plants with great care and thoroughness, covering past and current production of both plutonium and uranium. The conclusion reached was that even with the most rigorous powers a world-wide control organization with a complement of about 1,500 scientists, and a total with supporting staff of about 10,000, would not be able to guarantee in those countries which have had nuclear weapons programmes that some 10–20 per cent of the weapons had not been hidden, the percentage figure perhaps varying somewhat from country to country.

D.V.–F

These conclusions, relating of course solely to practical experiment in the United Kingdom, substantiate the view expressed by the Soviet government, and give it more precision. In so far as the conclusions are accurate and may be confirmed by further and future enquiry, they are both disturbing and important. The successful concealment of one nuclear weapon in five, or even one in ten, during the process of disarmament would entail serious risks for the security of those countries which carried out their obligations loyally. An estimate made in 1963 credited the United States with possessing a total of 384 Inter-Continental Ballistic Missiles and a total including these of 1,800 Strategic Missiles; the United Kingdom with 142; and the Soviet Union with over 1,000. These numbers take no account of interdiction strike weapons, of short range tactical atomic weapons, which might number over 2,000 on each side, of tactical nuclear weapons or of extra stocks of fissile material. If, for example, at the end of the disarmament process the United States had succeeded in concealing one in ten of her weapons she would possess thirty-eight ICBMs, a total (including these) of 180 Strategic Missiles, and numerous short range weapons in addition, without mentioning extra stocks of fissile material. Since it is considered likely that the national life of the United Kingdom could be paralysed and perhaps extinguished by less than ten missiles with megaton type warheads, it is obvious that the possession of a stock of concealed weapons of this order of magnitude would confer enormous power on a successful violator. The effect of such successful concealment would be considerable in the first years of the disarmament process, and would become more and more serious and dangerous as the point approached at which countries which loyally observed their treaty obligations ceased to have any nuclear weapons or fissile material at their disposal at all.

It is possible to draw several varying conclusions from these considerations. It can be argued that they show that there can never be an adequate system of verification, that without this there can be no disarmament agreement, and that consequently we must resign ourselves to the continuance of the arms race and to the spread of nuclear weapons. Alternatively, the reasoning can be that disarmament must wait, not necessarily for ever, but at least until the international climate changes radically for the better. Yet again, it has been maintained in some quarters that it will never be safe for the West to disarm until all closed societies and totalitarian regimes are eliminated. Any of these three lines of thought lead to counsels of varying degrees of despair.

But there is an entirely different approach which is given expression in the Western disarmament proposals, namely that the dangers of possible concealment of nuclear weapons can be sufficiently guarded against by improved peace-keeping machinery and in particular by the creation of an effective peace-keeping force. The possible nature of such machinery and the composition and command structure of a peace-keeping force will be examined in the next chapter. The point that arises here is the need for such a force, for without it there would exist in a fully disarmed world nothing except limited national militias to deal with concealed weapons and a threat to use them. If on the other hand a peace-keeping force existed together with adequate machinery for its employment the threat created by any concealment of weapons would be largely if not wholly removed. Even the knowledge of its existence would constitute a strong deterrent to attempts at concealment, and a guarantee of security to states which carried out their obligations loyally. But the force must be so equipped that no state could challenge it; and its employment must not be subject to obstruction or veto either by a guilty party or by a friend of a guilty party.

It is indeed evident that even if there were no substantial risk of successful concealment of nuclear or other weapons, improved peace-keeping machinery and a peace-keeping force would in any case be an essential component of international life in a fully or nearly disarmed world. The possibility of concealment of nuclear weapons does not alone create, but decisively confirms the need. Security in a disarmed or largely disarmed world can be likened to a three-legged stool, the three legs being destruction of weapons, adequate and bearable verification, and an effective peace-keeping force. The stool cannot stand solidly on two legs but only on all three.

The introduction of the element of improved peace-keeping machinery with an effective peace-keeping force alters the whole picture presented by disarmament and verification. First it offers a solution to the dilemma created by the possibility of concealment of nuclear or other weapons; second, it makes it possible to consider easing the burden of verification in a variety of ways,

since it so greatly diminishes both the temptation to conceal
weapons and the threat to the security of other states created by
concealment. Indeed, the emphasis in the American disarmament
proposals on a peace-keeping force enables the Western countries
to go a long way to meet the Soviet dislike of stringent verification. A major offer of this kind to the Russians is contained in the
American disarmament plan.[1] The proposal is that parties to
the treaty would divide their territory into an agreed number of
zones, and at the beginning of each stage of disarmament would
submit to the international disarmament organization a declaration stating the total level of armaments, forces, and specified
types of activities subject to verification within each zone. The
exact location of armaments and forces within a zone would not
be revealed prior to its selection for inspection. An agreed
number of these zones would be progressively inspected and
would thereafter remain open for further inspection while verification was being extended to additional zones. Zones to be
inspected would be selected by procedures which would ensure
their selection by parties to the treaty other than the party whose
territory was to be inspected, or conceivably by lot. In this way
verification in all its four aspects would begin gradually with a
random sampling process in a few areas in each country and
would only be fully extended to cover all parts of the territory of
parties to the treaty at the end of the whole process of disarmament. Over and above the zonal sampling proposal, it is possible
to contemplate additional or alternative easements of verification,
especially in the first and perhaps the second of the three stages
of disarmament, provided that in parallel improved peace-
keeping machinery and an effective peace-keeping force were
coming into being.

The Soviet Union for its part has included in its draft disarmament treaty proposals for strengthening the United Nations
and for a peace-keeping force. How far these proposals would
enable a peace-keeping force to be adequately equipped and
effectively used will be discussed in the next chapter. The point
to be noted here is that they include the concept in their plan.

But the regrettable fact remains that the Russians have so far
steadfastly refused either to embody in their disarmament proposals or to admit in the process of negotiation the principle laid
down by Mr. Gromyko, the Soviet Foreign Minister, on 15th

[1] See Stage I G.3(c) in Appendix V

March 1962 that there shall be 'no loopholes which will permit the clandestine production of aggressive armaments once the process of general and complete disarmament has begun'. They have persistently declined to accept during disarmament adequate verification that no illegal replacement or production is taking place, that no arms are being retained above agreed levels, and that no arms are being concealed. They have said that the Western compromise proffered for zonal sampling is unacceptable to them; and they have declined to put forward any alternative proposals to meet the difficulty that verification of nothing but the destruction of arms and of declared factories and sites provides no guarantee of observance of disarmament obligations. So long as this attitude is maintained the Soviet plan does not offer any means of checking the security claimed for it; in the language of prospectors it is a gold brick. It can of course be adapted and modified, but will it? If not, the outlook for general and complete disarmament will remain grim.

7

Peace-keeping Machinery and an International Force

IT is hard to picture what life and politics would be like in a totally or even nearly disarmed world. We are close enough to the nineteenth century to have an idea of how affairs were regulated when peace over a large part of the globe was kept by the strength and presence of the British navy. We have had more recent experience of peace resting upon an uneasy balance of conventional forces, and since World War II of living under the threat of nuclear warfare with peace dependent upon the balance of nuclear prudence. What would happen when all armaments, both nuclear and conventional, were destroyed? Would the world automatically become safe and peaceful, all disputes and rivalries laid aside? It has already been noted that the Soviet Union at Geneva has persistently declined to agree to the use of the phrase 'a disarmed and peaceful world', apparently because according to Communist doctrine a world in which states were disarmed would not be a world in which the use of force by Communist revolutionaries would be ruled out. In any case it would be completely fanciful to suppose that all human beings would suddenly eschew ambition, friction and quarrels. Large nations would still possess greater impact and exercise more influence than smaller nations. The threat of the use of weapons would at best be replaced by the threat of economic or other pressures. Moreover arms of sorts can always be improvised. If disarmament is not to end in chaos there must be agreed and improved forms of machinery for the settlement of disputes, and if necessary for the prevention or suppression of violence.

Provisions of this kind are of course already contained in the Charter of the United Nations, and in particular in Chapter V dealing with the composition, functions and powers of the Security Council; in Chapter VI dealing with the pacific settlement of disputes; and in Chapter VII dealing with action with respect to threats to the peace, breaches of the peace and acts of aggression. Article 43 lays down that all members of the United

Nations shall make available to the Security Council on its call and in accordance with a special agreement or agreements, armed forces, assistance and facilities (including rights of passage) for the purpose of maintaining international peace and security. Article 45 lays down that to enable the United Nations to take urgent military measures, members shall hold immediately available national air force contingents for combined international action. Article 47 provides for the establishment of a military staff committee to advise and assist the Security Council on all questions relating to the Security Council's military requirements for the maintenance of international peace and security, the employment and command of forces placed at its disposal, the regulation of armaments, and possible disarmament. The military staff committee was to be responsible to the Security Council for the strategic direction of any armed forces placed at the disposal of the Security Council. But Articles 43 and 45 have never been implemented.

It is important to note that any action by the Security Council under Chapter VII, that is to say with respect to threats to the peace, breaches of the peace, and acts of aggression, requires under Article 27 the concurring votes of the five permanent Members; in other words, the five permanent Members have a veto on action under Chapter VII. The question arises whether these provisions of the Charter would be applicable and adequate to deal with the pacific settlement of disputes and with threats to the peace in a disarmed world. In seeking an answer to this question it is desirable always to bear in mind that the Charter established the International Court of Justice but did not make acceptance of its judgement compulsory; and that any action by the Security Council can be blocked by a veto of any one of the five permanent Members but not by any other state alone.

Under the Soviet plan (Article 3) states parties to the disarmament treaty would solemnly confirm their resolve in the course of and after general and complete disarmament . . . 'to strengthen the United Nations as the principal institution for the maintenance of peace and for the settlement of international disputes by peaceful means.' But the plan makes no specific proposal for such strengthening. Indeed the Soviet negotiator at the 18-power Disarmament Conference at Geneva made it clear that Moscow was opposed to any alteration to the Charter. The

Soviet plan explicitly lays down in Article 40 that all questions connected with the safeguarding of international peace and security, including preventive and enforcement measures, shall be decided by the Security Council in conformity with its powers under the U.N. Charter. This clearly points to Chapter VII of the Charter and so to the maintenance of the veto by the five permanent Members. There is no mention in the plan of strengthening the International Court of Justice or of compulsory acceptance of its judgement. Where the Soviet plan is more specific is in the matter of a peace-keeping force. It provides in Article 18 that states who are parties to the treaty shall between the signing of the treaty and its entry into force conclude agreements with the Security Council by which they undertake to make available to the latter armed forces, assistance and facilities, including rights of passage, as provided for in Article 43 of the Charter; and further that the armed forces provided under the said agreement shall form part of the national armed forces of the corresponding states and shall be stationed within their territories. Article 37 (2) lays down that the command of these units shall be made up of representatives of the three principal groups of states existing in the world on the basis of equal representation, and that the commanding body shall decide on all questions by agreement among its members representing the three groups of states. The pattern is perfectly clear. The international force shall consist of national contingents stationed in their own country until needed in an emergency; the Soviet Union as one of the five permanent members could veto the use of the force; and as an additional safeguard against the taking of any action contrary to the wishes of the Soviet Union, the Communist member of the High Command would have a veto on all action by the force.

The United States proposals are more far reaching. They provide that 'as national armaments are reduced, the United Nations would be progressively strengthened in order to improve its capacity to ensure international security and the peaceful settlement of differences.' They provide for a study of measures to strengthen existing political or legal arrangements for the peaceful settlement of international disputes and to institute new procedures and arrangements where needed. They provide that parties to the treaty would agree to support measures to strengthen the structure, authority and operation of the United

Nations so as to improve its ability to maintain international peace and security. They lay down that parties to the treaty would undertake in stage II to accept without reservation the compulsory jurisdiction of the International Court of Justice to decide international legal disputes. They provide for a peace observation corps. They specify a U.N. peace force to be equipped with agreed types of arms necessary to ensure that the United Nations can effectively deter or suppress any threat or use of arms; that arrangements should be made in stage I for the establishment of the peace force in stage II: and that it be progressively strengthened during stages II and III until it had sufficient armed forces and armaments so that no state could challenge it. The United States plan does not stipulate where the contingents are to be stationed or how they should be composed; it does not contemplate a troika command. It points to the Security Council as the body which would decide upon the use of the force but specifically provides for an agreement to be concluded in stage II upon all problems concerning the force, including command and control. In other words, it does not provide for a veto within the High Command on action by the force; and it leaves the question of a veto in the Security Council by a permanent Member on the use of the force as a matter for further consideration and negotiation (Stage I H (5)).

When all these juridical niceties have been examined, as they must be, the plain fact remains that a peace-keeping force can only provide the ultimate assurance of security for states if it is capable of taking effective fire brigade action in a world in which no other force would exist which could offer resistance to a violator armed with concealed nuclear weapons or prepared to use other means of violence.

But to afford a valid hope of this kind a peace-keeping force must at least meet the following criteria. It must be a force whose loyalties in an emergency would be international and not national. It must have a command structure which is at once international and effective. It must be equipped with types of armaments capable of ensuring that it can effectively deter or suppress any threat or use of arms, or in other words, it must possess sufficient man-power and armaments so that no state could challenge it.

The question of armaments with which a peace-keeping force should be equipped is particularly difficult. If it is to fulfil the criteria of being capable of effectively deterring or suppressing any threat or use of arms, and of possessing such armaments that no state could challenge it, it must be so equipped as to be able to meet a challenge from a state which had concealed appreciable quantities of nuclear weapons. If so, it is hard to escape the conclusion that it must itself be armed with nuclear weapons, since to fight nuclear weapons with conventional weapons is almost certainly to fight a losing battle. In a world in which nuclear weapons and means of producing and delivering them had been or were in the process of being totally abolished, the problem of providing a peace-keeping force with nuclear weapons and means of delivering them would be complicated. These must be produced, kept in a state of readiness, and guarded. It might be that the force would only need to possess such weapons and means of delivery for a temporary period, until life in a disarmed world had more or less settled down. It is possible, although hardly credible, that the necessity could be avoided altogether. The Soviet Government at Geneva insisted that this must be the case, and that the retention of any nuclear weapons and means of their delivery after the completion of the disarmament process would be self-contradictory and unthinkable. The United States and the United Kingdom on the other hand have prudently taken the view that the question must not be prejudged one way or the other, and that the only common-sense course is to leave the question open for later decision. What is inexorably certain is that a peace-keeping force of the kind so far advocated by the Soviet Union, composed of national contingents and with no integrated international structure, with a veto at the troika command level, a veto in the Security Council upon its use, and debarred in advance from possessing any nuclear weapons, would be wholly ineffective. To advocate such a force is to advocate a deceitful sham which in Communist parlance is nothing but opium for the masses.

The American plan is different. It contemplates a peace-keeping force international in structure, with integrated and veto-free command, and if necessary possessing, at least for the time being, nuclear weapons which would enable it to deal with any potential violator or aggressor. Where it is less specific is over the question of the international body which would finance, equip, and direct the force. It refrains from pronouncing definitely one way or the other on the question whether this body should be the Security Council of the United Nations as at present constituted, that is to say a body of twelve members of which the five permanent Members possess a veto upon action under Chapter VII of the Charter. The drawback to such a system is obvious. It means that any of the five permanent members could block the use of the peace-keeping force against any state and in any circumstances which did not suit their interests, while other states, whether large, such as India, or small, such as Guinea, would possess no such privilege. But if there is to be some different arrangement, one of two consequences becomes inevitable; either the supreme body which will direct and decide upon the use of the force will be some new body which is not provided for in the U.N. Charter and which will by-pass the Security Council in dealing with threats to peace, as defined in Chapter VII of the Charter; or else the powers or voting system of the Security Council or of the Assembly of the United Nations will have to be changed, which would involve amending the Charter.

This question has not so far been fully explored. But on the face of it there are at least three possible alternatives to leaving to the Security Council, as at present constituted and with its present voting system, the power to use and direct a peace-keeping force in a disarmed world. The first is to amend the Charter so that in this context the Security Council could take a decision by a two-thirds or conceivably a majority vote, without the power of veto for any state. The second possibility is to place the responsibility upon the U.N. Assembly, perhaps by a two-thirds vote. This again would presumably involve amendment of the Charter since it would mean giving to the Assembly responsibilities placed by the Charter on the Security Council. The third alternative would be to agree upon some specially constituted body. This would entail by-passing the existing provisions of the United Nations Charter and perhaps even the U.N. Organization altogether.

It would be out of place to seek to push this analysis further in the present context. The essential point to note is that the United States and the United Kingdom have shown themselves willing to explore the various possibilities involved, while the Soviet Union has so far set its face rigidly against any amendment of the Charter, or any by-passing of the Charter which would involve the abolition or the weakening of the Soviet power of veto. Yet without agreement on precisely this, the whole concept of general and complete disarmament carried out in three consecutive and uninterrupted stages is most unlikely to be realized, and it is misleading to pretend otherwise.

8

Partial and Collateral Measures

INTRODUCTION

BOTH the United States and the United Kingdom on the one hand, and the Soviet Union on the other, have committed themselves to the goal of general and complete disarmament. All three are committed also to the United States-Soviet Statement of Agreed Principles of 20th September 1961. But when it comes to negotiations with the object of translating these agreed goals and principles into the text of a treaty, wide divergencies of view have arisen. These differences have been analyzed in the preceding chapters. They centre mainly round three issues; whether verification can be made what the West considers adequate and the Communist countries bearable, whether there is to be strengthened peace-keeping machinery with an effective international peace-keeping force, and how to maintain the balance of security while disarmament is proceeding.

The hope must be that if there is good faith and good will on both sides persistent negotiation will lead to a compromise which both will accept. The partial test ban agreed upon in August 1963 did not raise any of the three issues. On the question of a comprehensive test ban, which involves on-site inspection, the gap between the two nuclear sides has been narrowed but not bridged. The gulf separating the two sides over the means and conditions for far-reaching disarmament remains wide.

This does not mean that negotiations are by any means useless. On the contrary, the contacts between Communist and Western countries which they involve are valuable in themselves; so is the participation in the discussions of a representative cross-section of unaligned countries. Furthermore, open probing of the issues and confrontation in detail and in depth of the views of the respective sides helps to clear the ground. Even if little or no positive agreement is reached for the time being divergences get clarified and narrowed; if the political winds become favourable world leaders can then take the remaining decisions more easily either at a Summit meeting or otherwise.

PARTIAL AND COLLATERAL MEASURES

Meanwhile, if agreement on general and complete disarmament proves too difficult to negotiate all at once, the natural question to ask is whether it would not be sensible to take several bites at the cherry and to work up to the final result by successive steps, each creating confidence for the next step. Would it not be possible to agree upon partial measures of disarmament, perhaps accompanied by collateral steps which do not strictly speaking involve disarmament but may facilitate it, such as agreements to stop the spread of nuclear weapons, and measures against surprise attack and war by miscalculation? Would not agreement of such a kind on a first package of both partial and collateral measures encourage world opinion in the hope that disarmament is not an impossible dream, and that there is real sincerity in the search for it? Might not an atmosphere of modest achievement be thus created which would bring at least some relief of international tension, would help to restore confidence, and might perhaps render general and complete disarmament itself easier to negotiate? Above all, are there no partial measures of actual disarmament which, while having an appreciable value, would not require the degree or rigour of verification which has proved so formidable an obstacle to surmount?

Reasoning of this kind led to the inclusion as No. 8 of the agreed Soviet-American Statement of Principles of 20th September 1961, of the following clause:[1]

> 'States participating in the negotiations should seek to achieve and implement the widest possible agreement at the earliest possible date. Efforts should continue without interruption until agreement upon the total programme has been achieved, and efforts to ensure early agreement on and implementation of measures of disarmament should be undertaken without prejudicing progress on agreement on the total programme and in such a way that these measures would facilitate and form part of that programme.'

This joint formulation by the Soviet Union and the United States, which was endorsed by the U.N. Assembly, would appear on the face of it to dispose of any objection that to take partial measures would be a confession of failure and of reluctance ever to agree on general and complete disarmament. And indeed on 26th September 1961 the Soviet government followed up the adoption of the Agreed Principles by submitting a memorandum

[1] See Appendix II

to the General Assembly proposing that early steps might be taken on all or at least some of the following eight measures, adding that they did not regard the list as exhaustive. The eight measures were:

1. Freezing of the military budgets of states.
2. Renunciation of the use of nuclear weapons.
3. Prohibition of war propaganda.
4. Conclusion of a non-aggression pact between the N.A.T.O. countries and the Warsaw Treaty countries.
5. Withdrawal of troops from foreign territory.
6. Measures to prevent the further spread of nuclear weapons.
7. Establishment of nuclear-free zones.
8. Steps to decrease the danger of surprise attack.

Paragraph 3 of the memorandum reads as follows:

'While it regards general and complete disarmament as the principal means of securing a lasting peace, the Soviet Government at the same time does not exclude the possibility of reaching agreement on a number of measures that would contribute to the easing of international tension and the strengthening of confidence among states and thereby facilitate the implementation of general and complete disarmament. Needless to say both in selecting these measures and in putting them into effect the guiding principle must be that no state or group of states should gain military advantages and that all states should enjoy an equal measure of security. The application of these measures should not divert attention and effort from the solution of the main problem—that of general and complete disarmament. On the contrary, each of these measures individually and all of them in combination should help to create a situation conducive to the conclusion and effective application of such a treaty. Along with the consideration of the disarmament problem as a whole and of several other important international problems, steps can and must be taken towards the adoption of a number of simple decisions, comprehensible to millions of people, which would lessen the danger of the outbreak of war and on which states might reach agreement in the immediate future.'

With the view expressed by the Soviet Government in this paragraph the Western countries were at the time and remained consistently afterwards in full agreement. It will of course be noted that the eight measures do not strictly speaking involve the destruction of any weapons; they are measures in the field of keeping the peace rather than of actual disarmament; in other words, they are what have come to be known as collateral measures. At least some of them are not necessarily the less valuable for that.

When the 18-power Conference opened at Geneva in March 1962, both the Western and the unaligned countries considered from the outset that serious attention should be paid to No. 8 of the Agreed Principles and to the Soviet initiative of 26th September 1961; the former, of course, covered both partial and collateral measures, the latter covered only collateral measures. It was proposed that special days be set aside for their discussion in addition to encouragement of direct talks upon them between the American and Soviet delegates, or in informal group meetings.

Most unexpectedly, and contrary to No. 8 of the agreed Soviet-American principles, Soviet opposition at once developed to any talk of partial measures. It was clear that the Soviet leaders had changed their minds between September 1961 and March 1962. All measures of actual disarmament, they now maintained, should be kept strictly within the framework of general and complete disarmament and should not be negotiated outside it; to maintain otherwise was a sign of insincerity on general and complete disarmament and of a desire to shelve it. Throughout the following year the Soviet government continued with some acerbity to stifle any discussion on partial measures.

Complications of other kinds arose over collateral measures, some of which were found to raise special difficulties for one side, and some for the other. For example, it had been decided at Geneva in 1962 that the least controversial subject to handle first as a collateral measure was 'the prohibition of war propaganda', which had been No. 3 on the Soviet list. After over two months of difficult negotiation between the American and Soviet co-chairmen a text was agreed by both on behalf of their governments and officially endorsed in plenary session by Mr. Zorin on 25th May. But at the next plenary meeting two days later he read out instructions from Moscow repudiating the agreement; and the conference accordingly found itself for the time being back at square one over collateral measures.

A further case in point was 'withdrawal of troops from foreign territory' which figured as No. 5 on the Soviet list. This must inevitably occur at some stage in the process of general and complete disarmament, but was unacceptable to the Western countries as an isolated measure because it would clearly upset the balance of military security and lead to the breakdown of N.A.T.O. even before disarmament had started.

A third case was 'steps to decrease the danger of surprise attack', which had figured as No. 8 on the Soviet list of 26th September 1961. The Soviet memorandum included the following paragraphs:

'Naturally, any steps to avert surprise attack should lead to the elimination of suspicion among states and not to its intensification. It is important to ensure that they do not entail attempts to obtain military advantages for any group of countries or the collection of intelligence information and that the security of the participating states is not jeopardized.

The most practical steps which might be taken at an early date include the setting up of land control posts at railway junctions and major ports and on motor roads, the function of which would be to ensure that dangerous concentrations of armed forces and military equipment did not take place.

The Soviet Government is of the opinion that the establishment of such land control posts might constitute an effective means of lessening the danger of surprise attack. No one is likely to dispute that fact that, even in this age of nuclear weapons, preparations for a large-scale modern war inevitably call for the concentration of large military units with large quantities of armaments and equipment at certain specific points.

The above measure might be accompanied by an appropriate reduction in the armed forces and armaments in territories situated within a given distance of either side of the demarcation line and their withdrawal from such territories.

The measures proposed by the Soviet Union would provide adequate means of detecting early signs of troop concentrations in the most critical areas and would give timely warning that an attack was being mounted. At the same time, these measures take the security interests of the two sides equally into account. Their implementation would lay a useful foundation for wider co-operation among states in strengthening European security and would contribute to the realization of general and complete disarmament.'

Yet when the matter was raised in Geneva six months afterwards, in 1962, the Russians repudiated these proposals and said that they were no longer appropriate. After long discussion they were not prepared to go further than to discuss measures against war by miscalculation, leaving out the question of surprise attack.

D.V.–G

But in 1963 Soviet policy shifted back again. First, there emerged in June an agreement on direct means of communication by teleprinter or the like between Mr. Khrushchev and President Kennedy, so that in a sudden crisis there could be no miscalculation arising from failure to exchange messages quickly. This was not a very significant result in itself, but better than nothing. Next, Mr. Khrushchev in August accepted the partial test ban proposed by the West the year before. He also agreed that this should be followed up by an attempt to reach understandings on further questions, and among them the idea of observation posts against surprise attack. Indeed the Moscow statement of 3rd August in answer to attacks from Peking reverted to the Soviet line of 1961 in favour of partial measures and a gradual approach to total disarmament. (See chapter 9 on Soviet policy). Thus by the summer of 1963, after a year of Russian hesitation, the negotiation of agreements on collateral measures began to look more hopeful in practice, as it had always been in theory. In particular the questions of 'measures to prevent further spread of nuclear weapons' and 'the establishment of nuclear-free zones' offered promise; and not least the exchange of observation posts against surprise attack.

MEASURES TO PREVENT THE FUTURE SPREAD OF NUCLEAR WEAPONS

In 1963 the United States, the Soviet Union and the United Kingdom were nuclear powers possessing nuclear knowledge, nuclear weapons and, to a varying extent, effective means of delivery. France was making strides in the same direction and was, of course, already in a position to pass on to yet other countries such nuclear know-how as she had already acquired. There was thus a balance, however precarious, resulting from the mutual power of the N.A.T.O. countries and of the Soviet Union to inflict unacceptable damage on each other by the use of nuclear weapons.

Other countries were waiting uneasily and uncertainly in the wings. Communist China had declared her intention to become a nuclear power. If she did so, what would be the attitude of India, already a victim of a successful attack by Communist China with conventional weapons? How long would countries such as Sweden and Switzerland, whose neutrality precluded them from relying on the weapons of allies, refrain from becoming nuclear powers? If there were no nuclear test ban treaty in existence, how long might Israel and the United Arab Republic stay outside the ring?

President Kennedy in his broadcast of 28th July 1963 on the signature of the partial test ban said:

'This treaty can be a step towards preventing the spread of nuclear weapons to nations not now possessing them. During the next several years, in addition to the four current nuclear powers, a small but significant number of nations will have the intellectual, physical and financial resources to produce both nuclear weapons and the means of delivering them. In time, it is estimated, many other nations will have either this capacity or other ways of obtaining nuclear warheads, even as missiles can be commercially purchased today.

I ask you to stop and think for a moment what it would mean to have nuclear weapons in many hands—in the hands of countries large and small, stable and unstable, responsible and irresponsible, scattered throughout the world. There would be no rest for anyone then, no stability, no real security, and no chance of effective disarmament. There would only be increased chances of accidental war, and an increased necessity for the great powers to involve themselves in otherwise local conflicts.'

One of the dangers in the case of potential nuclear countries is that if any of their neighbours or old or new enemies obtain even a small nuclear armoury they may themselves feel compelled to do the same. To the Soviet Union it would be a matter of special concern and fear if West Germany became a nuclear power.

With these disturbing possibilities in view the idea of an international agreement to stop the spread of nuclear weapons has been under discussion for several years. The Government of Eire has given a lead in the U.N. Assembly since 1959, and in 1961 its resolution was passed unanimously. This resolution called for an international agreement, if possible subject to inspection and control, under which nuclear states would undertake to refrain from relinquishing control of nuclear weapons and from transmitting the information necessary for their manufacture to states not possessing such weapons; and states not possessing such weapons would undertake not to manufacture or otherwise acquire control of such weapons.

It might appear that a multinational or multilateral nuclear force for N.A.T.O. would run counter to the idea behind the Irish proposal. This is not necessarily the case. The essential points involved are, first, the ability to manufacture and, secondly, the power to take a decision to launch. So long as the creation of a N.A.T.O. nuclear force did not enable any N.A.T.O country to make nuclear weapons which cannot do so now, and so long as it did not confer on any country which cannot now launch a nuclear weapon the power to do so, or to decide that it should be done, then it would not conflict with the Irish resolution. There might be more fingers on the safety catch—that is to say the consent of more N.A.T.O. countries, including West Germany, might be required for the launch of a nuclear weapon, instead of the launch depending on the United States alone; but only if the creation of a N.A.T.O. nuclear force gave to West Germany or any other non-nuclear N.A.T.O. country the power to pull the trigger would the Irish proposal be undermined.

To sum up the matter, which is needed and needed urgently is a formal agreement to stop the spread of nuclear weapons. Not only major nuclear powers would have to adhere to such a treaty, but also the non-nuclear powers.

The partial test ban treaty itself constituted a step in this direction, since by Article II each of the parties undertakes 'to refrain from causing, encouraging, or in any way participating in, the carrying out of any nuclear weapon test explosion, or any other nuclear explosion anywhere, which would take place in any of the environments described.' Mr. Kennedy in his broadcast of 28th July said:

'We have a great obligation—all four nuclear powers have a great obligation—to use whatever time remains to prevent the spread of nuclear weapons, to persuade other countries not to test, transfer, acquire, possess or produce such weapons. This treaty can be the opening wedge in that campaign.'

A non-dissemination agreement would have to rest at least partly on goodwill and common interest, since by its very nature its observance would be difficult to verify. Nor would every country whose intentions might be important necessarily adhere at the outset. But this should not be a reason for failing to develop the possibility to the full.

ESTABLISHMENT OF NUCLEAR-FREE ZONES

There have been proposals from various quarters that even though some states continue to possess nuclear weapons, certain areas of the world might be declared nuclear-free zones, in which testing, manufacture, storage or transport of nuclear weapons would be prohibited. A number of African countries took the initiative in proposing at the United Nations in 1961 that Africa should be recognized as such an area; in 1962 Brazil took the lead in making a similar suggestion for Latin America; and there have been several proposals at different times for some arrangement of this kind in Europe. Presumably, any such agreement would need to contain provisions for international verification to ensure that its terms were observed. Such agreements would clearly have to depend upon the consent of all states in the area concerned. It is inevitable that one country standing out in any given area, for example Cuba in Latin America or Algeria in Africa (if France could bring sufficient pressure upon her) could block agreement for the whole area. There might be fewest difficulties in Africa and Latin America, and if so, no state outside the area ought to raise objection. The situation is different in Europe where countries such as Western Germany and France rely to a large extent for their defence upon nuclear weapons, strategic or tactical, even though these are possessed and controlled by the United States, and are strongly opposed to the withdrawal of such weapons except as part of a phased and agreed disarmament treaty.

NON-AGGRESSION PACT BETWEEN N.A.T.O. COUNTRIES AND THE WARSAW PACT COUNTRIES

This measure has been proposed on several occasions by the Soviet Union. It would not entail any new obligations which states members of the United Nations have not already assumed under the Charter. Moreover, the Federal Republic of Germany, although not a member of the United Nations, undertook in October 1954 to observe the obligations of the Charter never to use force to alter her frontiers, and to settle all disputes with other nations by peaceful means. It may accordingly be objected that such a pact would add nothing to existing international security. In addition, the objection has been voiced in France and West Germany that the Pact would tend to freeze the existing division of Europe and would bring to the foreground again the recognition of East Germany if only through her signature to the Pact. It may be therefore that the disadvantages outweigh the advantages.

A PACKAGE

It would be in full accordance with No. 8 of the agreed principles, namely that states participating in disarmament negotiations should seek to achieve and implement the widest possible agreement at the earliest possible date, for there to be an early agreement on a package deal. This might contain some actual measures of disarmament even if only partial, together with some collateral measures. Such a package could precede the signature of a more far-reaching agreement; for it would be intended to serve as an encouragement towards this, and in no way as a substitute. A tentative suggestion of this kind was put forward by the Swedish delegate at Geneva in the autumn of 1962. He suggested that among the elements could be the destruction of a certain number of weapons under international verification, some form of indirect budget control, prohibition of new production of weapons except for spare parts, and such collateral measures as might be chosen and agreed upon. A full nuclear test ban might accompany the other measures unless concluded before.

There is a considerable choice of elements which might be contained in such a package, and these would have to be so selected that the principle of balance was not infringed. But the possibilities are real and the advantages obvious. Even the modest agreement for direct communication by a so-called hot line between Chairman Khrushchev and President Kennedy was greeted with some acclaim as a safeguard against war by miscalculation. So was the agreement not to place nuclear weapons in orbiting satellites. A still more significant package would be a full nuclear test ban, an agreement to stop the spread of nuclear weapons, establishment of control posts and observers against surprise attack, and some physical destruction of armaments under international observation as a sign that weapons really can be scrapped. It would be yet better to add to this, as suggested by Sweden, some indirect budget controls, and some direct or indirect limitation and controls on production; and to include some destruction of fissile material, possibly in equal quantities by both sides. To some or all of these steps might further be added some trial experiment in verification procedures, perhaps in small selected zones, to test the number of staff required and the powers they would need, and to test also the degree to which verification could be made readily bearable. A verified freeze on all production of new quantities and types of nuclear delivery vehicles and verified cut-off of the production of fissile material for weapons use were suggested by the United States in January 1964.

While the attempt is pushed forward to break the deadlock over verification both for a full test ban and for full disarmament, the best hope must surely lie in widening the range of agreements on collateral measures and in trying to include some partial measures, particularly if these would serve to make a dent in the problem of verification. It has to be recognized that the reluctance of the Soviet Union to come to grips with the fundamental issues inherent in disarmament remains basically unaltered. But it must be hoped that Soviet willingness in the summer of 1963 to follow up the partial test ban by exploring collateral measures more actively will provide something on which to begin to build. There is a long way to go.

PART THREE

The Soviet Approach

A DELEGATE MUST try to make a fair assessment of the sincerity of the governments and individuals with whom he is negotiating. If he starts with the belief that all that is said and done by the other side is in complete good faith he may be gravely deceived and may fail to protect the interests of his own country. If on the other hand he assumes from the outset that the other side is always speaking and acting in bad faith he is bound to regard negotiation as an exercise in propaganda and nothing more; he may then fail to put the last ounce into the effort to reach a reasonable compromise, and may thereby forfeit any slender chance there may be of an agreement.

The judgement of sincerity is particularly difficult when negotiating with the Russians. In the background there is the Communist doctrine that world revolution and the triumph of Communism everywhere must be the unswerving aim, that sooner or later this aim will inevitably be attained, and that agreements with non-Communist countries are only tactical and temporary expedients. Moreover in any negotiation Communists, if we are to believe that they are the Marxist-Leninists they claim to be, are out to secure their total objectives and do not regard any compromise as a permanent solution.

It is even harder than usual to judge Soviet objectives over disarmament and a full test ban. There have been many utterances of Soviet leaders during the last few years in favour of both. Yet there is a body of Communist doctrine of a different character. Lenin wrote in 1916, 'To put disarmament in the programme is to say: we are against the use of arms. There is not one grain of Marxism in this, just as there isn't in saying: we are against the use of force'[1]. In 1919 he wrote of the 'slogan of struggling till victory is achieved over the bourgeoisie of the whole world and in the internal civil and international revolutionary wars'.[2] The Comintern laid down in 1928: '. . . The

[1] Lenin, 1916, *On the Slogan of Disarmament*, Second Russian edition of Collected Works, vol. 19, p. 315

[2] Lenin, 1919, *Draft Programme of the Russian Communist Party*, *loc. cit.*, vol. 24, p. 97

disarmament policy of the Soviet government must be utilized for purposes of agitation', and spoke of '. . . utilizing the results of the Soviet disarmament policy in the effort to eradicate all pacifist illusions and to carry on propaganda among the masses in support of the only way toward disarmament and abolition of war, viz.: arming of the proletariat, overthrowing the bourgeoisie and establishing the proletarian dictatorship'.[1]

These and other similar definitions of Communist policy have been superseded in Moscow, if latest Soviet pronouncements are to be believed, by the concept that in a nuclear world Communist aims can and must be secured by means other than war, since nuclear weapons render war too destructive for both sides. This thesis has been accepted by Russia's allies in the Warsaw Pact but not by Communist China and Albania. There will be further reference to these developments later in this chapter; the point to be made here is to note the existence of these changes and controversies within the Communist world as a complicating factor in making an accurate estimate of what Soviet policy towards disarmament really is now, and what it is likely to be in the future. It is perhaps fair to raise the additional point whether, if nuclear weapons and the means of delivering them were in fact to be abolished, the old Communist doctrine of the inevitability of war or the new Soviet doctrine that nuclear war is too destructive would prevail. Under the Soviet plan the future peace-keeping force would not possess nuclear weapons and its use would be subject to Soviet veto.

In trying to arrive at a fair balance of judgement it may be worth examining briefly some of the factors which must presumably be taken into consideration in the formulation of Soviet policy. There is the danger, apparent to all, of the manufacture and accumulation even by the present nuclear countries of increasingly powerful weapons of mass destruction. There is the even greater peril inherent in their spread to more and more countries with the multiplied risk of irresponsible use and of accident or miscalculation. There is the economic argument that the enormous sums spent on the nuclear arms race could with advantage be diverted to the improved well-being of their own or other peoples. Awareness of these issues is common to both

---

[1] Theses and Resolution of the VIth World Congress of the Communist International—International Press Correspondence, vol. VIII, no. 84, 28th November 1928, pp. 1596–7

nuclear sides. But in the case of the Soviet Union there may be the special and additional factor of their fear of West Germany becoming a nuclear power in its own right, or of having a finger on the trigger, or even the safety catch, of a N.A.T.O. nuclear force. Twice within this century Russia has suffered tremendous loss of life and wealth as the result of an attack by Germany. In World War II over twenty million Russians died. It is natural that every Russian should regard with misgiving the prospect of a West Germany, resentful of partition, able to manufacture and use nuclear weapons. It is now clear that the Soviet Union also dislikes the prospect of China becoming a nuclear power.

These various considerations would presumably make for a Soviet desire for a full and world-wide test ban. If at any moment they have appeared or should appear decisive to the Kremlin the natural consequence would be Soviet willingness to accept a certain amount of international verification in order to obtain Western agreement to such a ban. This would be the more logical since the amount of verification required would be minimal and could not possibly endanger Soviet defence security. In the Geneva negotiations from 1958 to May 1960 the Soviet government did indeed show signs of willingness to accept minimal and reasonable international verification; at least it accepted the principle, although leaving negotiating loopholes in practice. In fact, in 1958–60 the Russians may well have wanted an agreement, although they had their own ideas about the price they would pay for it. Britain also wanted an agreement, exerted all the influence she could both in Moscow and Washington to promote it, and saw these efforts on the brink of fruition when the U-2 incident and the failure of the Paris summit, like a turn of the game at snakes and ladders, meant going back to square one and starting the persistent effort afresh.

It was unfortunate that owing to scientific and political divergencies in Washington Soviet sincerity was never fully put to the test in 1958–60. While the scientists disputed and the Agencies bickered there was no strong central direction from the top, as later under President Kennedy, who insisted upon the sternest probing of the real Soviet intentions. As a result the American delegation was compelled, on instructions from Washington, to maintain for long periods initial negotiating positions which it was obvious to everyone would not be the final American stand, but which in the meantime enabled the Russians to claim that the Americans were unreasonable and wanted to put them in an inferior situation which they could never accept. A case in point was the delay, which lasted over two years until President Kennedy came into office, to admit equality for the Soviet Union on the Control Commission. A succession of British initiatives mitigated the effects of this slowness; but valuable time was lost, and from May 1960 when the U-2 incident occurred and the summit conference in Paris failed, Moscow began to stage a retreat from acceptance of international verification. It may be debated whether the U-2 incident was the true cause of or merely a pretext for this retreat, which may conceivably have been decided upon for other reasons. But at any rate the incident and the visible beginning of the retreat coincided in time. Early in 1963 when Mr. Khrushchev again offered two to three on-site inspections, to be combined with three unmanned seismic stations in the Soviet Union, he seemed to be flirting once more with the barest modicum of international verification to secure a full test ban; but that offer was in turn withdrawn in favour of signature in August 1963 of a partial test ban with no on-site inspection at all.

Whatever the truth of all this, there may well be certain factors tending to tilt the balance in Moscow either permanently or for given periods of time against a full test ban, especially if any on-site inspection is involved. There may be military advice on the Soviet as well as the American side against complete cessation of research into more powerful weapons of offence and into means of possible defence such as anti-missile missiles. It may also be that Moscow is inhibited by Communist China's determination to become a nuclear power, and by the knowledge that the Soviet Union alone can no longer speak for the whole of the world Communist movement. If these considerations have been operative the signature of a partial test ban could conceivably represent a useful half-way house. Time will show, and the best indication will be Soviet willingness to follow-up the partial test ban with other agreements. Is it in Russian eyes a sop to Cerberus or, as President Kennedy put it, a case of 'even a journey of a thousand miles begins with a single step'?

In the case of general and complete disarmament the considerations involved may be somewhat different. In the first place Russia occupies the central geographic position in the great land mass of Europe and Asia. The freedom and independence of

most non-Communist countries in this enormous area, including
western European countries, depends upon the certainty of military help from the United States in case of attack by the Soviet
Union. If the United States disarmed to the point where she
could no longer furnish this help, the Soviet Union, moving on
inner lines of communication, could concentrate decisive manpower on any point she wished. Thus a disarmed world without
an effective peace-keeping force might well suit the strategic and
political interests of Moscow. It can be argued that in such a
world some of the satellite Communist states might and would
leave the bloc. This possibility must have been weighed by
Russian planners, since a world of exactly this kind would in fact
be created by the Soviet disarmament plan, and if the plan is
sincere, must appear to them an acceptable risk. The political
situation in the satellites is, of course, subject to fluctuation, and
this in turn may lead to corresponding fluctuations in Soviet
disarmament attitudes.

In any case it would certainly be of clear strategic and political
advantage to the Soviet Union for all foreign bases to be liquid-
ated, for all American and British troops to be withdrawn from
foreign countries, and for all or most nuclear delivery vehicles to
be destroyed, at an early stage in the disarmament process and
before alternative forms of security had been established. These
measures do in fact figure in the first stage of the Soviet disarmament plan (subsequently modified somewhat in respect of
nuclear delivery vehicles). It may be that these considerations
explain the refusal of the Soviet Union at Geneva to admit the
use of the phrase 'a disarmed and peaceful world', since the
Soviet Union may not anticipate that a disarmed world would
be peaceful.

If Russian intentions are interpreted solely in terms of classic
Communist doctrine, the assessment of policy in the preceding
paragraph would almost certainly be accurate. But under the
new Moscow doctrine that nuclear war is too dangerous, the
only risk to Communism is successful war by non-Communist
countries. If therefore an agreement can be reached by which
non-Communist countries destroy their arms and are unable to
make war, then the future for Communism will be assured; and
if the possibility of successful and undetected evasion is preserved,
so much perhaps the better, since any means are justified which
lead to the achievement of world revolution and Communism.

The two sets of considerations outlined above may be regarded as opposite sides of the same coin. At different times either one may carry the greater weight, depending on extraneous factors such as political developments inside the United States, the state of Sino-Soviet relations, or the Cuban affair. It is response to such extraneous factors which may be largely responsible for the remarkable series of hesitations and contradictions in the conduct of Soviet nuclear and disarmament policy. It is interesting to look at the record.

Let it be said at once that on a subject of such importance to the security of nations as nuclear and conventional disarmament hesitations and even reversals of policy are understandable and perhaps natural. There have certainly been both hesitations and reversals on the Western side. There is nothing strange or reprehensible about this; what is important is that second thoughts should be better than first thoughts. Nonetheless the scope and character of Soviet retractions is striking; it is enough to cite a few of them between 1958–63 without going back earlier. Take first the case of a test ban. In 1958 Moscow pressed for a separate test ban agreement as a prelude to disarmament, without being linked with or conditioned upon a disarmament agreement or progress towards disarmament. Indeed on 30th August 1958 in an official Soviet note to the Western governments there was communicated the record of an interview of Mr. Khrushchev with a *Pravda* correspondent. Answering a question on what his views were about making a link with disarmament a condition for a nuclear test ban treaty, Mr. Khrushchev said 'Is there any surer way of sabotaging the suspension of nuclear tests than by such a condition?' This remained official Soviet policy for some three years. Indeed when Mr. Zorin led the other four Communist delegations, looking gravely embarrassed, out of the conference room at the 10-nation Disarmament Conference on 27th July 1960 (Jules Moch cried 'scandale'. What did de Gaulle think?) the Soviet delegate continued to participate in the three-nation nuclear test ban conference, saying 'a test ban is another subject'. But in 1961 the Russian attitude changed. In the Aide Memoire of 4th June which Mr. Khrushchev handed to President Kennedy during their meeting in Vienna, he suggested making a test ban and disarmament interdependent. This continued to be the Russian line until November 1961, when Moscow made a proposal for an independent test ban without any inspection.

When this was not accepted Moscow switched back to linking a test ban with disarmament and drafted the Soviet disarmament plan of March 1962 in this way. Yet on 5th August 1963 Mr. Khrushchev accepted the partial test ban treaty without any link with disarmament.

By the same token there were repeated changes of line over inspection. In August 1958 Soviet expert representatives signed a report saying that every unidentified underground seismic event could be inspected by an international control organization. Three months later the Soviet political representatives asked for a veto by the Soviet Union of any inspection of Soviet territory. Between December 1958 and the end of 1960 the Soviet Union had agreed to the text of seventeen treaty articles and two annexes which provided for permanent control posts in the Soviet Union largely manned by foreigners, and for a small number of on-site inspections in the Soviet Union every year. But in November 1961 they repudiated the whole of the experts' report of 1958 and all the agreed treaty articles and annexes.

A particularly interesting example of shift of position is afforded by Soviet acceptance of a partial test ban. Various forms of partial test ban had been offered by the West in the past; on each occasion Moscow had rejected them on the ground that nothing less than a treaty banning all tests was acceptable. The Soviet Aide Memoire of 4th June 1961 contained the sentence 'there can be no exceptions from the treaty: all kinds of nuclear weapon tests must be banned—in the air, underwater, underground, and in outer space'. When, immediately after Soviet resumption of testing, President Kennedy and Mr. Macmillan proposed on 3rd September 1961 a ban on atmospheric tests only and without inspection, Mr. Khrushchev replied on 9th September that 'cessation of one kind of test only—in the atmosphere—would be a disservice to the cause of peace. It would mean deceiving the peoples. Such agreement could create the harmful illusion among the peoples that steps were being taken to put an end to the arms race, while in reality nothing of the kind was being done. In fact states would continue in a sort of legalized way to improve existing types of atomic and hydrogen weapons, using for this purpose underground tests. . . .' Again, when in August 1962 the West proposed two alternative forms of test ban treaty, the first to ban all tests with the minimum of on-site inspection, and the second to ban all tests except underground without any on-site inspection at all, the Soviet government repeated these same arguments in rejecting a partial test ban, and Soviet delegates at the United Nations and at Geneva embroidered the theme with a good deal of eloquence. But in August 1963 Moscow accepted as a service to peace and a step full of hope for the world the same form of partial test ban they had been denouncing so persistently and emphatically.

There is a similar record over disarmament. On 16th September 1961 the Soviet Union joined with the United States in signing and presenting to the United Nations eight agreed principles to govern disarmament. Principle number 8 spoke of the importance of partial measures of disarmament as a step towards general and complete disarmament; but six months later, when the 18-power Disarmament Conference opened, the Soviet government repudiated this commitment. Mr. Gromyko's statement of 14th March 1962 at Geneva spoke of verification of non-concealment of weapons from the beginning of the disarmament process; yet the Soviet disarmament plan submitted the same day failed to provide for this, and Soviet representatives have since then consistently refused verification of non-concealment. But without verification of non-concealment the whole of the Soviet disarmament plan is a sham, because the plan provides for disarmament in three stages, each stage to be completed before embarking on the next; and if there is no means of verifying that arms are not being concealed, there can be no means of knowing that any stage has been completed. Then again Moscow has blown hot and cold several times over measures against surprise attack; in May 1962 it repudiated an agreement on anti-war propaganda which it had accepted at Geneva two days before; and these are far from exhausting the list of reversals.

The record, and it is a public record, is in fact one of a series of contradictions and retractions. All of them can be verified from the texts of public statements by Soviet statesmen and negotiators. The facts are not in dispute, only perhaps the interpretation to be placed upon them.

One possible interpretation is that the Soviet Union has never wanted a comprehensive nuclear test ban or a disarmament agreement. This finds support in the fact that, while admitting international verification in theory, Moscow has always drawn back when it came to translating the big words of principle into the small print of treaty commitments. It can also be said with some truth that when the Western countries move towards the Soviet Union and even a minor agreement appears possible, as over war propaganda, the Soviet Union has on more than one occasion moved backwards. If this interpretation is correct then Soviet policy over disarmament has been a gigantic exercise in propaganda, an exercise on the grand scale orchestrated by pressure groups of many kinds throughout the world, persuasive, vociferous, but totally insincere. Even the partial nuclear test ban treaty of August 1963 may be explicable in a propagandist context. It involves no inspection of Soviet territory, yet it has succeeded in creating the impression in the West that Mr. Khrushchev means business when he claims to want peace and disarmament. Moreover the non-participation of France and China gives Moscow the excuse to resume even atmospheric tests if it deems it militarily advantageous to do so.

The form and nature of Russian propaganda over disarmament is noteworthy; and it may perhaps be taken to support the interpretation that Soviet disarmament policy is insincere. Moscow has made an enormous effort to represent itself as the champion of disarmament, but it has either skated over or distorted the issue of verification to a point where the image of the problem becomes wholly defaced. It has long been Soviet policy to try and force issues on others by using Communists in Western and unaligned countries to repeat slogans representing Russian views. 'Second Front Now' was a favourite one during the last war. Pressure for disarmament on Russian terms, that is to say, without adequate verification, could obviously pay handsome dividends if in fact the Soviet Union has no intention of agreeing to adequate verification although knowing full well that without it disarmament is a will-of-the-wisp. And this is precisely the form which Russian propaganda has taken. This is a point of which honest members of organizations for peace and disarmament ought to be conscious and on their guard. Anyone who tries to secure the passage of resolutions or the adoption of slogans calling for disarmament without verification, is consciously or unconsciously playing the tune that the Communists are calling.

But it is possible to give a different and more sympathetic interpretation of Soviet policy, to say that it is a record not of sham but of vacillation, and that there has been some parallel vacillation upon the Western side. It is conceivable that different individuals in both civilian and military circles in the Kremlin have differing views, which gain and lose ascendancy under the stress of both internal and external events. It is indeed possible that Mr. Khrushchev wants a test ban and disarmament, but is obliged to shorten sail from time to time in response to shifting winds of internal opposition—much as an American President with an eye on the Senate. Communist policy may in fact be neither as monolithic nor as consistent beneath the surface as is sometimes supposed. The Viennese used to say: 'Es gibt nichts schlimmeres als ein Mädchen das weiss nicht was es will—there is nothing worse than a girl who does not know what she wants'. If that is the explanation, or part of it, the prospect for disarmament negotiations is less bleak; the indecision may after all prove to be only temporary. Certainly the example of the partial test ban demonstrates again what has so often proved to be the case before when negotiating with Moscow, that a Russian 'never' should never be taken to mean never.

This second interpretation, namely that Soviet policy vacillates and may evolve in the light of events, is lent colour by the Moscow statement of 3rd August 1963 in reply to criticism from Peking of the partial test ban treaty. The Moscow statement contains a number of passages of great interest. It says that 'science and technology are developing tempestuously and what was unacceptable only last night proves useful, even very useful, today'. It reverts to the thesis that an agreement on ending nuclear tests creates more favourable conditions for progress on disarmament; and it ridicules its own former argument that a partial treaty is bad because it does not cover underground nuclear tests. It goes out of the way in repeated passages to speak of the policy of peaceful co-existence between states with different social systems as 'Leninist', while claiming that the possession by the Soviet Union of nuclear weapons 'played a definite, one may even say the decisive, role in the fact that the socialist countries, including the Peoples Republic of China, have not become objects of imperialist aggression and are able to build Socialism and Communism successfully'. It reiterates Soviet desire for general and complete disarmament. It goes on to favour partial measures and a gradual approach to disarmament, saying 'We consider it better to achieve a part than to do nothing. . . . If in present day conditions it is not yet possible to solve the whole problem at once, the only reasonable way out is to solve it step by step. One must be absolutely out of touch with reality to advance the alternatives "all or nothing" in matters involving the fate of the world and the lives of millions of people. . . . The Chinese leaders, by the way, had to admit themselves in their statement, that the complete prohibition of nuclear weapons should be approached gradually. But if they recognize the need for this approach—and there is no other possible in present conditions—why then, one may ask, is the Soviet Union being reproached for not being able to secure the solution of the whole problem at one go?'

These and other passages involve some striking reversals of the attitude of the Russians at Geneva between March 1962 and August 1963, when they steadily refused either a partial test ban or the gradual approach to disarmament by successive partial measures. All this can be taken as pointing at least to the possibility of a more favourable evolution of Soviet policy in the field of disarmament and of related measures. Yet with the exception of hints of reverting after eighteen months of refusal to a discussion of observation posts against surprise attack, there was no indication at the end of August 1963 of Russian willingness to seek even a reasonable compromise over international verification, which is the key issue. Nor was there yet any proof that these signs of a thaw were necessarily more than tactical or temporary. What they certainly did was to justify the policy of keeping on negotiating with the Soviet Union, however frustrating and barren of results the talks may be for long periods. But as to the sincerity of Soviet disarmament policy, as to whether the right interpretation is sham or vacillation, the most charitable judgement is still to return an open verdict.

10

The American Approach

THE great moral and political strength of American policy over a nuclear test ban and disarmament derives from two firm positions. The first is that the United States has consistently offered to accept on its soil any requisite degree of international verification of American observance of treaty obligations, provided that other countries do the same; and this the Soviet Union declines. The second is that the United States is willing to consider the adoption of partial and balanced measures of disarmament, perhaps involving little or in some cases no international verification, as first steps towards more far-reaching measures; this also the Soviets for long declined, but gave some hope in the summer of 1963 of a less uncompromising response.

The point has already been made that open societies do not have the inhibitions about verification which Communist countries profess to feel; nonetheless no country enjoys having foreign inspectors stationed in its factories, visiting defence installations and free to question its citizens. Yet all these the United States and equally the United Kingdom are willing to accept during the process of disarmament; this is the test of sincerity, and this test the Soviet Union has not yet passed. To put it in other words, the United States and the United Kingdom have weighed the risk of the arms race and of the spread of nuclear weapons against any risk to national security inherent in adequate international verification; they have come down in favour of disarmament with verification however rigorous, provided peacekeeping machinery is improved and there is an adequate peacekeeping force armed with such weapons and so commanded that it could deal with any force brought against it. The Soviet Union, rather than make these sacrifices, has so far preferred the arms race.

But the American position has not been arrived at without doubt, hesitation and bitter internal controversy. A perpetual uncertainty is the attitude of the Senate to a precise treaty text; and a President who submitted for ratification by the Senate a treaty in the disarmament field signed with the Soviet Union, only to see it rejected, would be in much the same position as

President Wilson when the Senate voted against the Treaty of Versailles. No administration can afford to place itself in such a posture. What has been certain from the outset is that no control system can be 100 per cent foolproof. There will always be some danger of evasion, and this has to be balanced against the danger of the arms race. If nothing less than a treaty giving 100 per cent certainty would ever be acceptable to the Senate, then it would be more honest to abandon negotiation for a full test ban or a disarmament agreement once and for all. Since however the Senate contains practical politicians it must be supposed that a majority do not believe the absolute to be obtainable, and that the real issue in the minds of most senators is not whether there is any security risk at all, but what degree of security risk is acceptable when weighed against the opposite risk of having no agreement.

In the years under review, namely 1958-63, American policy fell into three phases. The first phase lasted from 1958 until John Foster Dulles retired as Secretary of State in the spring of 1959; the second covered the remaining eighteen months of the Eisenhower administration; the third was that of the Kennedy administration from January 1961 onwards.

Dulles at the end of his time as Secretary of State was a sick man fighting with great courage against a fatal illness. Perhaps for this reason he showed himself, at least where a test ban and disarmament were concerned, impatient and changeable. An example of his impatience was the haste with which he insisted, before the final text of the 1958 Experts' Report on a nuclear test ban had been studied or indeed even received in London, upon the issuing of a joint invitation from the United States and the United Kingdom governments to the Soviet government on 22nd August 1958 to join immediately in political negotiations upon the report. The invitation was sound in itself, but it was a mistake to set in motion political negotiations upon a technical document before all the relevant branches of the United States government had time to formulate and co-ordinate their views, and before a policy could be fully worked out between Washington and London. This haste made it impossible for all the governmental agencies concerned in Washington to raise points beforehand which they later brought up in mid-stream.

Certainly the unanimous findings of the experts that an adequate control system was possible, within acceptable limits, for a nuclear weapons test ban aroused immediate controversy in Washington. There were divisions of opinion, honestly held on both sides, whether a ban would be a security gain by putting an end to the future development and spread of nuclear weapons; or whether, because it might never be possible to monitor a ban reliably, the security of the West would be impaired. Broadly speaking, the State Department, the Central Intelligence Agency and the President's Scientific Advisor believed that if an adequately monitored ban could be achieved, the security of the West and of the world would gain; powerful influences in the Atomic Energy Commission and in the Pentagon inclined to the opposite view, and there were some who threw doubt on the validity of the experts' findings. So long as he was in the saddle Foster Dulles was able to cut through those disputes; but a piece of administrative machinery was set up to handle the matter which outlasted his tenure of office and whose working proved to be unfortunate. This was the Committee of Principals on which were represented the State Department, the C.I.A., the Atomic Energy Commission, the Defence Departments and the President's Special Scientific Advisor. Policy decisions about a nuclear test ban were made the responsibility of this Committee, of which the Secretary of State was an equal member. If the members were seriously divided, the divergence had to be referred to the President. The Committee could only normally be gathered together at intervals of several weeks and seldom found it easy to agree. So long as such disagreement remained unresolved the American negotiator in Geneva was inevitably left without instructions until the President, who was not always readily available at short notice, could turn his mind to the matter and give his decision. Furthermore, the Committee was a body ill adapted to formulating or approving fall-back positions or alternative negotiating tactics such as are required in an important and long drawn-out international conference. The American delegation was therefore left for lengthy periods temporarily incapable of negotiating, like a yacht with no wind in the sails. It is small exaggeration to say that for months on end instructions were doled out to them from Washington much as a Victorian workhouse master might dole out the gruel; and it is a tribute both to the State Department and to the American negotiators in Geneva that these handicaps were overcome or at least minimised with such composure and skill.

Yet handicaps they were. Examples are not difficult to find in the published proceedings of the Nuclear Test Ban Conference. Throughout 1959 and 1960, the Eisenhower administration was unable to make up its mind to modify a clearly untenable American position denying equality between the two nuclear sides on the control commission for a test ban; and indeed left office without having done so. It was President Kennedy who authorized on 21st March 1961 a proposal for equality which could and should have been made two years before. During all this time the American negotiator was continually pressed by the Soviet negotiator without having any adequate reply to give. This was no isolated case. One 10th July 1959 Technical Working Group I reported to the conference with agreed recommendations on ways of detecting high altitude tests. Although American proposals for a draft treaty text to follow up these recommendations was foreshadowed on 27th August 1959, it was not until 29th March 1961 under the Kennedy administration that specific American proposals were put forward. On a more important point, it took the Eisenhower administration nine months from May 1959 until February 1960 to decide to accept the proposal for a fixed annual inspection quota first floated by Mr. Macmillan and officially proposed by Mr. Khrushchev. There were similar delays over taking a decision about a moratorium on small underground tests, and on numerous other matters.

This slowness in taking decisions was the reflection of the struggle of varying ferocity between proponents and opponents of a treaty during the last eighteen months of the Eisenhower administration. No one was really able or willing to resolve the inter-agency disputes and to give that positive direction to United States policy which President Kennedy supplied in full measure as soon as he took office. Since the struggle between the protagonists was conducted to a considerable extent in public, and since the arguments on both sides were freely aired in the press and in Congressional hearings, all this is a matter of open record.

From first to last the opponents of a treaty derived much of their strength from the views of certain American scientists. Most of the American experts involved were open-minded and scrupulously objective. It is only necessary to mention such names as Dr. Fisk, Dr. Bacher, Dr. Ernest Lawrence, Dr. Bethe, Dr. Panofsky, Dr. Alvin Graves, Dr. Carl Romney and Dr. Press, to evoke the respect which their integrity, knowledge and commonsense commanded on all sides and at all times. But there were others who, while of the highest professional competence and to whom it would be unthinkable to suppress relevant data, whether favourable or unfavourable to a treaty, gave the impression (perhaps wrongly) that they found more pleasure in introducing sound technical arguments for putting a treaty out of court than for improving methods of detection. In the early days there was indeed so little practical experience of the phenomena involved in seismic and outer space controls, and the interpretation of the limited data involved such wide margins of error, that there was considerable room for allowing scientific conclusions to be coloured by political inclination or by other subjective considerations. These dangers were reduced when, by 1961, results began to be available from the massive VELA research programme into improved methods of detecting nuclear explosions which had been initiated by the Eisenhower administration in 1959 following upon recommendations of the Berkner panel and other study groups. It was a pity that the programme was not started earlier; it was a still greater pity that the Soviet Union refused repeated invitations to join in co-ordinated research with the United States and the United Kingdom, and when they did so in 1960 quickly retreated from their agreement.

There was at the same time a lack of grip in the procedure adopted for the gathering together of technical working groups. For example, on 5th January 1959 the United States asked for further expert discussions to revise and complete the Experts' Report of 1958. Five months later when the three powers agreed upon such a technical working group the United States were largely unprepared. An able team was assembled and sent to Geneva, but the members had received no full combined briefing in the United States and were unable to find time for prior consultation with their British colleagues. This was the result of a system whereby American scientific teams were chosen from widely scattered laboratories and institutions if the best talent was to be obtained. Because these busy and highly paid staff, not all of them government servants, were being taken away from other important work, they were usually in a hurry to get back to it; it was often difficult to prevent them from throwing in the sponge after a short time and leaving Geneva whatever the state of negotiations. Moreover, teams gathered in this way were inevitably resistant to any idea that politics and science might be interlocking.

As if this were not enough, an unfortunate influence was exercised by the system of Congressional Hearings in Washington. Hearings before Congressional Committees are of two kinds, closed and open. Any persons, including government servants, may be summoned to attend and to testify on oath. A grilling by a hostile Senator is a formidable ordeal which can intimidate the witness, who may feel that his prospects of promotion and future employment are liable to be affected by the impression he makes on the Committee, some of whose members may not be so much concerned to bring out all the facts as to justify preconceived views of their own. To appear at a closed session is less so, since the testimony is not supposed to become public and cannot therefore be attacked in the press by anyone who may disagree with it. But in an open session a witness may be and often is subjected to severe cross-examination, the answers to which may expose him to public criticism afterwards. Whether or not it was true that technical experts, who were often relatively junior, were hesitant to commit themselves to opinions which might expose them to hostile grilling by opponents in the Senate of any test ban or disarmament agreement is open to doubt. But in any case various Congressional Committees took an active hand in 1960, in 1961 and again in 1963 by holding elaborate public hearings on the technical possibility of detection and identification. Once publicly given and printed in the Congressional Committee Report, testimony even if speculative tended to acquire the status of doctrine. This for example is what happened over the mentioning of a figure of twenty for an annual deterrent quota of on-site inspections, this figure for a time becoming quite unnecessarily the word of the law in Senate circles. However all this may be, the impression was certainly left upon others that the ever-present possibility of public interrogations at Congressional Hearings made for hesitation in expressing sincerely held opinions; and that the ghost of Senator McCarthy still brooded over Capitol Hill.

In this matter of scientific advice the American administration found itself constantly on the horns of a dilemma. If a scientist is to be objective he must base his advice on the data available to him; the pace of nuclear and space research had become so fast by 1958 that the data were continually changing and objective scientific advice was bound to change with them. This made the formulation of a reasonably consistent political policy a matter of difficulty. It is true that the United States administration were fortunate in having at their disposal a large body of technical knowledge and research capabilities on which to call. But the problem was complicated by the open disagreements among experts. There were divergencies of view over the effectiveness of detection methods, that is to say in the field of seismology, and also about the dangers of fall-out, thus extending to biology and genetics. An account of these divergencies is given by Robert Gilpin in his valuable book *American Scientists and Nuclear Weapons Policy*.[1] The following passages (p. 167) in particular deserve quotation. He writes:

'The rancor and bitterness of the conflict among the scientists over the dangers of radioactive fall-out was unparalleled in the whole history of scientific conflict over nuclear weapons policy. While the chief protagonists in the struggle, Linus Pauling and Edward Teller, remained constantly within the bounds of the limited scientific evidence, their interpretations of this evidence ranged on occasion from the one extreme that fall-out was equivalent to the plague to the other that fall-out might even be beneficial.

An example of the way in which the debate was handled by the chief protagonists is found in the use by each side of the same data (from the research of Dr. Hardin Jones of the Donner Laboratory, University of California at Berkeley) on the harmful effects of fall-out. Whereas Pauling presented the danger in absolute terms, i.e. the number of individuals (especially children) who would probably die due to fall-out, Teller presented it in relative terms, i.e. the number of days lost per life for the American people as a whole due to fall-out relative to the shortening of life due to smoking.

Nevertheless the extremes to which the debates went and the apparent manipulation of scientific data for partisan purposes were such as to upset much of the scientific community. Equally disturbing was the view of many scientists that each side was guilty of intellectual dishonesty.'

In a field so experimental in character as that of nuclear tests such differences of view were perhaps natural. Natural also was the fact that American scientists made mistaken calculations on occasion. But these experiences ought to have been taken as a clearer warning than they always were that scientific views on the risks inherent in any system of international verification, and

[1] Princeton University Press, 1962

indeed on all aspects of nuclear weapons problems, should be regarded at any given moment as being relative or tentative rather than absolute, and that the final decision must be political.

Meanwhile between 1958 and the end of 1961 Russian policy had gone through at least two phases. From the endorsement by the Soviet government in the autumn of 1958 of the Experts' Report until the Summit Conference in the spring of 1960 the Soviet leaders gave the impression that they were anxious, at least up to a point, to secure a test ban treaty. During this period the Russians were in public agreement with the principle of on-site inspection; they accepted that there should be fifteen fixed control posts in the Soviet Union containing 100 American and British technicians and 100 other foreign technicians; and they accepted an annual quota of three on-site inspections. But in the period from May 1960 until 1962–3, they repudiated all they had agreed, resumed testing and rejected every Western offer either for a partial ban or a full ban.

While Great Britain since 1958 has been single-minded and consistent, the Russians have chopped and changed over verification, and Washington blew hot and cold before Kennedy. It is one of the tragedies of the story that when one side was trying for agreement the other side was often lukewarm and vice versa. In the United States there was opposition in some quarters to any treaty, partly in the Senate and partly from scientists such as Dr. Teller. There was also opposition from the Atomic Energy Commission where the argument that cessation of nuclear tests would involve the dispersal of research teams, which would be difficult to gather together again, was aired more freely than its merits deserved. This opposition, even if not numerous, was both vocal and determined. It had fastened upon the emergence of some new scientific data during the last few nuclear tests, made by the United States in October 1958 to check the accuracy of the Experts' Report in so far as underground tests were concerned. It was claimed by some, and the theory became associated with the name of Professor Albert Latter, that it might be possible to muffle underground nuclear tests by conducting them in large subterranean cavities or holes which would make them much more difficult, if not impossible, to detect. It was true that the Experts had based their recommendations in 1958 upon extremely slender data, because none other were available; and it would certainly have been wrong to conceal from the public or from the other nuclear side the fact that new and awkward data had arisen. Yet these new data were themselves slender. But because they represented an appreciable increase in the total of information at that time available, limited in scope as this total was, they became a powerful source in dividing American opinion about the feasibility of monitoring underground tests. Some of the conclusions drawn from these data were later found to have less validity than was at first claimed. But the controversy over them had the unfortunate result that in 1958–60 Soviet sincerity was never put to as searching a test by the Americans as it ought to have been. It was tested up to a point, but only up to a point. Had the energy and drive brought to bear on the problems of a test ban and disarmament in 1961 and later been available during the two preceding years, the issues would almost certainly have been clarified earlier, and there might well have been more progress earlier.

Moreover, on 29th December 1959 the United States administration issued a statement to the effect that, in the light of the equivocal attitude of the Soviet government, the United States government considered themselves free to resume nuclear weapons testing, although they would not do so without announcing their intention in advance of any resumption. The impression was given at the time that the statement was partly the result of pique at certain criticisms of American scientists by Soviet representatives at Geneva. These were regrettable, but hardly worse than what some American scientists have said publicly about each other. However this may be, by giving way to whatever pressures were in fact responsible for the issue of the statement at that juncture, the Eisenhower administration got the worst of both worlds. The United States government did not in fact resume testing until after the Russians had done so eighteen months later, but the statement enabled the Russians to claim that the West had been the first to speak of resuming.

The jolt given by this statement was severe. Yet in spite of these internal cross-currents and their effect on negotiations with the Russians, the Eisenhower administration embarked on a resolute effort in 1960 to make progress both over a test ban and disarmament. In the autumn of 1959 a study was initiated by the Secretary of State, Mr. Herter, at the request of the President, to investigate arrangements which would provide the United States with the most effective means of dealing with the increasingly complex disarmament problem. This resulted in September 1960 in the establishment of a special Disarmament Agency to develop and co-ordinate United States policies and activities in the field of arms limitation and control. Meanwhile the 10-nation Disarmament Conference met in Geneva on 15th March 1960. A Western paper with new disarmament proposals was submitted the following day, and a further American paper on 27th June. At the same time patient negotiation in Geneva had narrowed the outstanding issues over a test ban, and the Eisenhower-Macmillan declaration of 29th March[1] had opened the way for the conclusion of a comprehensive treaty. At the end of 1959 the United States, the United Kingdom, the Soviet Union and France had agreed to hold a meeting in Paris of the heads of government of the four powers, which opened on 16th May 1960. It was expected to deal primarily with the problems of Germany, Berlin and disarmament, and it was further hoped that the few points of difference on a test ban still persisting would be settled there, and a treaty initialled. But on 1st May 1960 an American U-2 'plane crashed in Soviet territory while on a reconnaissance mission, and on the ground that the incident was not cleared up to his satisfaction, Mr. Khrushchev declined, after his arrival in Paris, to participate in the proposed meeting. These occurrences put an end to hopes of a test ban in 1960, although the negotiations at Geneva were not actually suspended. The 10-nation Disarmament Conference on the other hand was brought to an end on 27th June by a walk-out of the Communist delegations.

In the deteriorated atmosphere which followed, the prospects of progress in the disarmament field for some time to come looked dim. Moreover, strong pressures were building up for a resumption of American nuclear tests. But when Mr. Kennedy was elected he immediately put the full weight which a new President can carry into a fresh and sustained attempt to find a constructive solution both to test ban and disarmament problems. Over a test ban he took decisions on the nature of the Control Commission and on other issues over which the previous administration had been hesitating, in some cases for a year or even two years. He joined with the United Kingdom in tabling new and

[1] *Geneva Conference on the Discontinuance of Nuclear Weapons Tests: History and Analysis of Negotiations*, U.S. Department of State publication 7258, Disarmament Series 4, October 1961

helpful treaty proposals in March 1961. In June 1961 he visited
Vienna for a personal talk with Mr. Khrushchev. He put his
authority behind the Vela research project with the intention of
pushing ahead vigorously with possible improvement in means
of detection and identification of underground events. It is
another sad page in the history of the effort for a nuclear test
ban that Mr. Khrushchev evidently under-estimated in 1961
both the goodwill and the effective mettle of President Kennedy.

When the Soviet Union resumed nuclear testing unilaterally
in August 1961 and conducted a massive series of tests, including
that of a 60-megaton bomb, of greater aggregate megatonnage
than all other previous tests put together, President Kennedy
showed remarkable restraint. He made an offer that autumn,
together with the United Kingdom, to disregard any advantage
which the Soviet Union might have gained by their new test
series, and to sign an agreement for a permanent test ban on the
same terms as previously offered, without any compensating test
series by the United States. This offer was rejected by the Soviet
Union; and only following upon that rejection did the United
States embark upon a further and significant test series.

Reference has already been made in an earlier chapter to the
initiative taken by the United States, together with the United
Kingdom, in August 1962, in tabling simultaneously two alternative draft treaties embodying two new compromise offers. The
first was for a ban on all tests with no on-site inspection except
for a minimum in underground environments. The second was
for a ban on all tests except those in underground media, thereby
avoiding the need for on-site inspection all together. Both offers
were turned down at the time by the Soviet government. But
following a yet further initiative by President Kennedy and Mr.
Macmillan in the spring of 1963 Mr. Khrushchev changed his
mind and agreed to follow up the second Western offer, namely
for a partial test ban, and a three-nation treaty on this basis
was signed in Moscow on Monday, 5th August 1963.

Full credit must go to the Kennedy administration for their
persistence and drive in this matter. Credit is also due to them
in the field of disarmament, first for the negotiation with the
Russians in September 1961 of the agreed American-Soviet disarmament principles, and second for the formulation of the new
American disarmament plan of 18th April 1962, as well as for
determined subsequent negotiation upon it.

But it must be firmly borne in mind that in the absence of a reliable disarmament agreement the United States bears the overall responsibility for the defence of the West, for the security and continued freedom of her friends and allies as well as her own. As Mr. Arthur Dean, the leader of the American delegation at Geneva, said on 14th December 1962:

'The United States is committed to world-wide arrangements for the defence of the free world, defensive arrangements brought into being by Soviet threats and by Soviet threats alone. The United States sees these co-operative world-wide arrangements as a shield to prevent any other nation from using its military strength either directly or indirectly, through threats and intimidation, or threats of destruction, to frustrate the freedom and independence which the United States shares with all the free peoples of the world. The United States favours complete and total disarmament in a peaceful world; but declines to accept obligations in the disarmament field which would diminish total free world security, or are not honest and beneficial to both sides at the same time.

If it is to remain faithful to these principles, it is clearly out of the question for the United States at any stage of the disarmament process to agree to the destruction of all nuclear weapons and all nuclear delivery vehicles, or to the withdrawal of all American forces from overseas, unless and until an alternative form of security for herself and her allies has begun to take concrete shape; and such alternative security can only rest upon disarmament adequately verified and accompanied by sufficiently reliable peace-keeping machinery.'

On Mr. Dean's statement there has been full Anglo-American agreement and solidarity.

11

The British Approach

UP until 1958 British policy over a nuclear test ban and disarmament had been subject to hesitations and fluctuations in the same way as Soviet and American policy, although to a less marked degree. But in 1958 Mr. Macmillan put his full weight behind a sustained drive for progress in both fields, and in this he received strong encouragement and support from Mr. Selwyn Lloyd and Mr. (then) Ormsby Gore at the Foreign Office. That his repeated initiatives took place mainly behind the scenes increased rather than diminished their effectiveness in a highly sensitive field of international action.

Among other steps, the United Kingdom took the lead behind the scenes at the end of 1958 in securing Western agreement to the Soviet proposal at that time that a nuclear test ban might be negotiated as a separate act, neither conditioned upon nor linked with progress over actual disarmament. This step was taken as part of the search for agreement with the Soviet Union. It was a substantial modification of earlier policy, both British and American, and was only agreed by Foster Dulles with reluctance.

Public opinion in the United Kingdom supported this move. Indeed with few if any serious notes of dissent it has consistently favoured a nuclear test ban, whether directly linked with disarmament, or as a separate act having value in itself but in addition constituting a step towards disarmament. It also desires an effective disarmament agreement, partial or total, despite the fact that had Great Britain possessed adequate arms in 1914 and again in 1939, and had it been known that they would be used, both world wars might well have been averted. It can be argued even more cogently that if the United States had been neither disarmed nor neutral in 1914 and 1939 neither world war would have occurred. But the dangers of weapons of mass destruction have broadly speaking led British opinion to the widespread view that in the nuclear age the best hope of safety lies in far-reaching disarmament adequately verified. This has been and remains the attitude of all three political parties and of Parliament, the churches and the country as a whole.

British statesmen have thus been in an easier position when handling disarmament problems than their American counterparts. In the United States distrust of Soviet policy and good faith is deep, widespread and vocal. It is accompanied by a consciousness of great nuclear weapon power and a fear that American strength, on which the survival of the whole free world depends, may be undermined by weak diplomacy and unsound agreements. Thus American political leaders, even if themselves convinced that a test ban or disarmament agreement is in the security interest of the United States, have to be constantly looking over their shoulders at opponents of a treaty of any kind with the Soviet Union. They have to weigh at every step the risk that any agreement may fail to be ratified by Congress on the allegation that it provides for inadequate verification or in some other way endangers American and Western security. What drag there may be upon the government in the United Kingdom is in the opposite direction, and comes from unilateral disarmers or those who want the West to go further to meet Russian dislike of verification than the Americans think it safe to do. This latter view can be advocated the more lightly since the United Kingdom does not bear the supreme responsibility for the security of the West, and the ultimate decision lies with Washington and not with London. Those who do not bear responsibility seldom find much discomfort in criticising those who do.

The belief that the safety of the West and of the world requires an early disarmament agreement leads some people to a desire based more on emotion than on reason that the United Kingdom should take spectacular public initiatives independently of the United States. Those who advocate this course overlook the fact that the United Kingdom is no longer one of the greatest military powers. It is of course still a nuclear power. But it has abolished conscription and cut down its manpower and conventional armaments to such a bare minimum that it is already being accused of not carrying its fair share of the defence effort of the North Atlantic Treaty Organization. Almost any disarmament proposal which London could put forward would thus involve greater defence sacrifices by the United States than by the United Kingdom; and what the latter may say can carry but limited weight. Only the fact that the United Kingdom is one of the three principal nuclear powers with nuclear know-how as well as nuclear weapons, and that it commands deep respect in the field of nuclear science, gives it a special influence over the issues of a nuclear test ban and to a lesser degree of disarmament. Yet by a curious mental quirk those who are most anxious that the government should take independent initiatives are often the same people who wish Great Britain to give up unilaterally her position as a nuclear power.

The argument is sometimes put forward that de Gaulle does not hesitate to take independent initiatives which prove effective, even if disagreeable to the partners of France, and that the United Kingdom might with advantage act in similar fashion. The benefit even to France and certainly to the security of the West of most of de Gaulle's initiatives in the field of defence is in fact debatable; but in any case as a stubborn realist he confines them to fields in which it lies in his own power to carry them through. Thus his example hardly offers a parellel to the concept of urging upon others a course it is clear in advance they will reject. The government of Canada under Mr. Diefenbaker had a penchant for making moves of this kind in the nuclear field. These achieved little beyond causing embarrassment to Canadian delegates, disarray within the North Atlantic Treaty Organization in their negotiations with others, and irritation in Washington.

This desire to attitudinise can often be ascribed merely to a wish to strike a moral pose or to court votes. But in some cases it is no doubt based upon a real belief that British compromise proposals might influence middle of the road or hesitant American opinion to support or even demand a more forthcoming attitude on the part of the administration in Washington. This latter argument is the only one which, if substantiated, could carry serious weight. There may indeed be occasions now and again when an open lead from the United Kingdom going beyond the public American position can serve a useful purpose. But such public moves are as a rule more likely to prove counterproductive, and merely to harden opinion in the United States against what may appear there as an attempt at appeasement by a country lacking overall responsibility for Western defence. Moreover public differences on defence matters can only weaken the North Atlantic Treaty Organization, as the actions of France have repeatedly shown. It may be tempting but it is never responsible and seldom productive for a member of a team to strike solitary poses to the gallery.

It is of course the case, as is natural and inevitable, that differences both of scientific assessment and of political appreciation frequently arise between the United States and the United Kingdom. But there is a better way of handling these differences, at least in the first instance, than by public confrontation and perhaps open dispute. Whether minor or major, there is no good reason why they should not be thoroughly but quietly discussed between the two administrations, and why either should not seek to convince the other of the justice and force of its views. This has, in fact, been the course adopted throughout the test ban and disarmament discussions. While at times the American view has prevailed even when the United Kingdom was not persuaded of its wisdom, there have been many occasions when British views have been gratefully and gracefully accepted on the American side.

It may be worth tracing briefly the part played by the United Kingdom in the search for a nuclear test ban. As an active factor in international politics the problem dates from early in 1954. Before that time nuclear tests were not regarded as a separate issue from that of atomic energy and atomic armaments. Certainly whilst the Soviet Union was catching up with the United States and developing its own nuclear weapons, Moscow showed no concern to restrict testing as an essential part of such development. The first United States thermo-nuclear device was exploded on 31st October 1952, and the first Soviet device was detonated unexpectedly soon afterwards on 12th August 1953. The greatly increased destructive power of these new weapons was at once apparent, but their potential danger to human health was first brought home to world opinion by the huge explosion at Bikini Atoll on 1st March 1954 when the crew of a Japanese fishing boat were caught by fall-out. A month later Mr. Nehru, basing himself on this incident, appealed for a standstill of all nuclear explosions. On 28th May the Communist-sponsored World Peace Council began to campaign for the cessation of nuclear weapon tests.

The Soviet government declared itself in favour of a test ban 'as one of the first measures' in the Soviet disarmament plan of 10th May 1955, accompanying the proposal with a vague offer of an international supervisory commission. The United States at that time took the line that nuclear testing was merely an aspect of nuclear armaments; if the latter could be restricted then so could the former; but so far there was no technical basis for controls capable of ensuring that a test ban would be observed. President Eisenhower, who had approved an inter-departmental recommendation against a separate test mora-torium in June 1954, confirmed this position after a further inter-agency review in June 1955 and again in October 1956. Nevertheless, the campaign against testing gathered momentum. By early 1956 the Soviet government was advocating immediate and unconditional test suspension, without control, as a pre-liminary to any disarmament plan.

The United Kingdom at that time shared the United States' opinion that suspension of tests would be unreal and unjustifiable unless linked with disarmament measures. Nevertheless, the United Kingdom can claim an important part of the credit for the trend of events which led to the Geneva Conference. Mr. Nutting, then Minister of State for Foreign Affairs, had already in October 1955 made a suggestion in the United Nations Dis-armament Sub-Committee for convening a group of scentists to work out controls for nuclear disarmament. In 1957 this idea was developed and applied specifically to the controls for a nuclear test suspension, notably by Mr. Selwyn Lloyd, then British Foreign Secretary, in a statement to the Disarmament Sub-Committee on 17th July. A month earlier, on 14th June, Mr. Zorin made a proposal for a two or three year suspension of tests, still as an independent preliminary to disarmament but under the wing of an international supervisory commission with control posts on the territories of the three nuclear powers and in the Pacific testing areas. The 1957 Western plan for partial disarmament took a significant step towards the Soviet Union by agreeing that tests should be suspended as soon as the plan was signed; that is to say when controls were agreed but before they were actually set up; but the suspension was still tied in with the whole disarmament plan and its length was made dependent upon implementation of the 'cut-off' in the pro-duction of fissile material for weapon purposes.

The failure of the 1957 General Assembly to agree a formula for continuing disarmament talks left nuclear tests as the main issue on which East-West understanding seemed possible although not very likely. There then began a series of somewhat compli-cated developments. Unilateral suspension of Soviet nuclear weapon tests on 31st March 1958 after completion of a massive

series led President Eisenhower and Mr. Macmillan to renew the
proposal for technical talks on controls, and this Mr. Khrushchev
accepted on 9th May. As a result the 'Conference of Experts to
study the possibility of detecting violations of a possible agreement on the cessation of nuclear tests' took place in Geneva from
1st July to 21st August 1958. Contrary to all expectations it
succeeded in presenting a report recommending the outline of a
control system which the experts considered capable of effectively
verifying the suspension of all nuclear weapon tests down to the
equivalent of one kiloton on the earth's surface and in the atmosphere, and five kilotons underground (no specific recommendations were made about controls over testing in outer space).

In the United Kingdom the pressure of public opinion against
nuclear testing had by this time become a serious factor; no
British government could afford to appear to drag its feet, even
if it had wanted to do so; but in fact the United Kingdom had
come to believe that the limited experiment of an adequately
controlled test ban might prove the key to the advantage which
real disarmament would subsequently bring.

The role of the United Kingdom in the test ban conference
was necessarily somewhat different from that of the two major
nuclear powers. But British public opinion was known to be
solidly in favour of an adequate agreement; British policy showed
none of the vacillations of Moscow or the hesitation of Washington; and the single-minded purpose behind it was of significant
influence in the shaping of the Western attitude and the course
of the negotiations. British resources could not match those of the
United States on the technical side; but the competence of
the limited number of British scientists in the field involved, and
above all the personality and high standing of Sir William
Penney, meant that the United Kingdom exercised an active and
helpful influence upon events. On the political side it was rightly
appreciated from the first, and events confirmed the appreciation, that the success of the negotiations was seldom promoted
by getting openly out of step with the United States. To do so
served no purpose except to encourage the Soviet Union to think
that the unified Western defence plans could be undermined at
the conference table in Geneva. Where Britain could play the
most valuable part was to help the United States to come to an
agreement with the Soviet Union which would safeguard
Western security and which the American Congress as well as

the British Parliament would ratify. To do this the need was for co-ordination of American and British policies during the stage of formulation, rather than for one side to reach a policy decision at cabinet level which was then opposed by the other at the conference table. Once a policy decision is approved at high level, particularly in the United States where a large number of government departments and agencies are involved, radical modification is a lengthy and difficult process.

In practice it was no easy matter to co-ordinate the formulation of American and British policies, however desirable this was, and considerable inner strain developed between the two sides at various moments. This was particularly the case during the last months of the tenure of John Foster Dulles. At the beginning of 1959 he gave the impression to the Russians that he wished to break off the negotiations, and to the British that he was not taking them into his confidence. He was certainly prone to change his mind without telling the British he had done so, and by no means believed in always keeping them fully informed of how his thoughts were developing. But in spite of this a relationship of increasing trust was built up at delegation level. Mr. (then) Ormsby Gore and Mr. Wadsworth on the two sides played a big part in this, and when Mr. Herter succeeded John Foster Dulles as Secretary of State the atmosphere developed into that of a confident collaboration which continued with Mr. Eaton, Mr. Dean and Mr. Stelle, and at cabinet level with Mr. Dean Rusk.

But the fact that the United Kingdom did not find it necessary to part company with the United States on a number of occasions on which it felt too strongly for compromise was primarily due to the close attention which Mr. Macmillan, as Prime Minister, paid to the negotiations and to his discussions with President Eisenhower and President Kennedy, as well as to his interventions with Mr. Khrushchev. Mr. Macmillan held the view from the outset that a nuclear test ban, as well as progress on disarmament, was of major importance both to the world and to Great Britain, and he spared no effort to bring them about. If it had not been for his active interventions the test ban negotiations would almost certainly have broken down early in 1959, and again in the spring of 1960, and testing by the West might have been resumed late in 1960. Without his sustained exertions and repeated initiatives there would not have been the successive Anglo-American test treaty offers in March 1961 and in August

1962 in the form they were made, the Western position on disarmament would not be as forthcoming as it is, and there would
have been no partial test ban signed in 1963.

A few instances among many will serve to give an idea of the
role he played in bringing agreement nearer, a role only made
possible by the fact that Great Britain was a nuclear power. In
March 1959 the negotiations in Geneva were deadlocked over
the Soviet demand for a veto on all on-site inspections in the
Soviet Union, and the American demand for all suspicious events
to be inspected. Mr. Macmillan saw that on-site inspection of all
suspicious events would be unworkable, and developed the idea
that a more practical approach, which would at the same time
go far to meet Soviet dislike of inspection, would be to have a
small annual deterrent quota of veto-free inspections. There was
considerable resistance to this idea in Washington and Mr.
Macmillan was asked by the Americans not to put it forward at
his meeting with Mr. Khrushchev in Moscow in March. He
floated the idea in Moscow nonetheless, and it appealed to Mr.
Khrushchev, who embodied it in a formal proposal to the conference in May 1959. Nine months later it was accepted by
Washington and became official American policy. A second
instance occurred in February–March 1960 when the negotiations were again in a critical state. On 11th February the
American negotiator introduced a new United States proposal
for a phased treaty, which accepted the principle of a deterrent
inspection quota for underground events above a certain magnitude but excluded smaller tests below the stated magnitude. On
19th March the Soviet government agreed to these proposals,
but only on condition that there was a moratorium on tests below
the threshold while the three governments instituted a programme on joint research and experiment. Mr. Macmillan
intervened with President Eisenhower, and on 29th March the
Eisenhower-Macmillan declaration was issued accepting a
voluntary moratorium of agreed duration while the three governments conducted a co-ordinated research programme. This
declaration opened the way for final agreement on a test ban
treaty at the proposed Summit Conference in Paris in May 1960,
a hope which was dashed by the U-2 incident and the failure of
the Summit Conference. During the deadlock which followed in
1960–1 the influence of Mr. Macmillan was again an important
contributory factor in securing that the West should go the last

mile in negotiation before being the first to resume testing. For
a year or more during this period, as emerged afterwards, the
Russians were preparing in secret their own unilateral resumption
of testing, and there is every reason to believe that they tried to
goad the Americans into resuming testing first; certain elements
in the United States were pressing for this and had they gained
their way the Western position would have been gravely undermined.

It was not only Mr. Macmillan. Mr. Selwyn Lloyd and Mr.
(then) Ormsby Gore could justly claim much credit for the fresh
impulse given to disarmament by the calling of the 10-power
Disarmament Conference in 1960. In 1961 and 1962 both Lord
Home and Mr. Godber played important parts, largely behind
the scenes, both over disarmament and a test ban, and not least
when it came to the Anglo-American treaty offers in March 1961
and in August 1962. It was against this background of sustained
effort that the final moves towards the partial test ban treaty of
5th August 1963 were worked out, beginning with the personal
messages of Mr. Macmillan and President Kennedy to Mr.
Khrushchev in April, and culminating in the agreement of the
Soviet government to open negotiations in Moscow in July 1963.
At a time when the negotiations in Geneva seemed once more
to be in a stalemate the new opportunity created was the result
of the joint determination of Mr. Macmillan and President
Kennedy, and of their intimate understanding of each other's
problems and objectives. None of this could have taken place
had Great Britain not been able to speak as a nuclear power in
her own right.

To cite these examples of active British intervention in the
formulation of Western policy, and there were many others both
over a test ban and disarmament, is not to imply that initiative
and drive were lacking on the American side. If there was some
lack of grip under the Eisenhower administration, the reverse
certainly became true when President Kennedy formed his
administration. The point to be made is that there grew up a
real working partnership between Great Britain and the United
States, and that although Great Britain was the junior partner
the Americans were generous in giving weight to British views.

In retrospect both partners would probably agree that the
British contributions were wise. They covered not only the field
of a test ban but also the preparations for the 10-power and the

18-power Disarmament Conferences and the evolution of Western policy throughout these negotiations. The underlying and consistent theme on the British side was that the West should be at least as forthcoming in political negotiation as the scientific and technical assessment of the risks involved warranted, since the contrary risks of the continuation of the arms race and of the spread of nuclear weapons were so great.

This theme was by no means supported by extreme right wing opinion in the United States, which either opposed any treaty whatever or was insistent that any verification system must be absolutely foolproof. Since such a system was impossible to devise the two positions amounted to the same thing. On the Russian side there was evidently a school which argued that to accept any form of international verification at all was a greater security risk than the arms race; just as there were those in the United States who argued that any possible form of treaty was a greater security risk than the arms race. It was ironical that the proponents of the extreme Russian view should thus find themselves allied with extreme right wing opinion in the United States in preferring the arms race to an agreement. Later on, when the partial test ban treaty was signed in August 1963, the opposition came from a no less curious alignment of schools of thought—the Communist Chinese, the Albanians, de Gaulle, and Dr. Teller. Disarmament makes strange bedfellows.

But the purposeful and sustained drive for a test ban and disarmament on the part of the United Kingdom was not based solely on the conviction that an international agreement was of importance to mankind as a whole; it derived also from a solid calculation of where the interest and security of the country lay. Great Britain has world-wide interests and commitments which for the sake of freedom and the daily bread of her people she must do her best to ensure are safeguarded. To do this she cannot in the world of 1963 rely upon the strength of her own national armed forces, if only because she no longer possesses the financial and economic strength to remain a major military power. The arms race is placing an almost prohibitive financial strain even upon the Soviet Union and the United States; Great Britain, like other medium and smaller powers with fewer national resources, cannot afford to match the effort of the giants, and must look to other means of assuring her safety. To rely upon a balance of terror which may at any moment be upset hardly seems to afford a satisfactory answer. She would almost certainly find herself in an economically stronger and military safer position, like most other countries, in a disarming and finally disarmed world, provided only that the permanent disarmament of others is adequately and internationally verified, and that there is adequate peace-keeping machinery.

If this is accepted the critical question is how Great Britain can most effectively contribute to bringing disarmament about. It is urged persuasively in many quarters that one step Great Britain can and should take is to renounce unilaterally the possession of nuclear weapons. This, so the argument runs, would diminish the number of nuclear powers, and would set an example of abnegation which would influence other nations, or at least nations other than the United States and the Soviet Union, to follow suit. But there is no evidence, rather the contrary, that unilateral action on the part of London would in fact help to induce Paris or Peking to give up the possession or desire to possess nuclear weapons. If any countries favour such action by Great Britain it is likely to be those who in any event have no intention of becoming nuclear powers themselves. The case of Switzerland is interesting. There the result of a plebiscite was to reject a pledge by Switzerland not to obtain nuclear weapons in the absence of agreement by all nuclear powers to cease being so. The real hope of preventing the spread of nuclear weapons is by the adoption of the Irish resolution under which nuclear powers would undertake not to give nuclear weapons or know-how to countries not yet possessing them, and countries not yet possessing them would agree not to acquire them. The partial test ban of August 1963 is in fact drafted so as to be a step in this direction. If there were any signs that Paris and Peking would agree to abjure nuclear weapons provided London did so there might be much to be said for such a course; but for Great Britain to give up nuclear weapons unilaterally in the mere hope that her example would be followed by others, and without securing any undertaking to this effect, would surely be empty and meaningless. There may be arguments in favour of Great Britain giving up nuclear weapons under some conditions and at some moment; these will be looked at further in the concluding chapter of this book. But it is hardly tenable to maintain that unilateral renunciation would bring a comprehensive test ban or a far-reaching disarmament agreement any nearer. The contrary is more likely to be true. In any case the record shows that Great Britain's possession of nuclear weapons has enabled her to exercise effective influence in favour of a test ban and disarmament to a degree which she could not otherwise have done. And to say that even if this has been the case in the past it will no longer be so in the future, is an assumption which may prove valid but is belied by what has happened so far.

12

The Role of the Scientist

WITHIN the past twenty years the scientist has come to play an essential role in matters of defence. It is he who has opened the way for the peaceful use of nuclear energy and for the exploration of space. But nuclear energy and space can be used by man either for peaceful or for warlike purposes, and it is the scientist who provides the know-how for both. He plans the development of nuclear weapons whether strategic or tactical, and for their means of delivery by rocket, aircraft, artillery, or otherwise; he is equally involved in devising forms of defence against these weapons, and is consulted on methods of achieving international arms control, and on the risks of evasion. In all these matters help and advice is essential from scientists familiar with the technical problems which, in the nuclear and space age, lie at the heart of all disarmament issues. But the concept of 'help and advice' generates a host of problems both for political leaders and for the scientist himself.

The scientist of course works in a variety of capacities. In an increasing number of cases, scientists serve as established or temporary government servants, for example in the Ministry of Defence in London, or in special institutions such as the Atomic Energy Research Establishment at Harwell and the Weapons Research Establishment at Aldermaston. In the United States scientists are frequently employed by the Government on contract for particular research or study purposes. Others again work in wholly or partly independent establishments such as universities or special laboratories. This variety of forms of employment involves varying degrees of obligation towards or independence of government. But one principle holds good in all cases, namely that the scientist, in so far as he is acting as a scientist and not as something else, must be completely objective in isolating and analysing the technical issues within any aspect of defence matters laid before him; and to be completely objective he must base himself on the scientific data available to him and on such data alone. And here the first of many problems arises. Nuclear and space research are advanced and rapidly developing fields of science; seismology, on the other hand, has been so neglected as to have barely emerged from the Stone Age. In all these cases intensive research is now proceeding and new discoveries are constantly emerging. Sometimes newly arrived data confirm, and sometimes alter previous scientific conclusions. In so far as conclusions must be changed, the advice given by scientists must change accordingly. If, therefore, a political leader has honest and objective scientific advisers, their advice is almost certain to change as time, and often only a very short time, goes by. There is an obvious parallel in a motor manufacturer who is constantly improving his product and whose models therefore become obsolete each year. But the politician, particularly if he is seeking to conclude a lasting international agreement, or to make sure of the observance of such an agreement once completed, can ill afford to be constantly shifting his ground. The Russians have some right on their side in saying that it is as difficult to negotiate from a constantly changing scientific position as from a constantly shifting political position. A second difficulty arises in that the scientist inevitably wants to be seeking fresh data to add to the sum of knowledge; he wishes to be able to conduct without hindrance an endless series of experiments, for example in the testing of nuclear weapons or anti-weapons. He is almost driven to say to his political leaders that if more knowledge can be gained by more weapon tests national security in offence or defence can be better assured.

If he is to remain in the field of science and not to stray outside it, the scientist must aim to be no less objective in specifying significant criteria governing issues involved in a problem, and in evaluating the effects or risks of departing from these criteria. For example, he should strictly speaking confine himself to stating objectively the risks inherent in any particular system of test ban or arms control without urging upon political leaders what system they should choose or what degree of risk is bearable in terms of national security, particularly when weighed against counter risks which may be political rather than scientific. If at any point he allows subjective considerations whether emotional or political, or indeed non-scientific assumptions of any kind, to enter into his advice he is straying beyond the field of science and to that extent ceases to behave as a scientist. Certainly his views can no longer be claimed to be based solely on scientific knowledge if he advises on the final weighing of the

overall balance of technical and political considerations. An
illustration in point is afforded by the views frequently expressed
by the eminent American scientist, Dr. Teller, the discoverer of
the hydrogen bomb (for example in some of the arguments in
the book in which he was the co-author with Professor Albert
Latter, *Our Nuclear Future* (Secker and Warburg, 1958)). Another
illustration is provided by the opinions voiced by the distinguished British mathematician and philosopher, Lord Russell.
Equally political are some of the views put forward by Professor
P. M. S. Blackett and Sir R. Watson Watt. Everyone in a free
society has the right to express any view they wish, a right not
shared by scientists, philosophers, or indeed anyone in a Communist society; and the views of public personalities of deep
learning and integrity rightly command attention and respect.
But if there is not to be confusion a clear distinction should be
drawn between the scientific and the political content of opinions
expressed.

Further, the fact that the scientific content of opinion is solidly
founded on knowledge and experience does not automatically
mean that the political content is equally so. A good scientist is
not necessarily a good and seldom an experienced politician. It
is sometimes assumed that because a man is an eminent and
professional scientist he is exceptionally qualified by his gifts of
mind to tender advice in other fields where his knowledge
remains that of an amateur however able. An interesting and
challenging study of this thesis has been made by Robert Gilpin
in his book *American Scientists and Nuclear Weapons Policy*.[1] The
argument is sometimes carried further to the point of saying that
both policy making and negotiation, at least in the field of
nuclear weapons, ought to be left to the scientist. Experience
does not confirm that this is sound or is fair to the scientist himself, if carried beyond the undisputed point that science should
have its rightful share in both. And theory apart, the hard fact
emerges in practice that scientists are in frequent disagreement
among themselves. If all is to be left to the scientist what is the
answer to the question 'which scientists?' Tizzard or Lindemann?
Bethe or Teller?

For scientific advice like other advice is often divergent and
sometimes fallible. Robert Gilpin gives a detailed and disturbing
account of the depth and persistence of these divergencies among

[1] Princeton University Press, 1962

American scientists over a nuclear test ban. The truth is that with good faith, and on occasion with vehemence, scientists can and do differ in their interpretation of the same set of facts. The differences are apt to be still more pronounced when they are called upon to advise on the consequences of a particular course of action. When Professor Van Allen, the discoverer of the Van Allen belt, was asked by President Kennedy whether an American high altitude test would risk interference with the belt, he predicted that it would not. Sir Bernard Lovell took the view that precise predictions were not possible and suggested a number of eventualities including that of a new radiation zone similar to that created by previous high altitude shots. In the event the latter did in fact occur. Obviously when two scientists disagree, both cannot be right; one or both views, however honestly held, must be mistaken. These considerations complicate still further the task of the political leader who has to choose between conflicting scientific advice on which he is not qualified himself to form a judgement.

All this poses challenging problems for the scientist himself, who is apt to be faced by a series of dilemmas. If he is involved in independent research he naturally has a vested technical interest in the continuation of that research. If he is a member of a team engaged in a project he may realize only too clearly that, for example, a permanent or even a temporary suspension of nuclear tests may involve the break-up of the team; its members will be transferred to other jobs, and the team may never get together again as a unit. Moreover, the very concept that the pursuit of scientific knowledge ought to be interrupted or permanently stifled on military or political grounds may go against the grain of his scientific convictions. If he is working temporarily or permanently for the government, where does he feel his responsibility to begin or end? Is he justified in refusing to participate in a project when asked to do so?

If he has taken part in the discovery or development of a weapon of mass destruction, must he necessarily acquiesce in having no more say than an ordinary citizen whether and in what circumstances it is to be used, controlled, or banned? A Communist scientist, unless he defects, can give no free reign to any such prompting of conscience; a Western scientist is free to quit government service and to give public voice to his views perhaps before and certainly after having done so. But if he enters the field of political controversy he ought to make a clear and public distinction between the scientific and political content of what he says. And in touching on politics at all he may impair his scientific future. These challenges he has to meet and resolve, perhaps only at the expense of intense inner conflict. This conflict may even extend to a direct clash in his mind between his duties as a scientist, as a citizen of his country, and as a citizen of the world.

But the dividing line between the scientific and political content of decisions is of course apt to become blurred, and perhaps necessarily so, in practice; and particularly when international negotiation is involved as distinct from the formulation of policy at home. A good illustration was afforded by the Conference of Experts in Geneva in 1958. There the political goal was to seek a treaty banning nuclear tests in all environments, that is to say, in the atmosphere, underground, underwater, and in space. Given the significance such a measure must comport for future military security on either side it was both right and reasonable that governments should first seek to determine whether there could be assurance that a ban was being observed by all parties who might agree to the ban. Consequently experts from eight nations assembled in Geneva in 1958 to examine the technical feasibility of monitoring a nuclear test ban. It was for these scientists to study the physical effects of a nuclear explosion in each of the environments mentioned, and then to enumerate methods by which any or all of these effects could be observed, together with the distances and efficiencies at which they could be observed. Strictly speaking, the role of the scientists would have been fulfilled by reporting factually whether or not nuclear explosions in the various environments would produce such effects as could be observed and monitored beyond the frontiers of a country within which a nuclear explosion had taken place. But additionally they were pressed by their governments to agree upon a particular monitoring system. A preference for one particular system among various possible systems could not be expressed without the exercise of an element of political judgement. As a scientist an individual could objectively suggest a varying number of monitoring systems, each having a different monitoring capability, a different degree of impact on national sovereignty, and a different financial cost. But if that same individual were to recommend which among the variants should be chosen he thereby inevitably exercised a degree of political judgement concerning financial, security, or political interests involved.

The point is made here not to condemn the double role enjoined upon and accepted by the scientists but to register it and to recognize it as marking a certain watershed. In this particular case although scientists were, as scientists, left to take the double decision, their unanimous judgement was accepted and endorsed by all the eight governments concerned. To this extent the scientists can be said to have completed their task successfully, since they reported affirmatively on the feasibility of monitoring a nuclear test ban. They recommended a specific system for such monitoring; and their recommendation was accepted by all the governments concerned as a basis for negotiating a political treaty for the discontinuance of nuclear weapon tests in all environments. In so doing they had been required to stray, and had in fact strayed, over the boundaries of science on to the Tom Tiddler's ground of politics.

The shaded area between science and politics is in fact constantly invaded in the course of international negotiation, and is likely to be so recurrently in the future. The fact is that in seeking a test ban or disarmament the scientist, if his special knowledge and skills are to be used effectively, should be a full partner of a team representing political, military, scientific, and administrative interests. He should be fully informed of the political objectives and with these in mind should carry responsibility for isolating technical issues, evaluating their significance, and specifying the technical means of monitoring them and the risks of evasion. In particular the task of evaluating risks of evasion is likely to involve some non-scientific assumptions and should be shared with political and sometimes military elements in the same team. There must in fact be a partnership between the scientific, military, and political representatives concerned both in formulating policy and negotiating agreements in the light of this formulation. This partnership cannot be achieved if there is failure of communication between scientists and the other elements concerned; and this danger will only be avoided if scientific, military and political experts are trained to communicate with each other and to work on a basis of mutual confidence. It is a failure in administration and a handicap to efficient negotiation if, as occurred on the American side in 1959, scientists are thrown haphazard into the front line of conference negotiation without having been taught the practice of close understanding and co-operation between scientists and political representatives, or perhaps without even having grasped the need for it.

This is especially true of negotiations between Western countries and Communist countries. To the Communist mind, negotiation is only useful in so far as it serves a political purpose to which technical facts and considerations will always be subordinated. It is tempting for Western participants either in official negotiations or in less formal gatherings such as Pugwash Conferences to fall into the error of assuming that Soviet scientific representatives will as a rule express independent views or, if they do so, will thereby be giving a valuable pointer to the form which Soviet policy will take. While such assumptions may prove to be well founded in the future, they have seldom been so in the past. Khrushchev is reported to have said when questioned on this point, 'In the Soviet Union those who talk do not make policy, and those who make policy do not talk'. Whether the story is apocryphal or not, events have so far confirmed the moral.

The conclusion to be drawn is that the extent to which the technical aspects of disarmament negotiations can in fact be divorced from the political is likely to be small. Western scientists participating in ostensibly technical meetings with the Soviet Union will almost inevitably find themselves negotiating politically as well as technically, and will only ignore this fact at considerable risk to the subsequent Western position. There is therefore a strong risk of disillusionment in the hope that real progress can be achieved in negotiation with Communist countries by strictly technical discussion. Either there should be political agreement beforehand upon the objectives of the technical discussions, or it should be recognized from the outset that even if there is agreement at the technical level it by no means follows either that there will be subsequent agreement at political level, or that in political discussions Communist governments will not disavow the statements of their scientists and repudiate the validity of any technical agreement reached by them. This happened at Geneva in 1960. It follows that when negotiating with the Russians it is the solution of political problems that will primarily determine the chances of agreement even on technical problems, and certainly of a technical agreement sticking. The greater the degree of prior political agreement, the more will the Soviet tendency to subordinate science to politics work in favour of a final overall accord.

It follows that the technique and preparation required for a successful technical meeting with the Russians are the same as that for a political meeting. Western political and scientific representatives at such meetings should be briefed beforehand to work as a team, trying not to overstep the boundaries of their respective competences but working together as closely as separate services in an amphibious operation. Above all the political implications of technical proposals should be examined before and not after they are put forward. It is unsafe, as Washington tended to do before the Kennedy administration took a firm grip of test ban and disarmament negotiations, to play things by ear. It is unsafe to hope that when the day of negotiation comes the very ablest representative at the conference table can secure the desired objectives if he has an insufficiently prepared brief and inadequate fall-back position; if differences between governments and agencies in his home capital have not been resolved; and if on top of this he is open to sniping from behind by Senators anxious to make a name for themselves or with an eye on the next Election. It is crucial that scientific, military, and political representatives, while strictly observing the limits of their respective functions, should work together as an integral team with integrated backing from home.

13

Choice of Risks

THE upshot of the matter is that we are faced with a choice of risks. To rely for peace upon the indefinite duration of a balance of nuclear forces and upon the self-restraint of a growing number of nuclear powers is an exercise in dangerous living comparable to building a permanent home on the slopes of Mount Etna. It is easy to say that disarmament is Utopian. But if the choice lies between Utopia and Nirvana, most of us would plump for Utopia. On the other hand there are risks in disarmament also. Disarmament without international verification and improved peace-keeping machinery can give us no assurance of security; yet verification of disarmament (not of a test ban) may involve interference with our way of life, and peace-keeping machinery may fail to function effectively. Which course involves the lesser risks?

Let us look first at the argument that we shall be safer if we rely on national armaments, or in other words on a form of arms race. This is the position here and now. We are living today in a state of balance—call it a balance of prudence or a balance of terror—kept by the possession of nuclear weapons, and by the knowledge that any use of conventional force may lead to escalation. And we have the official view of the Soviet government, twice expressed (see chapter 5), that any armed conflict, even insignificant at first, will inevitably grow into a universal rocket and nuclear war if the nuclear powers are drawn into it.

The result so far has been that no major war has occurred for nearly a generation, and that the Soviet government has been led to modify previous Communist doctrine that war is inevitable. Moscow has replaced this former doctrine by the new thesis that in a nuclear age war would inflict unacceptable damage upon both sides, and that Communism must and will now obtain its inevitable victory over capitalism by virtue of the greater merit of its economic and social system, and not through war. This redefinition underlined the rift between Moscow and Peking in 1963.

If this line of reasoning is pushed to its extreme limit it points to the conclusion that the best hope for the human race lies in the continued existence of nuclear weapons which could be used at any moment but never are. The survival of man would thus be guaranteed by the perpetual suspension over his head of a nuclear sword of Damocles. The weakness of the argument is of course the ease with which the thread suspending the sword can be severed. In other terms, the nuclear balance is highly precarious. It could be upset at any moment by a breakthrough on either side in the development of offensive weapons, or even of defensive weapons such as an effective anti-missile missile. Moreover, what solid assurance can there be that nuclear weapons will never be used? And once used by anyone, it may be too late to save a great part of civilization, if not of human life, from being destroyed within the first twenty-four hours. Non-use is dependent upon there being no accident, no miscalculation by subordinates, and no lapse of responsibility by rulers of nuclear countries. Further, if more countries acquire nuclear weapons it may soon cease to be a case of balance between two sides only. The wider the spread of nuclear weapons the greater the risk of their use by a ruthless or irresponsible hand. Twice in the last thirty years great nations have been ruled by men of unstable mentality and total lack of moral principle. Who can be sure that Hitler or Stalin would have exercised wisdom or restraint had they possessed equality or superiority in nuclear weapons? Who can feel certain that Soviet policy may not one day be re-Stalinized? Who can predict with confidence that the foreign policy of any country will be conducted for all time with responsibility and prudence; that no man with power in his hands will ever be carried away by ambition or feelings of national resentment? Who can warrant that no political leader will turn out to be a knave or a fool?

Only if one could feel assured on these scores would it be safe to dignify nuclear balance into an essential ingredient of security; to regard it as something so reliable and enduring as to form a satisfactory central pillar for a permanent structure of world peace. And the more closely such an assumption is examined, the more shaky it is seen to be.

But if we reject the idea of resting our hope of survival on a balance of nuclear weapons that exist but are never used, in what other direction are we to look for safety? If one nuclear nation or group of nations were to obtain the undisputed mastery of the world, the risk of nuclear war might of course disappear.

But this is unlikely to happen without the prior use of nuclear
weapons to decide which nation or group of nations it shall be.
What sort of world would then be left? Cum solitudinem faciunt
pacem appellant—they make a desert and call it peace. We are
accordingly driven back, as the only solution offering much hope,
to seeking international agreement to disarm and to verify. We
have already seen that an unverified ban on nuclear weapons
and delivery vehicles offers no way out, since without verification
no country, at least no Western country, can feel safe about what
others are doing. We have seen further that even with verification there will be dangerous margins of error, and that a
peace-keeping force is required to guard against these. Given
adequate verification and effective peace-keeping machinery,
what are the risks inherent in this course which have to be
weighed in the balance? The two most obvious are first, that
verification will leave too many loopholes, and second, that the
peace-keeping machinery will not work; in fact that the words
'adequate' and 'effective' will prove to be misnomers. Both risks
are real, not least the second. It is a big step for great powers to
agree to set up peace-keeping machinery that may be used
against their interests and their friends; and Mr. Khrushchev is
supposed to have said to Mr. McCloy that the Soviet Union
would never do so. Even if set up, the machinery may be open
to the two extremes of blocking on the one hand, and irresponsible exercise on the other.

Faced with these alternative risks, the United States and
Great Britain have come down in favour of the arms race being
the greater of the two sets of dangers, and have adopted as their
aim three practical steps—a full test ban, agreement to stop the
spread of nuclear weapons, and verified disarmament with
improved peace-keeping machinery. Specific proposals for the
latter are embodied in the American disarmament plan, which
represents official American and British policy. It is drafted in
such a way as to minimize as far as possible the risks of in-
adequacy and ineffectiveness; but it is precisely on these two
points that Soviet opposition centres.

Among the highest priorities for any responsible government,
and especially for the government of any nuclear country, ought
to be to bend its energies to forwarding the task of securing international agreement on these three steps, or on others in the same
field. The partial test ban is an encouraging beginning, but it

does not take us any distance in overcoming the main obstacle to progress, which is Soviet dislike of effective international verification and of veto-free international machinery. This is the principal hurdle to be'surmounted, and in the attempt we should surely be guided by two fixed principles. The first is that we must never waver on the simple proposition that there must be enough international verification to satisfy everyone that no one is cheating. The second is that international verification should not and need not involve any unacceptable risk to security or sovereignty. By being the pledge of safety it would not destroy security but create it. The United States and Great Britain have grasped this truth. We must continue to regard it as one of our main tasks to convince the other side that neither East nor West stand to lose from impartial verification, very much the contrary; to give assurance to the other side that we shall never seek any form of verification that would give more advantage to one side than to the other; and that we will consider any reasonable means of alleviating its incidence. We have already offered a major compromise in the form of a system of zonal sampling; we should continue to seek all methods we can devise to overcome unfounded suspicions that verification, even if conducted by neutrals, must be equivalent to some form of one-sided espionage.

In parallel with deploying every effort to overcome totally unjustified hesitations over a full test ban and verified disarmament, we should throw the full weight of our influence behind attempts to conclude agreements on partial and collateral measures; beginning perhaps with agreement against the spread of nuclear weapons, on observers and control posts against surprise attack, and possibly on the use of outer space. We should do our utmost to extend in breadth and depth the scope of understanding and compromise. But we must never for a moment slip into thinking that such measures are more than a form of second best, or accept them as a permanent answer.

They must not be regarded as ends in themselves, but as useful steps in the gradual approach. And if we are tempted to question the value of the gradual approach, it is well to note and to remember that the Soviet government in its important statement of 3rd August 1963 has declared the gradual approach to be the only possible and hopeful course, and has ridiculed those who advocate 'all now or nothing'.

If this represents the line of conduct incumbent on all governments with responsibility and influence, it is more particularly
the duty of governments of nuclear countries. And this brings us
to the question of the role which Great Britain can most effectively play. If the aim of British policy is to promote the kind of
agreements outlined above, what is the most helpful form of
contribution we can make? First let us be clear that we ought
to seek to make contributions that are positive. It will not help
to pretend that the danger of nuclear war does not exist, or that
unless positive action is taken the risk will not increase. It is
wiser to recognize the posture in which we have placed ourselves:

> Like one that on a lonesome road
> Doth walk in fear and dread
> And having once turned round, walks on
> And turns no more his head;
> Because he knows a frightful fiend
> Doth close behind him tread.

Having got ourselves to this pass by letting the fiend out of the
bottle, the instinct of those who urge positive effort of some kind
is surely right. 'Ban the bomb', unilateralism, peace rallies, these
and other movements and calls for action are expressions of a
truer instinct than the line of those who say that verified disarmament is too difficult, that it might involve diminution of
sovereignty for which no one is ready, and in short that it is just
not practical politics. The trouble is that most of the slogans call
for the wrong action, at least wrong in terms of getting the fiend
under control. To ban the bomb unless the ban can be verified
would be useless and indeed dangerous. But the day that Aldermaston marchers parade under the legend 'ban and verify' there
would be the foundation for the sort of unity on a basic national
aim which can so greatly strengthen the hands of a government
in working to achieve that aim.

What are the various courses of action open to us? One possibility is the unilateral and unconditional surrender by Great
Britain of her nuclear weapons. The moral aspect of this issue
has been under examination by the British Council of Churches.
This is no place to pronounce upon the dilemma of conscience
beyond pointing out that if we are unilaterally to renounce reliance on nuclear defence we ought logically to withdraw from
N.A.T.O. into a form of neutralism, and that such action by
Britain would certainly endanger the existing balance of peace.

If, however, the contention is that we should give up possessing nuclear weapons while remaining a partner in N.A.T.O., then it would be incumbent on us, unless there were a prior or simultaneous agreement between East and West on some degree of disarmament, to make an equivalent contribution to the defence of the West in conventional manpower or weapons. Those who advocate British surrender of nuclear weapons often prefer, whether for political or other reasons, to gloss over this point. Our present annual expenditure on nuclear weapons may be set at between £120 million and £200 million pounds. Even when this contribution to Western defence is included in the picture, we still fall short of taking as full a share as we ourselves should like, or is desired of us, in conventional weapons and manpower. Is it suggested that, in the absence of a disarmament agreement, we should abandon our nuclear contribution and merely continue to make an over-modest conventional effort? If not, we must devote to the latter at least what we should save on the former.

Experts differ on how the sum could best be allocated, but the probability is that it would involve raising and equipping more than one additional division, to be stationed on the continent. Without any form of compulsory military service Britain in 1963 was short by about 9,000 men of the target figure of 180,000 for the army. Any addition to our conventional forces, if it is to represent an appreciable and credible increase in our total conventional strength, must involve a considerable increase in manpower. It is unrealistic to suppose that this could be found without reintroducing a form of conscription in peace-time. This might or might not be desirable, and it might or might not be politically popular. But those who advocate the surrender of British weapons ought at least to be honest and to admit the consequences. The British defence contribution, about 7–8 per cent of our gross national product, is already considerably lower than the American proportion of about 10 per cent. The Soviet portion is believed to be larger still, perhaps 18 per cent. If we cease to be a nuclear power in the absence of a disarmament agreement, we must either reduce further our share of the cost of Western defence, or alternatively make a compensating addition to our conventional forces. If we choose the latter course, the surrender of nuclear weapons can hardly involve any economy, and may perhaps result in extra expenditure. Moreover, it is naïve in the extreme to suppose that the mere force of British example would induce France to follow suit or induce Communist China to refrain from becoming a nuclear power. Such decisions by these and other countries will be taken on quite different grounds. Even the Swiss people have decided, by two plebiscites, not to bind themselves not to possess nuclear weapons (so long as great nuclear powers exist). If the case is thus, our unilateral and unconditional surrender would not secure any positive advantage in the field of verified disarmament or of the spread of nuclear weapons. But it would have the negative consequence of depriving us of the right of speaking and acting as a nuclear power, and therefore of continuing as of right to play the authoritative part in negotiation for a test ban and nuclear disarmament which has been ours for the past five years.

The role of Britain has already been reviewed in chapter 9, and it is no minor consideration to weigh in the balance. Any denial that Britain has played this part can only stem either from inadequate knowledge of the facts, or from unwillingness to admit anything contrary to preconceived notions or to the policy of a particular political party. Britain's part was recognized by President Kennedy in his message to Mr. Macmillan published on 10th October 1963. The substance reads as follows:

'as I signed the instrument of ratification of the Nuclear Test Ban Treaty I could not but reflect on the extent to which your steadfastness of commitment and determined perseverance made this Treaty possible. Thanks to your never flagging interest, we were ready with our views when the Soviets decided they were ready to negotiate. If humanity is to be spared further radioactive contamination of the atmosphere, if the nuclear arms race is to be slowed down, if we are to make more rapid progress toward lasting stability in international affairs, it will be in no small measure due to your own deep concern and long labour. History will eventually record your indispensable role in bringing about the limitation of nuclear testing.'

The second possibility is to renounce the right to independent use of British nuclear weapons. Under the Nassau Agreement of the 21st December 1962, British nuclear forces have been placed at the disposal of N.A.T.O., except where Her Majesty's Government may decide that supreme national interests are at stake. Many people see no justification for Britain retaining a right of independent use, even for retaliation against a nuclear attack, independently either of N.A.T.O. or of the United States. They argue that it is inconceivable that the case would arise, or that if it did so such action would be inconceivably dangerous and should therefore be made impossible in advance. It is further argued that British retention of the right of independent use gives France a basis for her insistence on a similar right.

Let us look more closely at what is involved. There is in fact a distinction to be drawn between use independently of N.A.T.O. and use independently of the United States. It is one thing to say we will never use our nuclear weapons anywhere, even in retaliation, except in agreement with or after consultation with, the United States; it is another thing to say that in the event, for instance, of our wanting to put a deterrent umbrella of nuclear protection over a Commonwealth country, probably in agreement with, or in co-operation with the United States, we could not do so without the consent of all or a majority of N.A.T.O. powers. There is also a distinction between an obligation not to act without the consent of others and an obligation not to act without prior consultation.

The problem is further complicated by the unsatisfied desire of a number of N.A.T.O. countries for a more fully integrated N.A.T.O. defence policy, which might take the form either of a fuller share in planning, or of a share in the decision to use nuclear weapons, or both. To find means of satisfying this desire without running counter to the aim of preventing the spread of nuclear weapons is far from easy, whether the means to be adopted are a multilateral nuclear force, a share in settling in advance the principles which would guide the United States in the decision to use or not to use nuclear weapons in particular circumstances, or actual participation in the decision to use or not to use. Yet means can be found of doing so provided that non-nuclear N.A.T.O. countries are not thereby given possession of nuclear weapons, and provided also that no additional N.A.T.O. country is given the right of independent decision that nuclear weapons shall be used. Both these conditions can be met if use of a multi-lateral N.A.T.O. nuclear force requires the agreement of all or of a majority of N.A.T.O. countries, including the United States; in other words if, to take the most sensitive case, West Germany is given a finger on the safety catch, but not on the trigger. Both conditions would equally be met if final decision on the use of the multi-lateral force, after consultation with others, rested with the United States. A solution within these limits is what is at present contemplated, and this would not run counter to the principle of non-dissemination of nuclear weapons.

At the same time, any plan on these lines leaves much unsolved. Either it fails to meet the wish expressed by de Gaulle that France should in all respects be in the same position as the United States; or, if there is to be full fusion of authority for the control of nuclear weapons by N.A.T.O., then N.A T O. must be developed into some form of supra-national authority, which it is far from being today. Moreover, there is the further point that N.A.T.O. does not at present concern itself with the defence of countries outside the N.A.T.O. area. Prudence accordingly suggests caution, at the very least, in assigning British nuclear forces irrevocably to N.A.T.O. so long as these dilemmas remain unresolved, and so long as such a step would debar her from using any of her nuclear forces, even side by side with the United States, in defence, for example, of Australia or New Zealand, who have come to Britain's defence in two world wars in two generations. These grounds for hesitation do not apply to the revocable assignment to N.A.T.O. already made under the Nassau Agreement. Yet it is precisely on the fact that the assignment is revocable that superficial criticism fastens.

On the other hand, it is urged by many that retention by Britain and France, or by one of them, of any right of independent use militates against greater sharing, makes for discontent within the alliance, and may lead to Western Germany and perhaps others asking in due course for national possession and independent right of use of nuclear weapons The case of Western Germany is clearly a special one for two reasons. In the first place she has already bound herself not to manufacture nuclear weapons; secondly, possession and right of use of nuclear weapons by Western Germany is a particularly sensitive question both with the Soviet Union and with Soviet satellites. How far there is in fact a desire in Western Germany to possess nuclear weapons, despite the fact that this would strengthen the ties between the satellites and Russia which Western Germany wishes to see weakened, or how far such a desire may grow with time, is a moot point.

What then is the best course for Britain to adopt? Surely the sensible line to take in this context, as in others, is not to give up something in return for nothing, not to surrender or limit the right of independent use as a gesture to be made irrespective of whether France does the same, and irrespective of any other benefit; but on the contrary to see whether we can thereby obtain agreement and combined action upon some system of greater sharing within the alliance As a possible example, there might be a N A T O pool of nuclear weapons, for collective use by N.A.T.O. and for no other purpose, to which the United States, France, and Britain would each make their contribution; the United States would contribute only a part of her total nuclear weapons, while France and Britain might contribute either all or only a part of theirs Any proportion of French and British nuclear weapons withheld would be for possible use outside the N.A.T.O. area, but only after consultation with the United States. An alternative is to earmark the whole of French and British weapons to N.A.T.O. without retaining any portion for possible use outside N.A.T.O., but to recognize that a N.A.T.O. country has an inherent right, which has already been exercised on occasion, to withdraw conventional forces for use outside N.A.T.O.; and that the same inherent right pertains to nuclear weapons. This is in effect the arrangement already made by Britain under the Nassau Agreement whereby the British V-bomber force is assigned to N.A.T.O. An illuminating analysis of these and possible alternative arrangements will be found in *Arms and Stability in Europe* by Alastair Buchan and Philip Windsor published for the Institute for Strategic Studies.[1] The authors of this report of the views of a British-German-French study group come down in favour of a two-stage approach, beginning with increased allied planning in N.A.T.O., to be followed later by allied sharing in the operational decision to use nuclear weapons.

These particular examples of means of strengthening N.A.T.O. by increased sharing, but not in a manner which would lead to the spread of nuclear weapons, may or may not have merit; there may prove to be other and better ways. The basic point is that if Britain is to agree to surrender or limit her right of independent use of her own nuclear weapons, she should surely seek by so doing to accomplish something positive in terms of increased Western unity; or better still, in terms of the broader aim of verified disarmament. On the same principle, if Britain

[1] Chatto and Windus, London, 1963

is at any moment to give up possession of nuclear weapons it should be on conditions which would manifestly promote either greater Western unity, the acceptance of verified disarmament, or conceivably a general agreement that pending verified disarmament the possession of nuclear weapons will be confined to two powers only, the United States and the Soviet Union.

The political background against which British decisions on these matters have to be taken is constantly changing. Nye Bevan is credited with having said that there is no greater mistake in politics than to try to foresee and provide in advance for every contingency. In any case what was desirable yesterday may no longer be so tomorrow. What is clear is that most of the arguments for British renunciation of nuclear weapons have been as valid for a number of years as they are today. Had they prevailed in the past, two consequences would by now have ensued. First, as Mr. Macmillan said in the House of Commons on 3rd July 1963, we should not today possess the undertakings negotiated with two American Presidents under which the United States agreed never to use nuclear weapons anywhere in the world, whether in N.A.T.O. or outside, without prior consultation with the British government. Second, it is most unlikely that the prospects for advance in the field of disarmament opened up by the partial test ban would now lie before the world. Had Britain not been a nuclear power in her own right she would not have been able, either at the conference table or behind the scenes at Geneva, or by direct representations in Moscow or Washington, to make the repeated interventions which were a major factor in bringing about the treaty. How far Britain as a nuclear power may be able to continue in the future to influence nuclear disarmament discussions in the desired direction remains to be seen; but once she ceases to be a nuclear power, her ability to do so must diminish.

At this point we may glance at some final considerations. We have looked at the dangers inherent in failure to agree on verified disarmament, and on the probable need, as a second best, of beginning with partial and collateral measures not as ends in themselves but as steps in a gradual approach to the final aim. Yet we have to face the possibility that there will be failure to reach general agreement even on partial and collateral measures, or extreme slowness in doing so. We have examined the obstacles on the Russian side to progress. We must equally recognize that a limiting factor on the Western side is the lack of integrated and unified political policy on the part of N.A.T.O. as a whole. This may be largely because the principal emphasis has so far been placed on the military character of N.A.T.O. as a defensive alliance. Less effort, or less successful effort, has been made to develop the political and economic unity of N.A.T.O. Yet if N.A.T.O. is thought of mainly or entirely as a military alliance, the inevitable result is concentration on building up its military strength and increasing the size and quality of its resources in manpower and weapons; in other words, on more and better armaments rather than on disarmament. Unless and until there are agreements on disarmament this may in a sense be natural; but it has not so far made N.A.T.O. a forum well adapted for the discussion or promotion of disarmament, which may bring greater security than armaments.

However this may be, the lack of success in building up an integrated political policy within N.A.T.O. is reflected in the divergencies of view which exist over a wide range of possible collateral measures. On the one hand Continental European members of N.A.T.O. dislike the feeling that they may be drawn into a nuclear war over issues such as Cuba, without having had the opportunity of prior consultation or voice. This would logically point not only to a broadening of political consultation within N.A.T.O., but in parallel to the need for lessening East-West tension so that a crisis such as that over Cuba becomes less likely to arise. Yet when it comes to deciding on actual and practical measures to lessen East-West tension, agreement inside N.A.T.O. has so far proved very difficult to reach. For example, France and Western Germany dislike the idea of a non-aggression pact between the N.A.T.O. powers and the Warsaw powers, mainly because of the difficulty of the status of East Germany. They dislike any idea of de-militarized zones in Europe, as tending to freeze the division of Germany. They are hesitant for much the same reason over measures to limit the danger of surprise attack. France goes further, and stands out against joining a partial test ban, or even occupying the seat reserved for her at the 18-power Disarmament Conference. Unless and until these divergences can be resolved, it may be that the initiative in measures to lessen East-West tension will pass increasingly into the hands of the United States, and that the steps considered will lie to a large extent in fields, such as a test ban and outer space, which concern the United States more directly than they do the alliance as a whole. If matters were to go this way, a lessening of East-West tension bilaterally between Washington and Moscow might precede progress over disarmament itself, while at the same time helping to create better conditions for such progress. But this takes us into fields beyond the scope of this book.

Bibliography

THE HISTORICAL ASPECT

The following works deal with the history of recent disarmament negotiations and problems associated with arms control:

B. G. BECHHOEFER — *Post-War Negotiations for Arms Control* (Brookings Institute, Washington D.C., 1961). The most scholarly account, generally pro-West.

P. J. NOEL-BAKER — *The Arms Race* (Stevens, London, 1958). A British Labour view. Critical of both Washington and Moscow.

A. NUTTING — *Disarmament: An Outline of the Negotiations.* (Oxford University Press, London, 1958). A short account from the official British viewpoint.

J. P. MORRAY — *From Yalta to Disarmament; Cold War Debate* (M.R., New York, 1961). A distorted and lengthy apologia for the Soviet Union's record since 1945.

R. GILPIN — *American Scientists and Nuclear Weapons Policy* (Princeton University Press, Princeton, 1962). An outstanding and comprehensive survey.

Geneva Conference on the Discontinuance of Nuclear Weapon Tests. History and Analysis of Negotiations. (Department of State Publication, 1961).

International Negotiations on Ending Nuclear Weapon Tests. September 1961–September 1962 (U.S. Arms Control and Disarmament Agency Publication, 9.)

RECENT ANALYSIS

Among scores of important books in this field the following are chosen as representative rather than comprehensive:

JOHN STRACHEY — *On the Prevention of War* (Macmillan, London, 1962).

163

LEONARD BEATON
and
JOHN MADDOX
The Spread of Nuclear Weapons (Chatto & Windus, London, 1962).

SEYMOUR MELMAN (ed.)
Disarmament: its Politics and Economies (American Academy of Arts and Sciences, Boston, 1962).

ECONOMIC INTELLIGENCE UNIT
The Economic Effects of Disarmament (E.I.U., London, 1962).

D. G. BRENNAN (ed.)
Arms Control and Disarmament (Cape, London, 1961).

H. BULL
The Control of the Arms Race (Weidenfeld, London, 1961).

J. J. WADSWORTH
The Price of Peace (Praeger, New York, 1962).

Appendices

REPORT OF THE CONFERENCE OF EXPERTS TO STUDY
THE METHODS OF DETECTING VIOLATIONS OF A
POSSIBLE AGREEMENT ON THE SUSPENSION OF
NUCLEAR TESTS. GENEVA 1st JULY TO
21st AUGUST, 1958

. . . .

*IV.—Conclusions on a Control System for Detecting Violations of a
Possible Agreement on the Suspension of Nuclear Tests*

The Conference of Experts, having considered a control system for
detecting violations of a possible agreement on the suspension of
nuclear tests, has come to the conclusion that the methods for detecting nuclear explosions available at the present time, viz. the method of
collecting samples of radioactive debris, the methods of recording
seismic, acoustic and hydro-acoustic waves, and the radio-signal
method, along with the use of on-site inspection of unidentified events
which could be suspected of being nuclear explosions, make it possible
to detect and identify nuclear explosions, including low yield explosions
(1–5 kt.). The Conference has therefore come to the conclusion that
it is technically feasible to establish with the capabilities and limitations indicated below, a workable and effective control system to
detect violations of an agreement on the worldwide suspension of
nuclear weapons tests.

The Conference of Experts has come to the following conclusions
regarding such a system:

1. The control system should be under the direction of an international control organ which would ensure the co-ordination of the
activities of the control system in such a way that the system would
satisfy the following technical requirements and perform the functions
involved:

(a) The development, testing, and acceptance of the measuring
apparatus and of the equipment, and stating the criteria for the
siting, of the control posts;

(b) Carrying out at the control posts and on aircraft, mentioned in
items 3 and 5 of the present Conclusions, of continuous and
effective observations for the phenomena which make it

possible to detect nuclear explosions by the use of the methods recommended by the Conference;

(c) Reliable communication, with the aid of existing channels where they are suitable for this purpose, between the international control organ on the one hand and, on the other hand, the control posts and the bases from which the regular aircraft flights are carried out; communications and transportation should ensure the speedy transmission of the results of observations, of data (including samples), of reports, and of necessary supplies;

(d) Means of transport of personnel of the control posts in accordance with their duties and, so far as necessary, for the staff of the international control organ;

(e) Timely analysis and processing of the data from the observations of the control posts with the aim of speedily identifying events which could be suspected of being nuclear explosions, and in order to be able to report thereon in such manner as is considered by governments to be appropriate;

(f) Timely inspection of unidentified events which could be suspected of being nuclear explosions, in accordance with item 6 of the present Conclusions;

(g) Staffing of the control system (the network of control posts on land, on ships, and on aircraft, and also the staff of the international control organ) with qualified personnel having appropriate fields of specialization;

(h) Providing assistance in putting into effect a scientific research programme, with the aim of raising the scientific standard of the system.

2. A network of control posts is characterized by three main parameters:

(a) The minimum yield adopted for the nuclear explosion or the natural events giving equivalent signals;

(b) The number of control posts;

(c) The probability of correct identification of natural events, particularly earthquakes.

The dependence between these parameters is such that with an increase in the yield of the explosion or the number of control posts the probability of detection and identification increases, and the number of unidentified events suspected of being a nuclear explosion decreases. On the other hand, for the identification of the increased number of unidentified events resulting from a smaller number of control posts it would be necessary to increase the number of on-site inspections or to make greater use of information coming from sources not subordinate to the international control organ or, if necessary, both.

The Conference considers that the problem of detecting and identifying underground explosions is one of the most difficult, and that, to a large extent, it determines the characteristics of the network of control posts.

3. The network of control posts would include from 160 to 170 land-based control posts (equipped in accordance with Section III of this report) and about ten ships. Of these 160–170 control posts about 100–110 would be situated in continents, twenty on large oceanic islands, and forty on small oceanic islands: however, the exact number of control posts within the limits indicated above, can be determined only in the process of actually disposing them around the globe, taking into account the presence of noise at the sites at which they are located, and other circumstances.

The spacing between the control posts in continental aseismic areas would be about 1,700 kilometres, and in seismic areas about 1,000 kilometres. The spacing between the control posts in ocean areas would vary between 2,000 and more than 3,500 kilometres; the spacing between island control posts in seismic areas would be about 1,000 kilometres. This would lead to the following approximate distribution of control posts over the globe (with a network including 110 continental posts):

North America 24, Europe 6, Asia 37, Australia 7, South America 16, Africa 16, Antarctica 4; together with sixty control posts on islands and about ten ships.

4. The tasks of the personnel of the control posts would include the ensuring of the normal functioning of apparatus, the preliminary processing of data received, and the forwarding of these data to the international control organ and to the government of the country on whose territory the control post is located in such a manner as may be considered appropriate by governments.

In order to carry out the tasks required one might need for each control post about thirty persons with various qualifications and fields of specialization, and also some persons for the auxiliary servicing staff.

5. In addition to the basic network described, air sampling would be accomplished by aircraft carrying out regular flights along north–south routes over the oceans along the peripheries of the Atlantic and Pacific Oceans, and also over areas of the oceans which are remote from surface control posts.

When it is necessary to investigate whether a radioactive cloud is present, in the case of detection of an unidentified event which could be suspected of being a nuclear explosion, special aircraft flights would be organized in order to collect samples of radioactive debris in accordance with Section II B 10.

6. When the control posts detect an event which cannot be identified by the international control organ and which could be suspected of being a nuclear explosion, the international control organ can send an inspection group to the site of this event in order to determine whether a nuclear explosion had taken place or not. The group would be provided with equipment and apparatus appropriate to its task in each case. The inspection group would forward a report on the investigation it had carried out to the international control organ, and to the government of the country on the territory of which the investigation was made in such a manner as may be considered appropriate by governments.

7. The network of control posts disposed as described, together with the use of aircraft as described, would have the following effectiveness, subject to the qualifications discussed in items 8 and 9:

(a) Good probability of detecting and identifying nuclear explosions of yield down to about 1 kiloton, taking place on the surface of the earth and up to 10 kilometres altitude, and good probability of detecting but not always of identifying, explosions taking place at altitudes from 10 to 50 kilometres. In these cases the independent methods enumerated in Sections II A, II B and II D would be used.

(b) Good probability of detecting nuclear explosions of 1 kiloton yield set off deep in the open ocean. In this case use would be made of the independent hydro-acoustic and seismic methods described in Sections II A and II C.

   The identification of underwater explosions can, in comparatively rare cases, be made more difficult by natural events which give similar hydro-acoustic and seismic signals.

(c) Good probability of recording signals from deep underground nuclear explosions in continents equivalent to 1 kiloton and above. In this case use would be made of the seismic method described in Section II C.

The problem of identifying deep underground explosions is considered in item 8.

8. Along with the observation of signals of possible underground explosions the control posts would record at the same time a considerable number of similar signals from natural earthquakes. Although, with the present state of knowledge and techniques, the network of control posts would be unable to distinguish the signals from underground explosions from those of some earthquakes, it could identify as being of natural origin about ninety per cent of the

continental earthquakes, whose signals are equivalent to 5 kiloton, and a small percentage of continental earthquakes equivalent to 1 kiloton.[1]

It has been estimated on the basis of existing data that the number of earthquakes which would be undistinguishable on the basis of their seismic signals from deep underground nuclear explosions of about 5 kiloton yield could be in continental areas from 20 to 100 a year. Those unidentified events which could be suspected of being nuclear explosions would be inspected as described in item 6.

The capability of the control system to identify underground nuclear explosions of 1–5 kiloton yield depends on:

(a) The small fraction of earthquakes that can be identified on the basis of data obtained from the control posts alone;

(b) The fraction of earthquakes that can be identified with the aid of supplementary data obtained from existing seismic stations; and

(c) The fraction of events still left unidentified which could be suspected of being nuclear explosions and for which the international control organ carries out inspection in accordance with item 6.

Although the control system would have great difficulty in obtaining positive identification of a carefully concealed deep underground nuclear explosion, there would always be a possibility of detection of such a violation by inspection.

The on-site inspection carried out by the international control organ in accordance with item 6 would be able to identify with good probability underwater nuclear explosions with a yield of 1 kiloton and above.

9. The Conference notes that in certain special cases the capability of detecting nuclear explosions would be reduced; for instance, when explosions are set off in those areas of the ocean where the number of control posts is small and the meteorological conditions are unfavourable; in the case of shallow underground explosions; when explosions are set off on islands in seismic regions; and in some other cases when the explosion is carefully concealed. In some cases it would be impossible to determine exactly the area in which a nuclear explosion that had been detected took place.

However, the Conference considers that whatever the precautionary measures adopted by a violator he could not be guaranteed against

---

[1] The Conference notes that in order to increase the percentage of earthquakes of less than 5 kiloton yield which could be identified, it would be appropriate to supplement the data from the control posts by trustworthy data from the best existing seismic stations. The results of the observations of these seismic stations should, for this purpose, be made available to the international control organ, and the equipment of the seismic stations suitable for this purpose could be improved by using the best modern apparatus.

exposure, particularly if account is taken of the carrying out of inspection at the site of the suspected explosion.

10. The system described does not include specific means to detect and identify nuclear explosions at high altitudes (above 30–50 kilometres). The Conference has formulated its findings on the methods of detecting nuclear explosions set off at altitudes greater than 30–50 kilometres and has characterized these methods in Section II E.

11. The Conference of Experts recommends the control system described above for consideration by governments.

APPENDIX II

JOINT STATEMENT BY THE UNITED STATES AND THE U.S.S.R. OF AGREED PRINCIPLES FOR DISARMAMENT NEGOTIATONS 20TH SEPTEMBER 1961

Having conducted an extensive exchange of views on disarmament pursuant to their agreement announced in the General Assembly on 30th March 1961.

Noting with concern that the continuing arms race is a heavy burden for humanity and is fraught with dangers for the cause of world peace.

Reaffirming their adherence to all the provisions of the General Assembly resolution 1378 (XIV) of 20th November 1959.

Affirming that to facilitate the attainment of general and complete disarmament in a peaceful world it is important that all States abide by existing international agreements, refrain from any actions which might aggravate international tensions, and that they seek settlement of all disputes by peaceful means.

The United States and the U.S.S.R. have agreed to recommend the following principles as the basis for future multilateral negotiations on disarmament and to call upon other states to co-operate in reaching early agreement on general and complete disarmament in a peaceful world in accordance with these principles.

1. The goal of negotiations is to achieve agreement on a programme which will ensure that (a) disarmament is general and complete and war is no longer an instrument for settling international problems, and (b) such disarmament is accompanied by the establishment of reliable procedures for the peaceful settlement of disputes and effective arrangements for the maintenance of peace in accordance with the principles of the United Nations Charter.

2. The programme for general and complete disarmament shall ensure that states will have at their disposal only those non-nuclear armaments, forces, facilities, and establishments as are agreed to be necessary to maintain internal order and protect the personal security of citizens; and that states shall support and provide agreed manpower for a United Nations peace force.

3. To this end, the programme for general and complete disarmament shall contain the necessary provisions, with respect to the military establishment for every nation, for:

(a) Disbanding of armed forces, dismantling of military establishments, including bases, cessation of the production of armaments as well as their liquidation or conversion to peaceful uses;

(b) Elimination of all stockpiles of nuclear, chemical, bacteriological, and other weapons of mass destruction and cessation of the production of such weapons;

(c) Elimination of all means of delivery weapons of mass destruction;

(d) Abolishment of the organization and institutions designed to organize the military effort of states, cessation of military training, and closing of all military training institutions;

(e) Discontinuance of military expenditures.

4. The disarmament programme should be implemented in an agreed sequence, by stages until it is completed, with each measure and stage carried out within specified time-limits. Transition to a subsequent stage in the process of disarmament should take place upon a review of the implementation of measures included in the preceding stage and upon a decision that all such measures have been implemented and verified and that any additional verification arrangements required for measures in the next stage are, when appropriate, ready to operate.

5. All measures of general and complete disarmament should be balanced so that at no stage of the implementation of the treaty could any state or group of states gain military advantage and that security is ensured equally for all.

6. All disarmament measures should be implemented from beginning to end under such strict and effective international control as would provide firm assurance that all parties are honouring their obligations. During and after the implementation of general and complete disarmament, the most thorough control should be exercised, the nature and extent of such control depending on the requirements for verification of the disarmament measures being carried out in each stage. To implement control over and inspection of disarmament, an International Disarmament Organization including all parties to the agreement should be created within the framework of the United Nations. This International Disarmament Organization and its inspectors should be assured unrestricted access without veto to all places as necessary for the purpose of effective verification.

7. Progress in disarmament should be accompanied by measures to strengthen institutions for maintaining peace and the settlement of international disputes by peaceful means. During and after the implementation of the programme of general and complete disarmament, there should be taken, in accordance with the principles of the United Nations Charter, the necessary measures to maintain

international peace and security, including the obligation of states to place at the disposal of the United Nations agreed manpower necessary for an international peace force to be equipped with agreed types of armaments. Arrangements for the use of this force should ensure that the United Nations can effectively deter or suppress any threat or use of arms in violation of the purposes and principles of the United Nations.

8. States participating in the negotiations should seek to achieve and implement the widest possible agreement at the earliest possible date. Efforts should continue without interruption until agreement upon the total programme has been achieved, and efforts to ensure early agreement on and implementation of measures of disarmament should be undertaken without prejudicing progress on agreement on the total programme and in such a way that these measures would facilitate and form part of that programme.

APPENDIX III

LETTERS BETWEEN PRESIDENTIAL ADVISER McCLOY AND DEPUTY FOREIGN MINISTER ZORIN: VERIFICATION OF RETAINED FORCES AND ARMAMENTS, 20TH SEPTEMBER 1961

Dear Mr. Zorin,

At the 18th September 1961 session of our bilateral discussions on disarmament you indicated that the draft of a joint statement of agreed principles which I submitted to you on behalf of the United States Government on 14th September 1961 would be acceptable to the Government of the Soviet Union provided the following clause were omitted from paragraph 6:

'Such verification should ensure that not only agreed limitations or reductions take place but also that retained armed forces and armaments do not exceed agreed levels at any stage.'

This sentence expressed a key element in the United States position which we believe is implicit in the entire joint statement of agreed principles that whenever an agreement stipulates that at a certain point certain levels of forces and armaments may be retained, the verification machinery must have all the rights and power necessary to ensure that those levels are not exceeded.

It appears from your statements that the Soviet Union will be unwilling to agree to a joint statement of agreed principles unless the above-mentioned clause is omitted therefrom. My Government has authorized me to inform you that, in the interest of progress toward resuming disarmament negotiations, it is willing to remove the above-mentioned sentence from paragraph 6 of the joint statement of agreed principles since it is an item to which the Soviet Union has not agreed.

This is done upon the express understanding that the substantive position of the United States Government as outlined in the above-quoted sentence and in our memorandum of 14th September 1961 remains unchanged, and is in no sense prejudiced by the exclusion of this sentence from the joint statement of agreed principles.

The United States continues to adhere to and will continue to advance the principle contained in the omitted sentence as a necessary element in any comprehensive disarmament negotiations or agreement.

Very truly yours,
JOHN J. McCLOY

. . . . .

Dear Mr. McCloy,

I have received your letter of 20th September 1961, in which you express a reservation with regard to the position which the United States of America intends to adopt in subsequent negotiations on disarmament.

According to the agreement which we reached in the course of a bilateral exchange of views, the United States agreed not to include, in the joint statement by the Governments of the U.S.S.R. and the United States on the principles for disarmament negotiations, the proposal with which you are conversant and the adoption of which would imply acceptance of the concept of the establishment of control over armaments instead of control over disarmament. In your letter you say that this proposal 'expresses a key element in the United States position'.

In this connection I must state that, as you know, the position of the U.S.S.R. on the question of control over general and complete disarmament has been thoroughly and clearly explained in the statement of the Soviet Government and its leader N. S. Khrushchev. The Soviet Union favours the most thorough and strict international control over the mesaures of general and complete disarmament. While strongly advocating effective control over disarmament and wishing to facilitate as much as possible the achievement of agreement on this control, the Soviet Union is at the same time resolutely opposed to the establishment of control over armaments.

It appears from your letter that the United States is trying to establish control over the armed forces and armaments retained by states at any given stage of disarmament. However, such control, which in fact means control over armaments, would turn into an international system of espionage, which would naturally be unacceptable to any state concerned for its security and the interests of preserving peace throughout the world. The position of the United States on this question, if it insists on the proposal described above, will inevitably complicate agreement on a programme of general and complete disarmament, on the general principles of which we have agreed.

The Soviet Union will continue to make every effort towards the earliest preparation of a treaty on general and complete disarmament under effective international control.

I have the honour to be, etc.

V. ZORIN
Permanent Representative of the U.S.S.R.
to the United Nations.

APPENDIX IV

REVISED SOVIET DRAFT TREATY ON GENERAL AND COMPLETE DISARMAMENT UNDER STRICT INTERNATIONAL CONTROL, 24TH SEPTEMBER 1962

PREAMBLE

The States of the World,

Acting in accordance with the aspirations and will of the peoples,

Convinced that war cannot and must not serve as a method of settling international disputes, especially in the present circumstances of the precipitate development of means of mass annihilation such as nuclear weapons and rocket devices for their delivery, but must forever be banished from the life of human society.

Fulfilling the historic mission of saving all the nations from the horrors of war,

Basing themselves on the fact that general and complete disarmament under strict international control is a sure and practical way to fufil mankind's age-old dream of ensuring perpetual and inviolable peace on earth.

Desirous of putting an end to the senseless waste of human labour on the creation of the means of annihilating human beings and of destroying material values,

Seeking to direct all resources towards ensuring a further increase in prosperity and socio-economic progress in all countries in the world,

Conscious of the need to build relations among states on the basis of the principles of peace, good-neighbourliness, equality of states and peoples, non-interference and respect for the independence and sovereignty of all countries.

Reaffirming their dedication to the purposes and principles of the United Nations Charter,

Have resolved to conclude the present treaty and to implement forthwith general and complete disarmament under strict and effective international control.

PART I. GENERAL

ARTICLE 1

DISARMAMENT OBLIGATIONS

The states parties to the present treaty solemnly undertake:

1. To carry out, over a period of five years, general and complete disarmament entailing:

The disbanding of all armed forces and the prohibition of their re-establishment in any form whatsoever;

The prohibition and destruction of all stockpiles and the cessation of the production of all kinds of weapons of mass destruction, including atomic, hydrogen, chemical, biological and radiological weapons;

The destruction and cessation of the production of all means of delivering weapons of mass destruction to their targets;

The dismantling of all kinds of foreign military bases and the withdrawal and disbanding of all foreign troops stationed in the territory of any state;

The abolition of any kind of military conscription for citizens;

The cessation of military training of the population and the closing of all military training institutions;

The abolition of war ministries, general staffs and their local agencies, and all other military and paramilitary establishments and organizations;

The elimination of all types of conventional armaments and military equipment and the cessation of their production, except for the production of strictly limited quantities of agreed types of light firearms for the equipment of the police (militia) contingents to be retained by states after the accomplishment of general and complete disarmament;

The discontinuance of the appropriation of funds for military purposes, whether from state budgets or by organizations or private individuals.

2. To retain at their disposal, upon completion of general and complete disarmament, only strictly limited contingents of police (militia) equipped with light firearms and intended for the maintenance of internal order and for the discharge of their obligations with regard to the maintenance of international peace and security under the United Nations Charter and under the provisions of Article 37 of the present treaty.

3. To carry out general and complete disarmament simultaneously in three consecutive stages, as set forth in Parts II, III and IV of the present treaty. Transition to a subsequent stage of disarmament shall take place after adoption by the International Disarmament Organization of a decision confirming that all disarmament measures of the preceding stage have been carried out and verified and that any additional verification measures recognized to be necessary for the next stage have been prepared and can be put into operation when appropriate.

4. To carry out all measures of general and complete disarmament in such a way that at no stage of disarmament any state or group of states gains any military advantage and that the security of all states parties to the treaty is equally safeguarded.

ARTICLE 2

CONTROL OBLIGATIONS

1. The states parties to the treaty solemnly undertake to carry out all disarmament measures, from beginning to end, under strict international control and to ensure the implementation in their territories of all control measures set forth in Parts II, III and IV of the present treaty.

2. Each disarmament measure shall be accompanied by such control measures as are necessary for verification of that measure.

3. To implement control over disarmament, an International Disarmament Organization composed of all states parties to the treaty shall be established within the framework of the United Nations. It shall begin operating as soon as disarmament measures are initiated. The structure and functions of the International Disarmament Organization and its bodies are laid down in Part V of the present treaty.

4. In all states parties to the treaty the International Disarmament Organization shall have its own staff, recruited internationally and in such a way as to ensure the adequate representation of all three groups of states existing in the world.

This staff shall exercise control on a temporary or permanent basis, depending on the nature of the measure being carried out, over the compliance by states with their obligations to reduce or eliminate armaments and the production of armaments and to reduce or disband their armed forces.

5. The states parties to the treaty shall submit to the International Disarmament Organization in good time such information on their armed forces, armaments, military production and military appropriations as is necessary for the purpose of carrying out the measures of the stage concerned.

6. Upon completion of the programme of general and complete disarmament, the International Disarmament Organization shall be kept in being and shall exercise supervision over the fulfilment by states of the obligations they have assumed so as to prevent the re-establishment of the military potential of states in any form whatsoever.

ARTICLE 3

OBLIGATIONS TO MAINTAIN INTERNATIONAL PEACE AND SECURITY

1. The states parties to the treaty solemnly confirm their resolve in the course of and after general and complete disarmament:

    (a) to base relations with each other on the principles of peaceful and friendly coexistence and co-operation;

    (b) not to resort to the threat or use of force to settle any international disputes that may arise, but to use for this purpose the procedures provided for in the United Nations Charter;

    (c) to strengthen the United Nations as the principal institution for the maintenance of peace and for the settlement of international disputes by peaceful means.

2. The states parties to the treaty undertake to refrain from using the contingents of police (militia) remaining at the disposal upon completion of general and complete disarmament for any purpose other than the safeguarding of their internal security or the discharge of their obligations for the maintenance of international peace and security under the United Nations Charter.

PART II. FIRST STAGE OF GENERAL AND COMPLETE DISARMAMENT

ARTICLE 4

FIRST STAGE TASKS

The states parties to the treaty undertake, in the course of the first stage of general and complete disarmament, to effect the simultaneous elimination of all means of delivering nuclear weapons and of all foreign military bases in alien territories, to withdraw all foreign troops from these territories and to reduce their armed forces, their conventional armaments and production of such armaments, and their military expenditure.

CHAPTER I

Elimination of the Means of Delivering Nuclear Weapons and Foreign Military Bases in Alien Territories, and Withdrawal of Foreign Troops from those Territories. Control over such Measures

A. MEANS OF DELIVERY

ARTICLE 5

ELIMINATION OF ROCKETS CAPABLE OF DELIVERING NUCLEAR WEAPONS

1. All rockets capable of delivering nuclear weapons of any calibre and range, whether strategic, operational or tactical, and pilotless

aircraft of all types shall be eliminated from the armed forces and destroyed, except for an agreed and strictly limited number of inter-continental missiles, anti-missile missiles and anti-aircraft missiles in the ground to air category, to be retained by the Union of Soviet Socialist Republics and the United States of America, exclusively in their own territory, until the end of the second stage. A strictly limited number of rockets to be converted to peaceful uses under the provisions of Article 15 of the present treaty shall also be retained.

All launching pads, silos and platforms for the launching of rockets and pilotless aircraft, other than those required for the missiles to be retained under the provisions of this article, shall be completely demolished. All instruments for the equipment, launching and guidance of rockets and pilotless aircraft shall be destroyed. All underground depots for such rockets, pilotless aircraft and auxiliary facilities shall be demolished.

2. The production of all kinds of rockets and pilotless aircraft and of the materials and instruments for their equipment, launching and guidance referred to in paragraph 1 of this article shall be com-pletely discontinued. All undertakings or workshops thereof engaged in their production shall be dismantled; machine tools and equipment specially and exclusively designed for the production of such items shall be destroyed; the premises of such undertakings as well as general-purpose machine tools and equipment shall be converted to peaceful uses. All proving grounds for tests of such rockets and pilotless aircraft shall be demolished.

3. Inspectors of the International Disarmament Organization shall verify the implementation of the measures referred to in para-graphs 1 and 2 above.

4. The production and testing of appropriate rockets for the peaceful exploration of space shall be allowed, provided that the plants producing such rockets, as well as the rockets themselves, will be subject to supervision by the inspectors of the International Disarmament Organization.

ARTICLE 6

ELIMINATION OF MILITARY AIRCRAFT CAPABLE OF DELIVERING NUCLEAR WEAPONS

1. All military aircraft capable of delivering nuclear weapons shall be eliminated from the armed forces and destroyed. Military airfields serving as bases for such aircraft and repair and maintenance facilities and storage premises at such airfields shall be rendered inoperative or converted to peaceful uses. Training establishments for crews of such aircraft shall be closed.

2. The production of all military aircraft referred to in paragraph 1 of this article shall be completely discontinued. Undertakings or workshops thereof designed for the production of such military aircraft shall be either dismantled or converted to the production of civil aircraft or other civilian goods.

3. Inspectors of the International Disarmament Organization shall verify the implementation of the measures referred in paragraphs 1 and 2 above.

ARTICLE 7
ELIMINATION OF ALL SURFACE WARSHIPS CAPABLE OF BEING USED AS VEHICLES FOR NUCLEAR WEAPONS AND SUBMARINES

1. All surface warships capable of being used as vehicles for nuclear weapons and submarines of all classes or types shall be eliminated from the armed forces and destroyed. Naval bases and other installations for the maintenance of the above warships and submarines shall be demolished or dismantled and handed over to the merchant marine for peaceful uses.

2. The building of the warships and submarines referred to in paragraph 1 of this article shall be completely discontinued. Shipyards and plants, wholly or partly designed for the building of such warships and submarines, shall be dismantled or converted to peaceful production.

3. Inspectors of the International Disarmament Organization shall verify the implementation of the measures referred to in paragraphs 1 and 2 above.

ARTICLE 8
ELIMINATION OF ALL ARTILLERY SYSTEMS CAPABLE OF SERVING AS MEANS OF DELIVERING NUCLEAR WEAPONS

1. All artillery systems capable of serving as means of delivering nuclear weapons shall be eliminated from the armed forces and destroyed. All auxiliary equipment and technical facilities designed for controlling the fire of such artillery systems shall be destroyed. Surface storage premises and transport facilities for such systems shall be destroyed or converted to peaceful uses. The entire stock of non-nuclear munitions for such artillery systems, whether at the gun site or in depots, shall be completely destroyed. Underground depots for such artillery systems and for the non-nuclear munitions thereof shall be destroyed.

2. The production of the artillery systems referred to in paragraph 1 of this article shall be completely discontinued. To this end, all

plants or workshops thereof engaged in the production of such systems shall be closed and dismantled. All specialized equipment and machine tools at these plants and workshops shall be destroyed, the remainder being converted to peaceful uses. The production of non-nuclear munitions for these artillery systems shall be discontinued. Plants and workshops engaged in the production of such munitions shall be completely dismantled and their specialized equipment destroyed.

3. Inspectors of the International Disarmament Organization shall verify the implementation of the measures referred to in paragraphs 1 and 2 above.

B. Foreign Military Bases and Troops in Alien Territories

Article 9

Dismantling of Foreign Military Bases

1. Simultaneously with the destruction of the means of delivering nuclear weapons under Articles 5–8 of the present treaty the states parties to the treaty which have army, air force or naval bases in foreign territories shall dismantle all such bases, whether principal or reserve bases, as well as all depot bases of any types. All personnel of such bases shall be evacuated to their national territory. All installations and armaments existing at such bases and coming under Articles 5–8 of the present treaty shall be destroyed on the spot. Other armaments shall either be destroyed on the spot in accordance with Article 11 of the present treaty or evacuated to the territory of the state which owned the base. All installations of a military nature at such bases shall be destroyed. The living quarters and auxiliary installations of foreign bases shall be transferred for civilian use to the states in whose territory they are located.

2. The measures referred to in paragraph 1 of this article shall be fully applicable to military bases which are used by foreign troops but which may legally belong to the state in whose territory they are located. The said measures shall also be implemented with respect to army, air force and naval bases that have been set up under military treaties and agreements for use by other states or groups of states, regardless of whether any foreign troops are present at those bases at the time of the conclusion of the present treaty.

All previous treaty obligations, decisions of the organs of military blocs and any rights or privileges pertaining to the establishment or use of military bases in foreign territories shall lapse and may not be renewed. It shall henceforth be prohibited to grant military bases for use by foreign troops and to conclude any bilateral or multilateral treaties and agreements to this end.

3.   The legislatures and Governments of the states parties to the present treaty shall enact legislation and issue regulations to ensure that no military bases to be used by foreign troops are established in their territory. Inspectors of the International Disarmament Organization shall verify the implementation of the measures referred to in paragraphs 1 and 2 of this article.

ARTICLE 10

WITHDRAWAL OF FOREIGN TROOPS FROM ALIEN TERRITORIES

1.   Simultaneously with the elimination of the means of delivering nuclear weapons under Articles 5–8 of the present treaty, the states parties to the treaty which have troops or military personnel of any nature in foreign territories shall withdraw all such troops and personnel from such territories. All armaments and all installations of a military nature which are located at points where foreign troops are stationed and which come under Articles 5–8 of the present treaty shall be destroyed on the spot. Other armaments shall either be destroyed on the spot in accordance with Article 11 of the present treaty or evacuated to the territory of the state withdrawing its troops. The living quarters and auxiliary installations previously occupied by such troops or personnel shall be transferred for civilian use to the states in whose territory such troops were stationed.

2.   The measures set forth in paragraph 1 of this article shall be fully applicable to foreign civilians employed in the armed forces or engaged in the production of armaments or any other activities serving military purposes in foreign territory.

Such persons shall be recalled to the territory of the state of which they are citizens, and all previous treaty obligations, decisions by organs of military blocs, and any rights or privileges pertaining to their activities shall lapse and may not be renewed. It shall henceforth be prohibited to despatch foreign troops, military personnel or the above-mentioned civilians to foreign territories.

3.   Inspectors of the International Disarmament Organization shall verify the withdrawal of troops, the destruction of installations and the transfer of the premises referred to in paragraph 1 of this article. The International Disarmament Organization shall also have the right to exercise control over the recall of the civilians referred to in paragraph 2 of this article. The laws and regulations referred to in paragraph 3 of Article 9 of the present treaty shall include provisions prohibiting citizens of states parties to the treaty from serving in the

armed forces or from engaging in any other activities serving military purposes in foreign states.

CHAPTER II

Reduction of Armed Forces, Conventional Armaments and Military Expenditure Control over such Measures

Article 11

Reduction of Armed Forces and Conventional Armaments

1. In the first stage of general and complete disarmament the armed forces of the states parties to the treaty shall be reduced to the following levels:

The United States of America—1,900,000 enlisted men, officers and civilian employees;

The Union of Soviet Socialist Republics—1,900,000 enlisted men, officers and civilian employees.

....

(Agreed force levels for other states parties to the treaty shall be included in this article.)

2. The reduction of the armed forces shall be carried out in the first place through the demobilization of personnel released as a result of the elimination of the means of delivering nuclear weapons, the dismantling of foreign bases and the withdrawal of foreign troops from alien territories, as provided for in Articles 5–10 of the present treaty, but chiefly through the complete disbandment of units and ships' crews, their officers and enlisted men being demobilized.

3. Conventional armaments, military equipment, munitions, means of transportation and auxiliary equipment in units and depots shall be reduced by thirty per cent for each type of all categories of these armaments. The reduced armaments, military equipment and munitions shall be destroyed, and the means of transportation and auxiliary equipment shall be either destroyed or converted to peaceful uses.

All living quarters, depots and special premises previously occupied by units being disbanded, as well as the territories of all proving grounds, firing ranges and drill grounds belonging to such units, shall be transferred for peaceful uses to the civilian authorities.

4. Inspectors of the International Disarmament Organization shall exercise control at places where troops are being disbanded and released conventional armaments and military equipment are being destroyed, and shall also verify the conversion to peaceful uses of means of transportation and other non-combat equipment, premises, proving grounds, etc.

ARTICLE 12

REDUCTION OF CONVENTIONAL ARMAMENTS PRODUCTION

1. The production of conventional armaments and munitions not coming under Articles 5–8 of the present treaty shall be reduced proportionately to the reduction of armed forces provided for in Article 11 of the present treaty. Such reduction shall be carried out primarily through the elimination of undertakings engaged exclusively in the production of such armaments and munitions. These undertakings shall be dismantled, their specialized machine tools and equipment shall be destroyed, and their premises, and general-purpose machine tools and equipment shall be converted to peaceful uses.

2. Inspectors of the International Disarmament Organization shall exercise control over the measures referred to in paragraph 1 of this article.

ARTICLE 13

REDUCTION OF MILITARY EXPENDITURE

1. The states parties to the present treaty shall reduce their military budgets and appropriations for military purposes pro-portionately to the destruction of the means of delivering nuclear weapons and the discontinuance of their production, to the dis-mantling of foreign military bases and the withdrawal of foreign troops from alien territories as well as to the reduction of armed forces and conventional armaments and to the reduction of the production of such armaments, as provided for in Articles 5–12 of the present treaty.

The funds released through the implementation of the first-stage measures shall be used for peaceful purposes, including the reduction of taxes on the population and the subsidizing of the national economy. A certain portion of the funds thus released shall also be used for the provision of economic and technical assistance to under-developed countries. The size of this portion shall be subject to agreement between the parties to the treaty.

2. The International Disarmament Organization shall verify the implementation of the measures referred to in paragraph 1 of this article through its financial inspectors, to whom the states parties to the treaty undertake to grant unimpeded access to the records of central financial institutions concerning the reduction in their budgetary appropriations resulting from the elimination of the means of delivering nuclear weapons, the dismantling of foreign military bases and the reduction of armed forces and conventional armaments and to the relevant decisions of their legislative and executive bodies.

CHAPTER III

Measures to Safeguard the Security of States

ARTICLE 14

RESTRICTIONS ON THE MOVEMENT OF MEANS OF
DELIVERING NUCLEAR WEAPONS

1.   From the beginning of the first stage until the final destruction of all means of delivering nuclear weapons in accordance with Articles 5–8 of the present treaty, it shall be prohibited for any special devices capable of delivering weapons of mass destruction beyond the limits of their national territory to be placed in orbit or stationed in outer space, for warships to leave their territorial waters and for military aircraft capable of carrying weapons of mass destruction to fly to.

2.   The International Disarmament Organization shall exercise control over compliance by the states parties to the treaty with the provisions of paragraph 1 of this article. The states parties to the treaty shall provide the International Disarmament Organization with advance information on all launchings of rockets for peaceful purposes provided for in Article 15 of the present treaty, as well as on all movements of military aircraft within their national frontiers and of warships within their territorial waters.

ARTICLE 15

CONTROL OVER LAUNCHINGS OF ROCKETS FOR PEACEFUL PURPOSES

1.   The launching of rockets and space devices shall be carried out exclusively for peaceful purposes.

2.   The International Disarmament Organization shall exercise control over the implementation of the provisions of paragraph 1 of this article through the establishment, at the sites for peaceful rocket launchings of inspection teams, which shall be present at the launchings and shall thoroughly examine every rocket or satellite before its launching.

ARTICLE 16

PREVENTION OF THE FURTHER SPREAD OF NUCLEAR WEAPONS

The states parties to the treaty which possess nuclear weapons undertake to refrain from transferring control over nuclear weapons and from transmitting information necessary for their production to states not possessing such weapons.

The states parties to the treaty not possessing nuclear weapons undertake to refrain from producing or otherwise obtaining nuclear weapons and shall refuse to admit the nuclear weapons of any other state into their territories.

ARTICLE 17
PROHIBITION OF NUCLEAR TESTS

The conducting of nuclear tests of any kind shall be prohibited (if such a prohibition has not come into effect under other international agreements by the time this treaty is signed).

ARTICLE 17A
MEASURES TO REDUCE THE DANGER OF OUTBREAK OF WAR

1. From the commencement of the first stage large-scale joint military movements or manoeuvres by armed forces of two or more states shall be prohibited.

The states parties to the treaty agree to give advance notification of large-scale military movements or manoeuvres by their national armed forces within their national frontiers.

2. The states parties to the treaty shall exchange military missions between states or groups of states for the purpose of improving relations and mutual understanding between them.

3. The states parties to the treaty agree to establish swift and reliable communication between their Heads of Government and with the Secretary-General of the United Nations.

4. The measures set forth in this article shall remain in effect after the first stage until the completion of general and complete disarmament.

ARTICLE 18
MEASURES TO STRENGTHEN THE CAPACITY OF THE UNITED NATIONS TO MAINTAIN INTERNATIONAL PEACE AND SECURITY

1. With a view to ensuring that the United Nations is capable of effectively protecting states against threats to or breaches of the peace, all states parties to the treaty shall, between the signing of the treaty and its entry into force, conclude agreements with the Security Council by which they undertake to make available to the latter armed forces, assistance and facilities, including rights of passage, as provided in Article 43 of the United Nations Charter.

2.   The armed forces specified in the said agreements shall form part of the national armed forces of the states concerned and shall be stationed within their territories. They shall be kept up to full strength and shall be fully equipped and prepared for combat. When used under Article 42 of the United Nations Charter, these forces, serving under the command of the military authorities of the states concerned, shall be placed at the disposal of the Security Council.

CHAPTER IV

Time-limits for First-Stage Measures Transition from the First to the Second Stage

ARTICLE 19

TIME-LIMITS FOR FIRST-STAGE MEASURES

1.   The first stage of general and complete disarmament shall be initiated six months after the treaty comes into force (in accordance with Article 46), within which period the International Disarmament Organization shall be set up.

2.   The duration of the first stage of general and complete disarmament shall be eighteen months.

ARTICLE 20

TRANSITION FROM THE FIRST TO THE SECOND STAGE

In the course of the last three months of the first stage the International Disarmament Organization shall review the implementation of the first-stage measures of general and complete disarmament with a view to submitting a report on the matter to the states parties to the treaty as well as to the Security Council and the General Assembly of the United Nations.

PART III.   SECOND STAGE OF GENERAL AND COMPLETE DISARMAMENT

ARTICLE 21

SECOND STAGE TASKS

The states parties to the treaty shall undertake, in the course of the second stage of general and complete disarmament, to effect the complete elimination of nuclear and other weapons of mass destruction, to conclude the destruction of all military rockets capable of delivering nuclear weapons which were retained by the Union of Soviet Socialist Republics and the United States of America after the implementation of the first stage, and to make a further reduction in their armed forces, conventional armaments and production of such armaments, and military expenditure.

CHAPTER V

Elimination of Nuclear, Chemical, Biological and Radiological Weapons. Control over such Measures

ARTICLE 22

ELIMINATION OF NUCLEAR WEAPONS

1. (a) Nuclear weapons of all kinds, types and capacities shall be eliminated from the armed forces and destroyed. Fissionable materials extracted from such weapons, whether directly attached to units or stored in various depots, shall be appropriately processed to render them unfit for direct reconstitution into weapons and shall form a special stock for peaceful uses, belonging to the state which previously owned the nuclear weapons. Non-nuclear components of such weapons shall be completely destroyed.

All depots and special storage spaces for nuclear weapons shall be demolished.

(b) All stockpiles of nuclear materials intended for the production of nuclear weapons shall be appropriately processed to render them unfit for direct use in nuclear weapons and shall be transferred to the above-mentioned special stocks.

(c) Inspectors of the International Disarmament Organization shall verify the implementation of the measures to eliminate nuclear weapons referred to above in sub-paragraphs (a) and (b) of this paragraph.

2. (a) The production of nuclear weapons and of fissionable materials for weapons purposes shall be completely discontinued. All plants, installations and laboratories specially designed for the production of nuclear weapons or their components shall be eliminated or converted to production for peaceful purposes. All workshops, installations and laboratories for the production of the components of nuclear weapons at plants that are partially engaged in the production of such weapons shall be destroyed or converted to production for peaceful purposes.

(b) The measures for the discontinuance of the production of nuclear weapons and of fissionable materials for weapons purposes referred to in sub-paragraph (a) above shall be implemented under the control of inspectors of the International Disarmament Organization.

The International Disarmament Organization shall have the right to inspect all undertakings which extract raw materials for atomic production or which produce or use fissionable materials or atomic energy.

The states parties to the treaty shall make available to the International Disarmament Organization documents pertaining to the extraction and process of nuclear raw materials and to their utilization for military or peaceful purposes.

3. Each state party to the treaty shall, in accordance with its constitutional procedures, enact legislation completely prohibiting nuclear weapons and making any attempt by individuals or organizations to reconstitute such weapons a criminal offence.

ARTICLE 23

ELIMINATION OF CHEMICAL, BIOLOGICAL AND RADIOLOGICAL WEAPONS

1. All types of chemical, biological and radiological weapons, whether directly attached to units or stored in various depots and storage places, shall be eliminated from the arsenals of states and destroyed (neutralized). All instruments and facilities for the combat use of such weapons, all special facilities for their transportation, and all special devices and facilities for their storage and conservation shall simultaneously be destroyed.

2. The production of all types of chemical, biological and radiological weapons and of all means and devices for their combat use, transportation and storage shall be completely discontinued. All plants, installations and laboratories that are wholly or partly engaged in the production of such weapons shall be destroyed or converted to production for peaceful purposes.

3. The measures referred to in paragraphs 1 and 2 above shall be implemented under the control of inspectors of the International Disarmament Organization.

CHAPTER VA

The Destruction of Rockets Capable of Delivering Nuclear Weapons which were Retained after the First Stage

ARTICLE 23A

1. All intercontinental missiles, anti-missilemis siles and anti aircraft missiles in the ground to air category retained by the Union of Soviet Socialist Republics and the United States of America under paragraph 1 of Article 5 shall be destroyed, together with their launching installations and guidance systems.

2. Inspectors of the International Disarmament Organization shall verify the implementation of the measures referred to in paragraph 1 above.

CHAPTER VI

Further Reduction of Armed Forces, Conventional Armaments and Military Expenditures, Control over such Measures

ARTICLE 24

FURTHER REDUCTION OF ARMED FORCES AND CONVENTIONAL ARMAMENTS

1. In the second stage of general and complete disarmament the armed forces of the states parties to the treaty shall be further reduced to the following levels:

The United States of America — One million enlisted men, officers and civilian employees;

The Union of Soviet Socialist Republics .... — One million enlisted men, officers and civilian employees.

....

(Agreed force levels for other states parties to the treaty shall be included in this article.)

The reduction of the armed forces shall be carried out in the first place through the demobilization of personnel previously manning the nuclear or other weapons subject to elimination under Articles 22 and 23 of the present treaty, but chiefly through the complete disbandment of units and ships' crews, their officers and enlisted men being demobilized.

2. Conventional armaments, military equipment, munitions, means of transportation and auxiliary equipment in units and depots shall be reduced by thirty-five from the original levels for each type of all categories of these armaments. The reduced armaments, military equipment and munitions shall be destroyed, and the means of transportation and auxiliary equipment shall be either destroyed or converted to peaceful uses.

All living quarters, depots and special premises previously occupied by units being disbanded, as well as the territories of all proving grounds, firing ranges and drill grounds belonging to such units shall be transferred for peaceful uses to the civilian authorities.

3. As in the implementation of such measures in the first stage of general and complete disarmament, inspectors of the International Disarmament Organization shall exercise control at places where troops are being disbanded and released conventional armaments and military equipment are being destroyed, and shall also verify the conversion to peaceful uses of means of transportation and other non-combat equipment, premises, proving grounds, etc.

ARTICLE 25
FURTHER REDUCTION OF CONVENTIONAL ARMAMENTS PRODUCTION

1. The production of conventional armaments and munitions shall be reduced proportionately to the reduction of armed forces provided for in Article 24 of the preseent treaty. Such reduction shall, as in the first stage of general and complete disarmament, be carried out primarily through the elimination of undertakings engaged exclusively in the production of such armaments and munitions. These undertakings shall be dismantled, their specialized machine tools and equipment shall be destroyed, and their premises and general purpose machine tools and equipment shall be converted to peaceful uses.

2. The measures referred to in paragraph 1 of this article shall be carried out under the control of inspectors of the International Disarmament Organization.

ARTICLE 26
FURTHER REDUCTION OF MILITARY EXPENDITURE

1. The states parties to the treaty shall further reduce their military budgets and appropriations for military purposes proportionately to the destruction of nuclear, chemical, biological and radiological weapons and the discontinuance of the production of such weapons as well as to the further reduction of armed forces and conventional armaments and the reduction of the production of such armaments, as provided for in Articles 22–25 of the present treaty.

The funds released through the implementation of the second-stage measures shall be used for peaceful purposes, including the reduction of taxes on the population and the subsidizing of the national economy. A certain portion of the funds thus released shall also be used for the provision of economic and technical assistance to under-developed countries. The size of this portion shall be subject to agreement between the parties to the treaty.

2. Control over the measures referred to in paragraph 1 of this article shall be exercised in accordance with the provisions of para-

graph 2 of Article 13 of the present treaty. Financial inspectors of the International Disarmament Organization shall also be granted unimpeded access to records concerning the reduction in the budgetary appropriations of states resulting from the elimination of nuclear, chemical, biological and radiological weapons.

CHAPTER VII

Measures to Safeguard the Security of States

ARTICLE 27

CONTINUED STRENGTHENING OF THE CAPACITY OF THE UNITED NATIONS TO MAINTAIN INTERNATIONAL PEACE AND SECURITY

The states parties to the treaty shall continue to implement the measures referred to in Article 18 of the present treaty regarding the placing of armed forces at the disposal of the Security Council for use under Article 42 of the United Nations Charter.

CHAPTER VIII

Time-limits for Second Stage Measures
Transition from the Second to the Third Stage

ARTICLE 28

TIME-LIMITS FOR SECOND STAGE MEASURES

The duration of the second stage of general and complete disarmament shall be twenty-four months.

ARTICLE 29

TRANSITION FROM THE SECOND TO THE THIRD STAGE

In the course of the last three months of the second stage the International Disarmament Organization shall review the implementation of this stage.

Measures for the transition from the second to the third stage of general and complete disarmament shall be similar to the corresponding measures for the first stage, as laid down in Article 20 of the present treaty.

D.V.–N

PART IV. THIRD STAGE OF GENERAL AND COMPLETE DISARMAMENT

ARTICLE 30

THIRD STAGE TASKS

The states parties to the treaty undertake, in the course of the third stage of general and complete disarmament, fully to disband all their armed forces and thereby to complete the elimination of the military machinery of states.

CHAPTER IX

Completion of the Elimination of the Military Machinery of States Control over such Measures

ARTICLE 31

COMPLETION OF THE ELIMINATION OF ARMED FORCES AND CONVENTIONAL ARMAMENTS

1. With a view to completing the process of the elimination of armed forces, the states parties to the treaty shall disband the entire personnel of the armed forces which remained at their disposal after the accomplishment of the first two stages of disarmament. The system of military reserves of each state party to the treaty shall be completely abolished.

2. The states parties to the treaty shall destroy all types of armaments, military equipment and munitions, whether held by the troops or in depots, that remained at their disposal after the accomplishment of the first two stages of the treaty. All military equipment which cannot be converted to peaceful uses shall be destroyed.

3. Inspectors of the International Disarmament Organization shall exercise control over the disbanding of troops and over the destruction of armaments and military equipment, and shall control the conversion to peaceful uses of transport and other non-combat equipment, premises, proving grounds, etc.

The International Disarmament Organization shall have access to documents pertaining to the disbanding of all personnel of the armed forces of the states parties to the treaty.

ARTICLE 32

COMPLETE CESSATION OF MILITARY PRODUCTION

1. Military production at factories and plants shall be discontinued, with the exception of the production of agreed types and quantities of light firearms for the purposes referred to in Article 36,

paragraph 2, of the present treaty. The factories and plants subject to elimination shall be dismantled, their specialized machine tools and equipment shall be destroyed, and the premises, general purpose machine tools and equipment shall be converted to peaceful uses. All scientific research in the military field at all scientific and research institutions and at designing offices shall be discontinued. All blueprints and other documents necessary for the production of the weapons and military equipment subject to elimination shall be destroyed.

All orders placed by military departments with national or foreign government undertakings and private firms for the production of armaments, military equipment, munitions and material shall be cancelled.

2. Inspectors of the International Disarmament Organization shall exercise control over the measures referred to in paragraph 1 of this article.

ARTICLE 33

ABOLITION OF MILITARY ESTABLISHMENTS

1. War ministries, general staffs and all other military and paramilitary organizations and institutions for the purpose of organizing the military effort of states parties to the treaty shall be abolished. The states parties to the treaty shall:

(a) demobilize all personnel of these institutions and organizations;
(b) abrogate all laws, rules and regulations governing the organization of the military effort and the status, structure and activities of such institutions and organizations;
(c) destroy all documents pertaining to the planning of the mobilization and operational deployment of the armed forces in time of war.

2. The entire process of the abolition of military and paramilitary institutions and organizations shall be carried out under the control of inspectors of the International Disarmament Organization.

ARTICLE 34

ABOLITION OF MILITARY CONSCRIPTION AND MILITARY TRAINING

In accordance with their respective constitutional procedures, the states parties to the treaty shall enact legislation prohibiting all military training, abolishing military conscription and all other forms of recruiting the armed forces, and discontinuing all military courses for reservists. All establishments and organizations dealing with military training shall simultaneously be disbanded in accordance with Article 33 of the present treaty. The disbanding of all military training institutions and organizations shall be carried out under the control of inspectors of the International Disarmament Organization.

ARTICLE 35
PROHIBITION OF THE APPROPRIATION OF FUNDS FOR MILITARY PURPOSES

1.   The appropriation of funds for military purposes in any form, whether by Government bodies or private individuals and social organizations, shall be discontinued.

The funds released through the implementation of general and complete disarmament shall be used for peaceful purposes, including the reduction or complete abolition of taxes on the population and the subsidizing of the national economy. A certain portion of the funds thus released shall also be used for the provision of economic and technical assistance to underdeveloped countries. The size of this portion shall be subject to agreement between the parties to the treaty.

2.   For the purpose of organizing control over the implementation of the provisions of this Article, the International Disarmament Organization shall have the right to access to the legislative and budgetary documents of the states parties to the present treaty.

CHAPTER X
Measures to Safeguard the Security of States and to Maintain International Peace

ARTICLE 36
CONTINGENTS OF POLICE (MILITIA)

1.   After the complete abolition of armed forces, the states parties to the treaty shall be entitled to have strictly limited contingents of police (militia), equipped with light firearms, to maintain internal order, including the safeguarding of frontiers and the personal security of citizens, and to provide for compliance with their obligations in regard to the maintenance of international peace and security under the United Nations Charter.

The strength of these contingents of police (militia) for each state party of the treaty shall be as follows:

....

....

2.   The states parties to the treaty shall be allowed to manufacture strictly limited quantities of light firearms intended for such con-

tingents of police (militia). The list of plants producing such arms, the quotas and types for each party to the treaty shall be specified in a special agreement.

3. Inspectors of the International Disarmament Organization shall exercise control over compliance by the states parties to the treaty with their obligations with regard to the restricted production of the said light firearms.

ARTICLE 37

POLICE (MILITIA) UNITS TO BE MADE AVAILABLE TO THE SECURITY COUNCIL

1. The states parties to the treaty undertake to place at the disposal of the Security Council, on its request, units from the contingents of police (militia) retained by them, as well as to provide assistance and facilities, including rights of passage. The placing of such units at the disposal of the Security Council shall be carried out in accordance with the provisions of Article 43 of the United Nations Charter. In order to ensure that urgent military measures may be undertaken, the states parties to the treaty shall maintain in a state of immediate readiness those units of their police (militia) contingents which are intended for joint international enforcement action. The size of the units which the states parties to the treaty undertake to place at the disposal of the Security Council as well as the areas where such units are to be stationed shall be specified in agreements to be concluded by those states with the Security Council.

2. The command of the units referred to in paragraph 1 shall be composed of representatives of the three principal groups of states existing in the world on the basis of equal representation. It shall decide all questions by agreement among its members representing all three groups of states.

ARTICLE 38

CONTROL OVER THE PREVENTION OF THE RE-ESTABLISHMENT OF ARMED FORCES

1. The police (militia) contingents retained by the states parties to the treaty after the completion of general and complete disarmament shall be under the control of the International Disarmament Organization, which shall verify the reports by states concerning the areas where such contingents are stationed, concerning the strength and armaments of the contingents in each such area, and concerning all movements of substantial contingents of police (militia).

2. For the purpose of ensuring that armed forces and armaments abolished as a result of general and complete disarmament are not re-established, the International Disarmament Organization shall have the right of access at any time to any point within the territory of each state party to the treaty.

3. The International Disarmament Organization shall have the right to institute a system of aerial inspection and aerial photography over the territories of the states parties to the treaty.

CHAPTER XI
Time-limits for Third-Stage Measures
ARTICLE 39

The third stage of general and complete disarmament shall be completed over a period of one year. During the last three months of this stage the International Disarmament Organization shall review the implementation of the third-stage measures of general and complete disarmament with a view to submitting a report on the matter to the states parties to the treaty as well as to the Security Council and the General Assembly of the United Nations.

PART V. STRUCTURE AND FUNCTIONS OF THE INTERNATIONAL DISARMAMENT ORGANIZATION

ARTICLE 40
FUNCTIONS AND MAIN BODIES

The International Disarmament Organization to be set up under Article 2, paragraph 3, of the present treaty, hereinafter referred to as the 'Organization', shall consist of a Conference of all states parties to the treaty, hereinafter referred to as the 'Conference', and a Control Council, hereinafter referred to as the 'Council'.

The Organization shall deal with questions pertaining to the supervision of compliance by states with their obligations under the present treaty. All questions connected with the safeguarding of international peace and security which may arise in the course of the implementation of the present treaty, including preventive and enforcement measures, shall be decided by the Security Council in conformity with its powers under the United Nations Charter.

ARTICLE 41
THE CONFERENCE

1. The Conference shall comprise all states parties to the treaty. It shall hold regular sessions at least once a year and special sessions, which may be convened by decision of the Council or at the request of

a majority of the states parties to the treaty with a view to considering matters connected with the implementation of effective control over disarmament. The sessions shall be held at the headquarters of the Organization, unless otherwise decided by the Conference.

2. Each state party to the treaty shall have one vote. Decision on questions of procedure shall be taken by a simple majority and on all other matters by a two-thirds majority. In accordance with the provisions of the present treaty, the Conference shall adopt its own rules of procedure.

3. The Conference may discuss any matters pertaining to measures of control over the implementation of general and complete disarmament and may make recommendations to the states parties to the treaty and to the Council on any such matter or measure.

4. The Conference shall:

(a) Elect non-permanent members of the Council;
(b) Consider the annual, and any special, reports of the Council;
(c) Approve the budget recommended by the Council;
(d) Approve reports to be submitted to the Security Council and the General Assembly of the United Nations;
(e) Approve amendments to the present treaty in accordance with Article 47 of the present treaty;
(f) Take decisions on any matter specifically referred to the Conference for this purpose by the Council;
(g) Propose matters for consideration by the Council and request from the Council reports on any matter relating to the functions of the Council.

ARTICLE 42
THE CONTROL COUNCIL

1. The Council shall consist of:
(a) The five states which are permanent members of the United Nations Security Council;
(b) . . . (number) other states parties to the treaty, elected by the Conference for a period of two years.

The composition of the Council must ensure proper representation of the three principal groups of states existing in the world.

2. The Council shall:

(a) Provide practical guidance for the measures of control over the implementation of general and complete disarmament; set up such bodies at the headquarters of the Organization as it deems necessary for the discharge of its functions; establish procedures for their operation, and devise the necessary rules and regulations in accordance with the present treaty;

(b) Submit to the Conference annual reports and such special reports as it deems necessary to prepare;

(c) Maintain constant contact with the United Nations Security Council as the organ bearing the primary responsibility for the maintenance of international peace and security; periodically inform it of the progress achieved in the implementation of general and complete disarmament, and promptly notify it of any infringements by the states parties to the treaty of their disarmament obligations under the present treaty;

(d) Review the implementation of the measures included in each stage of general and complete disarmament with a view to submitting a report on the matter to the states parties to the treaty and to the Security Council and the General Assembly of the United Nations;

(e) Recruit the staff of the Organization on an international basis so as to ensure that the three principal groups of states existing in the world are adequately represented. The personnel of the Organization shall be recruited from among persons who are recommended by Governments and who may or may not be citizens of the country of the recommending Government;

(f) Prepare and submit to the Conference the annual budget estimates for the expenses of the Organization;

(g) Draw up instructions by which the various control bodies are to be guided in their work;

(h) Make a prompt study of incoming reports;

(i) Request from states such information on their armed forces and armaments as may be necessary for control over the implementation of the disarmament measures provided for by the present treaty;

(j) Perform such other functions as are envisaged in the present treaty.

3. Each member of the Council shall have one vote. Decisions of the Council on procedural matters shall be taken by a simple majority, and on other matters by a two-thirds majority.

4. The Council shall be so organized as to be able to function continuously. The Council shall adopt its own rules of procedure and shall be authorized to establish such subsidiary organs as it deems necessary for the performance of its functions.

Article 43

Privileges and Immunities

The Organization, its personnel and representatives of the states parties to the treaty shall enjoy in the territory of each state party to the treaty such privileges and immunities as are necessary for the exercise of independent and unrestricted control over the implementation of the present treaty.

ARTICLE 44
FINANCES

1.   All the expenses of the Organization shall be financed from the funds allocated by the states parties to the treaty. The budget of the Organization shall be drawn up by the Council and approved by the Conference in accordance with Article 41, paragraph 4 (c), and Article 42, paragraph 2 (f), of the present treaty.

2.   The states parties to the treaty shall contribute funds to cover the expenditure of the Organization according to the following scale:

....

(The agreed scale of contributions shall be included in the present article.)

ARTICLE 45
PREPARATORY COMMISSION

Immediately after the signing of the present treaty, the states represented in the 18-nation Disarmament Committee shall set up a Preparatory Commission for the purpose of taking practical steps to establish the International Disarmament Organization.

PART VI. FINAL CLAUSES

ARTICLE 46
RATIFICATION AND ENTRY INTO FORCE

The present treaty shall be subject to ratification by the signatory states in accordance with their constitutional procedures within a period of six months from the date of its signature, and shall come into force upon the deposit of instruments of ratification with the United Nations Secretariat by all the states which are permanent members of the Security Council, as well as by those states that are their allies in bilateral and multilateral military alliances, and by . . . (number) non-aligned states.

ARTICLE 47
AMENDMENTS

Any proposal to amend the text of the present treaty shall come into force after it has been adopted by a two-thirds majority at a conference of all states parties to the treaty and has been ratified by the states referred to in Article 46 of the present treaty in accordance with their constitutional procedures.

ARTICLE 48
AUTHENTIC TEXTS

The present treaty, done in the Russian, English, French, Chinese and Spanish languages, all texts being equally authentic, shall be deposited with the United Nations Secretariat, which shall transmit certified copies thereof to all the signatory states.

In witness whereof, the undersigned, duly authorized, have signed the present treaty.

Done at . . .

CORRECTION TO THE REVISED SOVIET DRAFT, 20TH DECEMBER 1962

Replace Article 14, paragraph 1, by the following:

ARTICLE 14
RESTRICTION OF DISPLACEMENTS OF THE MEANS OF DELIVERING NUCLEAR WEAPONS

1. From the very beginning of the first-stage and until the final destruction of all means of delivering nuclear weapons under Articles 5–8 of the present treaty, the placing into orbit or stationing in outer space of any special devices capable of delivering weapons of mass destruction, the leaving of their territorial waters by warships, and the flying beyond the limits of their national territory by military aircraft capable of carrying weapons of mass destruction, shall be prohibited.

APPENDIX V

UNITED STATES' OUTLINE OF BASIC PROVISIONS OF A TREATY ON GENERAL AND COMPLETE DISARMAMENT IN A PEACEFUL WORLD, OF 18TH APRIL 1962

In order to assist in the preparation of a treaty on general and complete disarmament in a peaceful world, the United States submits the following outline of basic provisions of such a treaty.

. . . .

A. *Objectives*

1. To ensure that (a) disarmament is general and complete and war is no longer an instrument for settling international problems, and (b) general and complete disarmament is accompanied by the establishment of reliable procedures for the settlement of disputes and by effective arrangements for the maintenance of peace in accordance with the principles of the Charter of the United Nations.

2. Taking into account paragraphs 3 and 4 below, to provide, with respect to the military establishment of every nation, for:

(a) Disbanding of armed forces, dismantling of military establishments, including bases, cessation of the production of armaments as well as their liquidation or conversion to peaceful uses;

(b) Elimination of all stockpiles of nuclear, chemical, biological and other weapons of mass destruction and cessation of the production of such weapons;

(c) Elimination of all means of delivery of weapons of mass destruction;

(d) Abolition of the organizations and institutions designed to organize the military efforts of states, cessation of military training, and closing of all military training institutions;

(e) Discontinuance of military expenditures.

3. To ensure that, at the completion of the programme for general and complete disarmament, states would have at their disposal only those non-nuclear armaments, forces, facilities and establishments as are agreed to be necessary to maintain internal order and protect the personal security of citizens.

4. To ensure that during and after implementation of general and complete disarmament, states also would support and provide agreed manpower for a United Nations Peace Force to be equipped with agreed types of armaments necessary to ensure that the United Nations can effectively deter or suppress any threat or use of arms.

5. To establish and provide for the effective operation of an International Disarmament Organization within the framework of the United Nations for the purpose of ensuring that all obligations under the disarmament programme would be honoured and observed during and after implementation of general and complete disarmament; and to this end to ensure that the International Disarmament Organization and its inspectors would have unrestricted access without veto to all places as necessary for the purpose of effective verification.

B. *Principles*

The guiding principles during the achievement of these objectives are:

1. Disarmament would be implemented until it is completed by stages to be carried out within specified time limits.

2. Disarmament would be balanced so that at no stage of the implementation of the treaty could any state or group of states gain military advantage, and so that security would be ensured equally for all.

3. Compliance with all disarmament obligations would be effectively verified during and after their entry into force. Verification arrangements would be instituted progressively as necessary to ensure throughout the disarmament process that agreed levels of armaments and armed forces were not exceeded.

4. As national armaments are reduced, the United Nations would be progressively strengthened in order to improve its capacity to ensure international security and the peaceful settlement of differences as well as to facilitate the development of international co-operation in common tasks for the benefit of mankind.

5. Transition from one stage of disarmament to the next would take place upon decision that all measures in the preceding stage had been implemented and verified and that any additional arrangements required for measures in the next stage were ready to operate.

INTRODUCTION

The treaty would contain three stages designed to achieve a permanent state of general and complete disarmament in a peaceful world. The treaty would enter into force upon the signature and ratification of the United States of America, the Union of Soviet Socialist Republics and such other states as might be agreed. Stage II would begin when all militarily significant states had become parties to the treaty and other transition requirements had been satisfied. Stage III would begin when all states possessing armed forces and armaments had become parties to the treaty and other transition requirements had been satisfied. Disarmament, verification, and measures for keeping the peace would proceed progressively and proportionately beginning with the entry into force of the treaty.

STAGE I

Stage I would begin upon the entry into force of the treaty and would be completed within three years from that date.

During stage I the parties to the treaty would undertake:

(1) To reduce their armaments and armed forces and to carry out other agreed measures in the manner outlined below;

(2) To establish the International Disarmament Organization upon the entry into force of the treaty in order to ensure the verification in the agreed manner of the obligations undertaken; and

(3) To strengthen arrangements for keeping the peace through the measures outlined below.

A. ARMAMENTS

1. *Reduction of Armaments*

(a) Specified parties to the treaty, as a first stage toward general and complete disarmament in a peaceful world, would reduce by thirty per cent the armaments in each category listed in subparagraph (b) below. Except as adjustments for production would be permitted in stage I in accordance with paragraph 3 below, each type of armament in the categories listed in subparagraph (b) would be reduced by thirty per cent of the inventory existing at an agreed date.

(b) All types of armaments within agreed categories would be subject to reduction in stage I (the following list of categories, and of types within categories, is illustrative):

(1) Armed combat aircraft having an empty weight of 40,000 kilograms or greater; missiles having a range of 5,000 kilometres or greater, together with their related fixed launching pads; and submarine-launched missiles and air-to-surface missiles having a range of 300 kilometres or greater.

(Within this category, the United States, for example, would declare as types of armaments: the B-52 aircraft; Atlas missiles together with their related fixed launching pads; Titan missiles together with their related fixed launching pads; Polaris missiles; Hound Dog missiles; and each new type of armament, such as Minuteman missiles, which came within the category description, together with, where applicable, their related fixed launching pads. The declared inventory of types within the category by other parties to the treaty would be similarly detailed.)

(2) Armed combat aircraft having an empty weight of between 15,000 kilograms and 40,000 kilograms and those missiles not included in category (1) having a range between 300 kilometres and 5,000 kilometres, together with any related fixed launching pads. (The parties would declare their armaments by types within the category.)

(3) Armed combat aircraft having an empty weight of between 2,500 and 15,000 kilograms. (The parties would declare their armaments by types within the category.)

(4) Surface-to-surface (including submarine-launched missiles) and air-to-surface aerodynamic and ballistic missiles and free rockets having a range of between 10 kilometres and 300 kilometres, together with any related fixed launching pads. (The parties would declare their armaments by types within the category.)

(5) Anti-missile missile systems, together with related fixed launching pads. (The parties would declare their armaments by types within the category.)

(6) Surface-to-air missiles other than anti-missile missile systems, together with any related fixed launching pads. (The parties would declare their armaments by types within the category.)

(7) Tanks. (The parties would declare their armaments by types within the category.)

(8) Armoured cars and armoured personnel carriers. (The parties would declare their armaments by types within the category.)

(9) All artillery, and mortars and rocket launchers having a calibre of 100 mm. or greater. (The parties would declare their armaments by types within the category.)

(10) Combatant ships with standard displacement of 400 tons or greater of the following classes: Aircraft carriers, battleships, cruisers, destroyer types and submarines. (The parties would declare their armaments by types within the category.)

2. *Method of Reduction*

(a) Those parties to the treaty which were subject to the reduction of armaments would submit to the International Disarmament Organization an appropriate declaration respecting inventories of their armaments existing at the agreed date.

(b) The reduction would be accomplished in three steps, each consisting of one year. One-third of the reduction to be made during stage I would be carried out during each step.

(c) During the first part of each step, one-third of the armaments to be eliminated during stage I would be placed in depots under supervision of the International Disarmament Organization. During the second part of each step, the deposited armaments would be destroyed or, where appropriate, converted to peaceful uses. The number and location of such depots and arrangements respecting their establishment and operation would be set forth in an annex to the treaty.

(d) In accordance with arrangements which would be set forth in a treaty annex on verification, the International Disarmament Organization would verify the foregoing reduction and would provide assurance that retained armaments did not exceed agreed levels.

3. *Limitation on Production of Armaments and on Related Activities*

(a) Production of all armaments listed in subparagraph (b) of paragraph 1 above would be limited to agreed allowances during stage I and, by the beginning of stage II, would be halted except for production within agreed limits of parts for maintenance of the agreed retained armaments.

(b) The allowances would permit limited production in each of the categories of armaments listed in sub-paragraph (b) of paragraph 1 above. In all instances during the process of eliminating production of armaments:

(1) any armament produced within a category would be compensated for by an additional armament destroyed within that category to the end that the ten per cent reduction in numbers in each category in each step, and the resulting thirty per cent reduction in stage I, would be achieved; and furthermore

(2) in the case of armed combat aircraft having an empty weight of 15,000 kilograms or greater and of missiles having a range of 300 kilometres or greater, the destructive capability of any such armaments produced within a category would be compensated for by the destruction of sufficient armaments within that category to the end that the ten per cent reduction in destructive capability as well as numbers in each of these categories in each step, and the resulting thirty per cent reduction in stage I, would be achieved.

(c) Should a party to the treaty elect to reduce its production in any category at a more rapid rate than required by the allowances provided in sub-paragraph (b) above, that party would be entitled to retain existing armaments to the extent of the unused portion of its production allowance. In any such instance, any armament so retained would be compensated for in the manner set forth in sub-paragraph (b) (1) and, where applicable, (b) (2) above, to the end that the ten per cent reduction in numbers and, where applicable, destructive capability in each category in each step, and the resulting thirty per cent reduction in stage I would be achieved.

(d) The flight testing of missiles would be limited to agreed annual quotas.

(e) In accordance with arrangements which would be set forth in the annex on verification, the International Disarmament Organization would verify the foregoing measures at declared locations and would provide assurance that activities subject to the foregoing measures were not conducted at undeclared locations.

4. *Additional Measures*

The parties to the treaty would agree to examine unresolved questions relating to means of accomplishing in stages II and III the reduction and eventual elimination of production and stockpiles of chemical and biological weapons of mass destruction. In light of this examination, the parties to the treaty would agree to arrangements concerning chemical and biological weapons of mass destruction.

B.   ARMED FORCES

1. *Reduction of Armed Forces*

Force levels for the United States of America and the Union of Soviet Socialist Republics would be reduced to 2.1 million each and for other specified parties to the treaty to agreed levels not exceeding 2.1 million each. All other parties to the treaty would, with agreed exceptions, reduce their force levels to 100,000 or one per cent of their population, whichever were higher, provided that in no case would the force levels of such other parties to the treaty exceed levels in existence upon the entry into force of the treaty.

2. *Armed Forces Subject to Reduction*

Agreed force levels would include all full-time, uniformed personnel maintained by national Governments in the following categories:

(a) Career personnel of active armed forces and other personnel serving in the active armed forces on fixed engagements or contracts.

(b) Conscripts performing their required period of full-time active duty as fixed by national law.

(c) Personnel of militarily organized security forces and of other forces or organizations equipped and organized to perform a military mission.

3. *Method of Reduction of Armed Forces*

The reduction of force levels would be carried out in the following manner:

(a) Those parties to the treaty which were subject to the foregoing reductions would submit to the International Disarmament Organization a declaration stating their force levels at the agreed date.

(b) Force level reductions would be accomplished in three steps, each having a duration of one year. During each step force levels would be reduced by one-third of the difference between force levels existing at the agreed date and the levels to be reached at the end of stage I.

(c) In accordance with arrangements that would be set forth in the annex on verification, the International Disarmament Organization would verify the reduction of force levels and provide assurance that retained forces did not exceed agreed levels.

4. *Additional Measures*

The parties to the treaty which were subject to the foregoing reductions would agree upon appropriate arrangements, including procedures for consultation, in order to ensure that civilian employment by military establishments would be in accordance with the objectives of the obligations respecting force levels.

C. NUCLEAR WEAPONS

1. *Production of Fissionable Materials for Nuclear Weapons*

(a) The parties to the treaty would halt the production of fissionable materials for use in nuclear weapons.

(b) This measure would be carried out in the following manner:

(1) The parties to the treaty would submit to the International Disarmament Organization a declaration listing by name, location and production capacity of every facility under their jurisdiction capable of producing and processing fissionable materials at the agreed date.

(2) Production of fissionable materials for purposes other than use in nuclear weapons would be limited to agreed levels. The parties to the treaty would submit to the International Disarmament Organization periodic declarations stating the amounts and types of fissionable materials which were still being produced at each facility.

(3) In accordance with arrangements which would be set forth in the annex on verification, the International Disarmament Organization would verify the foregoing measures at declared facilities and would provide assurance that activities subject to the foregoing limitations were not conducted at undeclared facilities.

2. *Transfer of Fissionable Material to Purposes Other than Use in Nuclear Weapons*

(a) Upon the cessation of production of fissionable materials for use in nuclear weapons, the United States of America and the Union of Soviet Socialist Republics would each transfer to purposes other than use in nuclear weapons an agreed quantity of weapons-grade U-235 from past production. The purposes for which such materials would be used would be determined by the state to which the material belonged, provided that such materials were not used in nuclear weapons.

(b) To ensure that the transferred materials were not used in nuclear weapons, such materials would be placed under safeguards and inspections by the International Disarmament Organization either in stockpiles or at the facilities in which they would be utilized for purposes other than use in nuclear weapons. Arrangements for such safeguards and inspection would be set forth in the annex on verification.

3. *Transfer of Fissionable Materials Between States for Peaceful Uses of Nuclear Energy*

(a) Any transfer of fissionable materials between states would be for purposes other than for use in nuclear weapons and would be subject to a system of safeguards to ensure that such materials were not used in nuclear weapons.

(b) The system of safeguards to be applied for this purpose would be developed in agreement with the International Atomic Energy Agency and would be set forth in an annex to the treaty.

4. *Non-Transfer of Nuclear Weapons*

The parties to the treaty would agree to seek to prevent the creation of further national nuclear forces. To this end the parties would agree that:

(a) Any party to the treaty which had manufactured, or which at any time manufactures, a nuclear weapon would:

　(1) Not transfer control over any nuclear weapons to a state which had not manufactured a nuclear weapon before an agreed date;

　(2) Not assist any such state in manufacturing any nuclear weapons.

(b) Any party to the treaty which had not manufactured a nuclear weapon before the agreed date would:

　(1) Not acquire, or attempt to acquire, control over any nuclear weapons;

(2) Not manufacture, or attempt to manufacture, any nuclear weapons.

5. *Nuclear Weapons Test Explosions*

(a) If an agreement prohibiting nuclear weapons test explosions and providing for effective international control had come into force prior to the entry into force of the Treaty, such agreement would become an annex to the treaty, and all the parties to the treaty would be bound by the obligations specified in the agreement.

(b) If, however, no such agreement had come into force prior to the entry into force of the treaty, all nuclear weapons test explosions would be prohibited, and the procedures for effective international control would be set forth in an annex to the treaty.

6. *Additional Measures*

The parties to the treaty would agree to examine remaining un-resolved questions relating to the means of accomplishing in stages II and III the reduction and eventual elimination of nuclear weapons stockpiles. In the light of this examination, the parties to the treaty would agree to arrangements concerning nuclear weapons stockpiles.

D. OUTER SPACE

1. *Prohibition of Weapons of Mass Destruction in Orbit*

The parties to the treaty would agree not to place orbit weapons capable of producing mass destruction.

2. *Peaceful Co-operation in Space*

The parties to the treaty would agree to support increased inter-national co-operation in peaceful uses of outer space in the United Nations or through other appropriate arrangements.

3. *Notification and Pre-Launch Inspection*

With respect to the launching of space vehicles and missiles:

(a) Those parties to the treaty which conducted launchings of space vehicles or missiles would provide advance notification of such launchings to other parties to the treaty and to the International Disarmament Organization together with the track of the space vehicle or missile. Such advance notification would be provided on a timely basis to permit pre-launch inspection of the space vehicle or missile to be launched.

(b) In accordance with arrangements which would be set forth in the annex on verification, the International Disarmament Organization would conduct pre-launch inspection of space vehicles and missiles and would establish and operate any arrangements necessary for detecting unreported launchings.

4. *Limitations on Production and on Related Activities*

The production, stockpiling and testing of boosters for space vehicles would be subject to agreed limitations. Such activities would be monitored by the International Disarmament Organization in accordance with arrangements which would be set forth in the annex on verification.

E. MILITARY EXPENDITURES

1. *Report on Expenditures*

The parties to the treaty would submit to the International Disarmament Organization at the end of each step of each stage a report on their military expenditures. Such reports would include an itemization of military expenditures.

2. *Verifiable Reduction of Expenditures*

The parties to the treaty would agree to examine questions related to the verifiable reduction of military expenditures. In the light of this examination, the parties to the treaty would consider appropriate arrangements respecting military expenditures.

F. REDUCTION OF THE RISK OF WAR

In order to promote confidence and reduce the risk of war, the parties to the treaty would agree to the following measures:

1. *Advance Notification of Military Movements and Manoeuvres*

Specified parties to the treaty would give advance notification of major military movements and manoeuvres to other parties to the treaty and to the International Disarmament Organization. Specific arrangements relating to this commitment, including the scale of movements and manoeuvres to be reported and the information to be transmitted, would be agreed.

2. *Observation Posts*

Specified parties to the treaty would permit observation posts to be established at agreed locations, including major ports, railway centres, motor highways, river crossings, and air bases to report on concentrations and movements of military forces. The number of such posts could be progressively expanded in each successive step of stage I. Specific arrangements relating to such observation posts, including the location and staffing of posts, the method of receiving and reporting information, and the schedule for installation of posts would be agreed.

3. *Additional Observation Arrangements*

The parties to the treaty would establish such additional observation arrangements as might be agreed. Such arrangements could be extended in an agreed manner during each step of stage I.

4. *Exchange of Military Missions*

Specified parties to the treaty would undertake the exchange of military missions between states or groups of states in order to improve communications and understandings between them. Specific arrangements respecting such exchanges would be agreed.

5. *Communications between Heads of Government*

Specified parties to the treaty would agree to the establishment of rapid and reliable communications among their Heads of Government and with the Secretary-General of the United Nations. Specific arrangements in this regard would be subject to agreement among the parties concerned and between such parties and the Secretary-General.

6. *International Commission on Reduction of the Risk of War*

The parties to the treaty would establish an International Commission on Reduction of the Risk of War as a subsidiary body of the International Disarmament Organization to examine and make recommendations regarding further measures that might be undertaken during stage I or subsequent stages of disarmament to reduce the risk of war by accident, miscalculation, failure of communications, or surprise attack. Specific arrangements for such measures as might be agreed to by all or some of the parties to the treaty would be subject to agreement among the parties concerned.

G. The International Disarmament Organization

1. *Establishment of the International Disarmament Organization*

The International Disarmament Organization would be established upon the entry into force of the treaty and would function within the framework of the United Nations and in accordance with the terms and conditions of the treaty.

2. *Co-operation of the Parties to the Treaty*

The parties to the treaty would agree to co-operate promptly and fully with the International Disarmament Organization and to assist the International Disarmament Organization in the performance of its functions and in the execution of the decision made by it in accordance with the provisions of the treaty.

3. *Verification Functions of the International Disarmament Organization*

The International Disarmament Organization would verify disarmament measures in accordance with the following principles which would be implemented through specific arrangements set forth in the annex on verification:

(a) Measures providing for reduction of armaments would be verified by the International Disarmament Organization at agreed depots and would include verification of the destruction of armaments and, where appropriate, verification of the conversion of armaments to peaceful uses. Measures providing for reduction of armed forces would be verified by the International Organization either at the agreed depots or other agreed locations.

(b) Measures halting or limiting production, testing, and other specified activities would be verified by the International Disarmament Organization. Parties to the treaty would declare the nature and location of all production and testing facilities and other specified activities. The International Disarmament Organization would have access to relevant facilities and activities where located in the territory of such parties.

(c) Assurance that agreed levels of armaments and armed forces were not exceeded and that activities limited or prohibited by the treaty were not being conducted clandestinely would be provided by the International Disarmament Organization through agreed arrangements which would have the effect of providing that the extent of inspection during any step or stage would be related to the amount of disarmament being undertaken and to the degree of risk to the parties to the treaty of possible violations. This might be accomplished, for example, by an arrangement embodying such features as the following:

  (1) All parts of the territory of those parties to the treaty to which this form of verification was applicable would be subject to selection for inspection from the beginning of stage I as provided below.

  (2) Parties to the treaty would divide their territory into an agreed number of appropriate zones and at the beginning of each step of disarmament would submit to the International Disarmament Organization a declaration stating the total level of armaments, forces, and specified types of activities subject to verification within each zone. The exact location of armaments and forces within a zone would not be revealed prior to its selection for inspection.

(3) An agreed number of these zones would be progressively inspected by the International Disarmament Organization during stage I according to an agreed time schedule. The zones to be inspected would be selected by procedures which would ensure their selection by parties to the treaty other than the party whose territory was to be inspected or any party associated with it. Upon selection of each zone, the party to the treaty whose territory was to be inspected would delcare the exact location of armaments, forces and other agreed activities within the selected zone. During the verification process, arrangements would be made to provide assurance against undeclared movements of the objects of verification to or from the zone or zones being inspected. Both aerial and mobile ground inspection would be employed within the zone being inspected. In so far as agreed measures being verified were concerned access within the zone would be free and unimpeded, and verification would be carried out with the full co-operation of the state being inspected.

(4) Once a zone had been inspected it would remain open for further inspection while verification was being extended to additional zones.

(5) By the end of stage III, when all disarmament measures had been completed, inspection would have been extended to all parts of the territory of parties to the treaty.

4. *Composition of the International Disarmament Organization*

(a) The International Disarmament Organization would have:

(1) A General Conference of all the parties to the treaty;

(2) A Control Council consisting of representatives of all the major signatory powers as permanent members and certain other parties to the treaty on a rotating basis; and

(3) An Administrator who would administer the International Disarmament Organisation under the direction of the Control Council and who would have the authority, staff, and finances adequate to ensure effective and impartial implementation of the functions of the International Disarmament Organization.

(b) The General Conference and the Control Council would have power to establish such subsidiary bodies, including expert study groups, as either of them might deem necessary.

5. *Functions of the General Conference*

The General Conference would have the following functions, among others which might be agreed:

(a) Electing non-permanent members to the Control Council;

(b) Approving certain accessions to the treaty;

(c) Appointing the Administrator upon recommendation of the Control Council;

(d) Approving agreements between the International Disarmament Organization and the United Nations and other international organizations;

(e) Approving the budget of the International Disarmament Organization;

(f) Requesting and receiving reports from the Control Council and deciding upon matters referred to it by the Control Council;

(g) Approving reports to be submitted to bodies of the United Nations;

(h) Proposing matters for consideration by the Control Council;

(i) Requesting the International Court of Justice to give advisory opinions on legal questions concerning the interpretation or application of the treaty, subject to a general authorization of this power by the General Assembly of the United Nations;

(j) Approving amendments to the treaty for possible ratification by the parties to the treaty;

(k) Considering matters of mutual interest pertaining to the treaty or disarmament in general.

6. *Functions of the Control Council*

The Control Council would have the following functions, among others which might be agreed:

(a) Recommending appointment of the Administrator;

(b) Adopting rules for implementing the terms of the treaty;

(c) Establishing procedures and standards for the installation and operation of the verification arrangements, and maintaining supervision over such arrangements and the Administrator;

(d) Establishing procedures for making available to the parties to the treaty data produced by verification arrangements;

(e) Considering reports of the Administrator on the progress of disarmament measures and of their verification, and on the installation and operation of the verification arrangements;

(f) Recommending to the Conference approval of the budget of the International Disarmament Organization;

(g) Requesting the International Court of Justice to give advisory opinions on legal questions concerning the interpretation or application of the treaty, subject to a general authorization of this power by the General Assembly of the United Nations;

(h) Recommending to the Conference approval of certain accessions to the treaty;

(i) Considering matters of mutual interest pertaining to the treaty or to disarmament in general.

7. *Functions of the Administrator*

The Administrator would have the following functions, among others which might be agreed:

(a) Administering the installation and operation of the verification arrangements, and serving as Chief Executive Officer of the International Disarmament Organization;

(b) Making available to the parties to the treaty data produced by the verification arrangements:

(c) Preparing the budget of the International Disarmament Organization.

(d) Making reports to the Control Council on the progress of disarmament measures and of their verification, and on the installation and operation of the verification arrangements.

8. *Privileges and Immunities*

The privileges and immunities which the parties to the treaty would grant to the International Disarmament Organization and its staff and to the representatives of the parties to the International Disarmament Organization, and the legal capacity which the International Disarmament Organization should enjoy in the territory of each of the parties to the treaty would be specified in an annex to the treaty.

9. *Relations with the United Nations and Other International Organizations*

(a) The International Disarmament Organization, being established within the framework of the United Nations, would conduct its activities in accordance with the purposes and principles of the United Nations. It would maintain close working arrangements with the United Nations, and the Administrator of the International Disarmament Organization would consult with the Secretary-General of the United Nations on matters of mutual interest.

(b) The Control Council of the International Disarmament Organization would transmit to the United Nations annual and other reports on the activities of the International Disarmament Organization.

(c) Principal organs of the United Nations could make recommendations to the International Disarmament Organization, which would consider them and report to the United Nations on action taken.

NOTE: The above outline does not cover all the possible details or aspects of relationships between the International Disarmament Organization and the United Nations.

H. Measures to Strengthen Arrangements for Keeping the Peace

1. *Obligations Concerning Threat or Use of Force*

The Parties to the Treaty would undertake obligations to refrain, in their international relations, from the threat or use of force of any type—including nuclear, conventional, chemical or biological means of warfare—contrary to the purposes and principles of the United Nations Charter.

2. *Rules of International Conduct*

(a) The parties to the treaty would agree to support a study by a subsidiary body of the International Disarmament Organization of the codification and progressive development of rules of international conduct related to disarmament.

(b) The parties to the treaty would refrain from indirect aggression and subversion. The subsidiary body provided for in sub-paragraph (a) would also study methods of assuring states against indirect aggression or subversion.

3. *Peaceful Settlement of Disputes*

(a) The parties to the treaty would utilize all appropriate processes for the peaceful settlement of all disputes which might arise between them and any other state, whether or not a party to the treaty, including negotiation, inquiry, mediation, conciliation, arbitration, judicial settlement, resort to regional agencies or arrangements, submission to the Security Council or the General Assembly of the United Nations, or other peaceful means of their choice.

(b) The parties to the treaty would agree that disputes concerning the interpretation or application of the treaty which were not settled by negotiation or by the International Disarmament Organization would be subject to referral by any party to the dispute to the International Court of Justice, unless the parties concerned agreed on another mode of settlement.

(c) The parties to the treaty would agree to support a study under the General Assembly of the United Nations of measures which should be undertaken to make existing arrangements for the peaceful settlement of international disputes, whether legal or political in nature, more effective; and to institute new procedures and arrangements where needed.

4. *Maintenance of International Peace and Security*

The parties to the treaty would agree to support measures strengthening the structure, authority, and operation of the United Nations so as to improve its capability to maintain international peace and security.

5. *United Nations Peace Force*

The parties to the treaty would undertake to develop arrangements during stage I for the establishment in stage II of a United Nations Peace Force. To this end, the parties to the treaty would agree on the following measures within the United Nations:

(a) Examination of the experience of the United Nations leading to a further strengthening of United Nations forces for keeping the peace;

(b) Examination of the feasibility of concluding promptly the agreements envisaged in Article 43 of the United Nations Charter;

(c) Conclusion of an agreement for the establishment of a United Nations Peace Force in stage II, including definitions of its purpose, mission, composition and strength, disposition, command and control, training, logistical support, financing, equipment and armaments.

6. *United Nations Peace Observation Corps*

The parties to the treaty would agree to support the establishment within the United Nations of a Peace Observation Corps, staffed with a standing cadre of observers who could be despatched promptly to investigate any situation which might constitute a threat to or a breach of the peace. Elements of the Peace Observation Corps could also be stationed as appropriate in selected areas throughout the world.

I. TRANSITION

1. Transition from stage I to stage II would take place at the end of stage I, upon a determination that the following circumstances existed:

(a) All undertakings to be carried out in stage I had been carried out;

(b) All preparations required for stage II had been made; and

(c) All militarily significant states had become parties to the treaty.

2. During the last three months of stage I, the Control Council would review the situation respecting these circumstances with a view to determining whether these circumstances existed at the end of stage I.

3. If, at the end of stage I, one or more permanent members of the Control Council should declare that the foregoing circumstances did not exist, the agreed period of stage I would, upon the request of such permanent member or members, be extended by a period or periods totalling no more than three months for the purpose of bringing about the foregoing circumstances.

4. If, upon the expiration of such period or periods, one or more of the permanent members of the Control Council should declare that the foregoing circumstances still did not exist, the question would be placed before a special session of the Security Council; transition to stage II would take place upon a determination by the Security Council that the foregoing circumstances did in fact exist.

STAGE II

Stage II would begin upon the transition from stage I and would be complete within three years from that date.

During stage II, the parties to the treaty would undertake:

(1) To continue all obligations undertaken during stage I;

(2) To reduce further the armaments and armed forces reduced during stage I and to carry out additional measures of disarmament in the manner outlined below;

(3) To ensure that the International Disarmament Organization would have the capacity to verify in the agreed manner the obligations undertaken during stage II; and

(4) To strengthen further the arrangements for keeping the peace through the establishment of a United Nations Peace Force and through the additional measures outlined below.

A. ARMAMENTS

1. *Reduction of Armaments*

(a) Those parties to the treaty which had during stage I reduced their armaments in agreed categories by thirty per cent would during stage II further reduce each type of armaments in the categories listed in Section A, sub-paragraph 1 (b) of stage I by fifty per cent of the inventory existing at the end of stage I.

(b) Those parties to the treaty which had not been subject to measures for the reduction of armaments during stage I would submit to the International Disarmament Organization an appropriate declaration respecting the inventories by types, within the categories listed in stage I, of their armaments existing at the beginning of stage II. Such parties to the treaty would during stage II reduce the inventory of each type of such armaments by sixty-five per cent in order that such parties would accomplish the same total percentage of reduction by the end of stage II as would be accomplished by those parties to the treaty which had reduced their armaments by thirty per cent in stage I.

2. *Additional Armaments Subject to Reduction*

(a) The parties to the treaty would submit to the International Disarmament Organization a declaration respecting their inventories existing at the beginning of stage II of the additional types of armaments in the categories listed in sub-paragraph (b) below, and would during stage II reduce the inventory of each type of such armaments by fifty per cent.

(b) All types of armaments within further agreed categories would be subject to reduction in stage II (the following list of categories is illustrative):

(1) Armed combat aircraft having an empty weight of up to 2,500 kilograms (declarations by types).

(2) Specified types of unarmed military aircraft (declarations by types).

(3) Missiles and free rockets having a range of less than 10 kilometres (declarations by types).

(4) Mortars and rocket launchers having a calibre of less than 100 mm. (declarations by types).

(5) Specified types of unarmoured personnel carriers and transport vehicles (declarations by types).

(6) Combatant ships with standard displacement of 400 tons or greater which had not been included among the armaments listed in stage I, and combatant ships with standard displacement of less than 400 tons (declarations by types).

(7) Specified types of non-combatant naval vessels (declarations by types).

(8) Specified types of small arms (declarations by types).

(c) Specified categories of ammunition for armaments listed in stage I, Section A, sub-paragraph 1 (b), and in sub-paragraph (b) above would be reduced to levels consistent with the levels of armaments agreed for the end of stage II.

3. *Method of Reduction*

The foregoing measures would be carried out and would be verified by the International Disarmament Organization in a manner corresponding to that provided for in stage I, section A, paragraph 2.

4. *Limitation on Production of Armaments and on Related Activities*

(a) The parties to the treaty would halt the production of armaments in the specified categories except for production, within agreed limits, of parts required for maintenance of the agreed retained armaments.

(b) The production of ammunition in specified categories would be reduced to agreed levels consistent with the levels of armaments agreed for the end of stage II.

(c) The parties to the treaty would halt development and testing of new types of armaments. The flight testing of existing types of missiles would be limited to agreed annual quotas.

(d) In accordance with arrangements which would be set forth in the annex on verification, the International Disarmament Organization would verify the foregoing measures at declared locations and would provide assurance that activities subject to the foregoing measures were not conducted at undeclared locations.

5. *Additional Measures*

(a) In the light of their examination during stage I of the means of accomplishing the reduction and eventual elimination of production and stockpiles of chemical and biological weapons of mass destruction, the parties to the treaty would undertake the following measures respecting such weapons:

(1) The cessation of all production and field testing of chemical and biological weapons of mass destruction.

(2) The reduction, by agreed categories, of stockpiles of chemical and biological weapons of mass destruction to levels fifty per cent below those existing at the beginning of stage II.

(3) The dismantling or conversion to peaceful uses of all facilities engaged in the production or field testing of chemical and biological weapons of mass destruction.

(b) The foregoing measures would be carried out in an agreed sequence and through arrangements which would be set forth in an annex to the treaty.

(c) In accordance with arrangements which would be set forth in the annex on verification the International Disarmament Organization would verify the foregoing measures and would provide assurance that retained levels of chemical and biological weapons did not exceed agreed levels and that activities subject to the foregoing limitations were not conducted at undeclared locations.

B. ARMED FORCES

1. *Reduction of Armed Forces*

(a) Those parties to the treaty which have been subject to measures providing for reduction of force levels during stage I would further reduce their force levels on the following basis:

(1) Force levels of the United States of America and the Union of Soviet Socialist Republics would be reduced to levels fifty per cent below the levels agreed for the end of stage I.

(2) Force levels of other parties to the treaty which had been subject to measures providing for the reduction of force levels during stage I would be further reduced, on the basis of an agreed percentage, below the levels agreed for the end of stage I to levels which would not in any case exceed the agreed level for the United States of America and the Union of Soviet Socialist Republics at the end of stage II.

(b) Those parties to the treaty which had not been subject to measures providing for the reduction of armed forces during stage I would reduce their force levels to agreed levels consistent with those to be reached by other parties which had reduced their force levels during stage I as well as stage II. In no case would such agreed levels exceed the agreed level for the United States of America and the Union of Soviet Socialist Republics at the end of stage II.

(c) Agreed levels of armed forces would include all personnel in the categories set forth in section B, paragraph 2, of stage I.

2. *Method of Reduction*

The further reduction of force levels would be carried out and would be verified by the International Disarmament Organization in a manner corresponding to that provided for in section B, paragraph 3, of stage I.

3. *Additional Measures*

Agreed limitations consistent with retained force levels would be placed on compulsory military training, and on refresher training for reserve forces of the parties of the treaty.

C. NUCLEAR WEAPONS

1. *Reduction of Nuclear Weapons*

In the light of their examination during stage I of the means of accomplishing the reduction and eventual elimination of nuclear weapons stockpiles, the parties to the treaty would undertake to reduce in the following manner remaining nuclear weapons and fissionable materials for use in nuclear weapons:

(a) The parties to the treaty would submit to the International Disarmament Organization a declaration stating the amounts, types, and nature of utilization of all their fissionable materials.

(b) The parties to the treaty would reduce the amounts and types of fissionable materials declared for use in nuclear weapons to minimum levels on the basis of agreed percentages. The foregoing reduction would be accomplished through the transfer of such materials to purposes other than use in nuclear weapons. The purposes for which such materials would be used would be determined by the state to which the materials belonged, provided that such materials were not used in nuclear weapons.

(c) The parties to the treaty would destroy the non-nuclear components and assemblies of nuclear weapons from which fissionable materials had been removed to effect the foregoing reduction of fissionable materials for use in nuclear weapons.

(d) Production or refabrication of nuclear weapons from any remaining fissionable materials would be subject to agreed limitations.

(e) The foregoing measures would be carried out in an agreed sequence and through arrangements which would be set forth in an annex to the treaty.

(f) In accordance with arrangements that would be set forth in the verification annex to the treaty, the International Disarmament Organization would verify the foregoing measures at declared locations and would provide assurance that activities subject to the foregoing limitations were not conducted at undeclared locations.

2. *Registration of Nuclear Weapons for Verification Purposes*

To facilitate verification during stage III that no nuclear weapons remained at the disposal of the parties to the treaty, those parties to the treaty which possessed nuclear weapons would, during the last six months of stage II, register and serialize their remaining nuclear weapons and would register remaining fissionable materials for use in such weapons. Such registration and serialization would be carried out with the International Disarmament Organization in accordance with procedures which would be set forth in the annex on verification.

D. MILITARY BASES AND FACILITIES

1. *Reduction of Military Bases and Facilities*

The parties to the treaty would dismantle or convert to peaceful uses agreed military bases and facilities wherever they might be located.

2. *Method of Reduction*

(a) The list of military bases and facilities subject to the foregoing measures and the sequence and arrangements for dismantling or converting them to peaceful uses would be set forth in an annex to the treaty.

(b) In accordance with arrangements which would be set forth in the annex on verification, the International Disarmament Organization would verify the foregoing measures.

E. REDUCTION OF THE RISK OF WAR

In the light of the examination by the International Commission on Reduction of the Risk of War during stage I the parties to the treaty would undertake such additional arrangements as appeared desirable to promote confidence and reduce the risk of war. The parties to the treaty would also consider extending and improving the measures undertaken in stage I for this purpose. The Commission would remain in existence to examine extensions, improvements or additional measures which might be undertaken during and after stage II.

F. THE INTERNATIONAL DISARMAMENT ORGANIZATION

The International Disarmament Organization would be strengthened in the manner necessary to ensure its capacity to verify the measures undertaken in stage II through an extension of the arrangements based upon the principles set forth in Section G, paragraph 3, of stage I.

G. MEASURES TO STRENGTHEN ARRANGEMENTS FOR KEEPING THE PEACE

1. *Peaceful Settlement of Disputes*

(a) In light of the study of peaceful settlement of disputes conducted during stage I, the parties to the treaty would agree to such additional steps and arrangements as were necessary to assure the just and peaceful settlement of international disputes, whether legal or political in nature.

(b) The parties to the treaty would undertake to accept without reservation, pursuant to Article 36, paragraph (1) of the Statute of the International Court of Justice, the compulsory jurisdiction of that Court to decide international legal disputes.

2. *Rules of International Conduct*

(a) The parties to the treaty would continue their support of the study by the subsidiary body of the International Disarmament Organization initiated in stage I to study the codification and progressive development of rules of international conduct related to disarmament. The parties to the treaty would agree to the establishment of procedures whereby rules recommended by the subsidiary

D.V.–P

body and approved by the Control Council would be circulated to all parties to the treaty and would become effective three months thereafter unless a majority of the parties to the treaty signified their disapproval, and whereby the parties to the treaty would be bound by rules which had become effective in this way unless, within a period of one year from the effective date, they formally notified the International Disarmament Organization that they did not consider themselves so bound. Using such procedures, the parties to the treaty would adopt such rules of international conduct related to disarmament as might be necessary to begin stage III.

(b) In the light of the study of indirect aggression and subversion conducted in stage I, the parties to the treaty would agree to arrangements necessary to assure states against indirect aggression and subversion.

3. *United Nations Peace Force*

The United Nations Peace Force to be established as the result of the agreement reached during stage I would come into being within the first year of stage II and would be progressively strengthened during stage II.

4. *United Nations Peace Observation Corps*

The parties to the treaty would conclude arrangement for the expansion of the activities of the United Nations Peace Observation Corps.

5. *National Legislation*

Those parties to the treaty which had not already done so would, in accordance with their constitutional processes, enact national legislation in support of the treaty imposing legal obligations on individuals and organizations under their jurisdiction and providing appropriate penalties for non-compliance.

H. TRANSITION

1. Transition from stage II to stage III would take the place at the end of stage II, upon a determination that the following circumstances existed:

(a) All undertakings to be carried out in stage II had been carried out;

(b) All preparations required for stage III had been made; and

(c) All states possessing armed forces and armaments had become parties to the treaty.

2.   During the last three months of stage II, the Control Council would review the situation respecting these circumstances with a view to determining at the end of stage II whether they existed.

3.   If, at the end of stage II, one or more permanent members of the Control Council should declare that the foregoing circumstances did not exist, the agreed period of stage II would, upon the request of such permanent member or members, be extended by a period or periods totalling no more than three months for the purpose of bringing about the foregoing circumstances.

4.   If, upon the expiration of such period or periods, one or more of the permanent members of the Control Council should declare that the foregoing circumstances still did not exist, the question would be placed before a special session of the Security Council; transition to stage III would take place upon a determination by the Security Council that the foregoing circumstances did in fact exist.

STAGE III

Stage III would begin upon the transition from stage II and would be completed within an agreed period of time as promptly as possible.

During stage III, the parties to the treaty would undertake:

(1) To continue all obligations undertaken during stages I and II;
(2) To complete the process of general and complete disarmament in the manner outlined below;
(3) To ensure that the International Disarmament Organization would have the capacity to verify in the agreed manner the obligations undertaken during stage III and of continuing verification subsequent to the completion of stage III; and
(4) To strengthen further the arrangements for keeping the peace during and following the achievement of general and complete disarmament through the additional measures outlined below.

A.   ARMAMENTS

1.   *Reduction of Armaments*

Subject to agreed requirements for non-nuclear armaments of agreed types for national forces required to maintain internal order and protect the personal security of citizens, the parties to the treaty should eliminate all armaments remaining at their disposal at the end of stage II.

2.   *Method of Reduction*

(a) The foregoing measure would be carried out in an agreed

sequence and through arrangements that would be set forth in an annex to the treaty.

(b) In accordance with arrangements that would be set forth in the annex on verification, the International Disarmament Organization would verify the foregoing measures and would provide assurance that retained armaments were of the agreed types and did not exceed agreed levels.

3. *Limitations on Production of Armaments and on Related Activities*

(a) Subject to agreed arrangements in support of national forces required to maintain internal order and protect the personal security of citizens and subject to agreed arrangements in support of the United Nations Peace Force, the parties to the treaty would halt all applied research, development, production, and testing of armaments and would cause to be dismantled or converted to peaceful uses all other facilities for such purposes.

(b) The foregoing measures would be carried out in an agreed sequence and through arrangements which would be set forth in an annex to the treaty.

(c) In accordance with arrangements which would be set forth in the annex on verification, the International Disarmament Organization would verify the foregoing measures at declared locations and would provide assurance that activities subject to the foregoing measures were not conducted at undeclared locations.

B. ARMED FORCES

1. *Reduction of Armed Forces*

To the end that upon completion of stage III they would have at their disposal only those forces and organizational arrangements necessary for agreed forces to maintain internal order and protect the personal security of citizens and that they would be capable of providing agreed manpower for the United Nations Peace Force, the parties to the treaty would complete the reduction of their force levels, disband systems of reserve forces, cause to be disbanded organizational arrangements comprising and supporting their national military establishment, and terminate the employment of civilian personnel associated with the foregoing.

2. *Method of Reduction*

(a) The foregoing measures would be carried out in an agreed sequence through arrangements which would be set forth in an annex to the treaty.

(b) In accordance with arrangements which would be set forth in the annex on verification, the International Disarmament Organization would verify the foregoing measures and would provide assurance that the only forces and organizational arrangements retained or subsequently established were those necessary for agreed forces required to maintain internal order and to protect the personal security of citizens and those for providing agreed manpower for the United Nations Peace Force.

3. *Other Limitations*

The parties to the treaty would halt all military conscription and would undertake to annul legislation concerning national military establishments or military service inconsistent with the foregoing measures.

C. Nuclear Weapons

1. *Reduction of Nuclear Weapons*

In the light of the steps taken in stages I and II to halt the production of fissionable material for use in nuclear weapons and to reduce nuclear weapons stockpiles, the parties to the treaty would eliminate all nuclear weapons remaining at their disposal, would cause to be dismantled or converted to peaceful use all facilities for production of such weapons, and would transfer all materials remaining at their disposal for use in such weapons to purposes other than use in such weapons.

2. *Method of Reduction*

(a) The foregoing measures would be carried out in an agreed sequence and through arrangements which would be set forth in an annex to the treaty.

(b) In accordance with arrangements which would be set forth in the annex on verification, the International Disarmament Organization would verify the foregoing measures and would provide assurance that no nuclear weapons or materials for use in such weapons remained at the disposal of the parties to the treaty and that no such weapons or materials were produced at undeclared facilities.

D. Military Bases and Facilities

1. *Reduction of Military Bases and Facilities*

The parties to the treaty would dismantle or convert to peaceful uses the military bases and facilities remaining at their disposal, wherever they might be located, in an agreed sequence except for such agreed bases or facilities within the territory of the parties to the treaty for agreed forces required to maintain internal order and protect the personal security of citizens.

2. *Method of Reduction*

(a) The list of military bases and facilities subject to the foregoing measure and the sequence and arrangements for dismantling or converting them to peaceful uses during stage III would be set forth in an annex to the treaty.

(b) In accordance with arrangements which would be set forth in the annex on verification, the International Disarmament Organization would verify the foregoing measure at declared locations and provide assurance that there were no undeclared military bases and facilities.

E.   RESEARCH AND DEVELOPMENT OF MILITARY SIGNIFICANCE

1. *Reporting Requirement*

The parties to the treaty would undertake the following measures respecting research and development of military significance subsequent to stage III:

(a) The parties to the treaty would report to the International Disarmament Organization any basic scientific discovery and any technological invention having potential military significance.

(b) The Control Council would establish such expert study groups as might be required to examine the potential military significance of such discoveries and inventions and, if necessary, to recommend appropriate measures for their control. In the light of such expert study, the parties to the treaty would, where necessary, establish agreed arrangements providing for verification by the International Disarmament Organization that such discoveries and inventions were not utilized for military purposes. Such arrangements would become an annex to the treaty.

(c) The parties to the treaty would agree to appropriate arrangements for protection of the ownership rights of all discoveries and inventions reported to the International Disarmament Organization in accordance with sub-paragraph (a) above.

2. *International Co-operation*

The parties to the treaty would agree to support full international co-operation in all fields of scientific research and development, and to engage in free exchange of scientific and technical information and free interchange of views among scientific and technical personnel.

F.   REDUCTION OF THE RISK OF WAR

1. *Improved Measures*

In the light of the stage II examination by the International

Commission on Reduction of the Risk of War, the parties to the treaty would undertake such extensions and improvements of existing arrangements and such additional arrangements as appeared desirable to promote confidence and reduce the risk of war. The Commission would remain in existence to examine extensions, improvements or additional measures which might be taken during and after stage III.

2. *Application of Measures to Continuing Forces*

The parties to the treaty would apply to national forces required to maintain internal order and protect the personal security of citizens those applicable measures concerning the reduction of the risk of war that had been applied to national armed forces in stages I and II.

G. INTERNATIONAL DISARMAMENT ORGANIZATION

The International Disarmament Organization would be strengthened in the manner necessary to ensure its capacity (1) to verify the measures undertaken in stage III through an extension of arrangements based upon the principles set forth in Section G, paragraph 3, of stage I so that by the end of stage III, when all disarmament measures had been completed, inspection would have been extended to all parts of the territory of parties to the treaty; and (2) to provide continuing verification of disarmament after the completion of stage III.

H. MEASURES TO STRENGTHEN ARRANGEMENTS FOR KEEPING THE PEACE

1. *Peaceful Change and Settlement of Disputes*

The parties to the treaty would undertake such additional steps and arrangements as were necessary to provide a basis for peaceful change in a disarmed world and to continue the just and peaceful settlement of all international disputes, whether legal or political in nature.

2. *Rules of International Conduct*

The parties to the treaty would continue the codification and progressive development of rules of international conduct related to disarmament in the manner provided in stage II and by any other agreed procedure.

3. *United Nations Peace Force*

The parties to the treaty would progressively strengthen the United Nations Peace Force established in stage II until it had sufficient armed forces and armaments so that no state could challenge it.

I. Completion of Stage III

1. At the end of the time period agreed for stage III, the Control Council would review the situation with a view to determining whether all undertakings to be carried out in stage III had been carried out.

2. In the event that one or more of the permanent members of the Control Council should delcare that such undertakings had not been carried out, the agreed period of stage III would, upon the request of such permanent member or members, be extended for a period or periods totalling no more than three months for the purpose of completing any uncompleted undertakings. If, upon the expiration of such period or periods, one or more of the permanent members of the Control Council should declare that such undertakings still had not been carried out, the question would be placed before a special session of the Security Council, which would determine whether stage III had been completed.

3. After the completion of stage III, the obligations undertaken in stages I, II and III would continue.

General Provisions Applicable to all Stages

1. *Subsequent Modifications or Amendments of the Treaty*

The parties to the treaty would agree to specific procedures for considering amendments or modifications of the treaty which were believed desirable by any party to the treaty in the light of experience in the early period of implementation of the treaty. Such procedures would include provision for a conference on revision of the treaty after a specified period of time.

2. *Interim Agreement*

The parties to the treaty would undertake such specific arrangements, including the establishment of a Preparatory Commission, as were necessary between the signing and entry into force of the treaty to ensure the initiation of stage I immediately upon the entry into force of the treaty, and to provide an interim forum for the exchange of views and information on topics relating to the treaty and to the achievement of a permanent state of general and complete disarmament in a peaceful world.

3. *Parties to the Treaty, Ratification, Accession and Entry into Force of the Treaty*

(a) The treaty would be open to signature and ratification, or accession by all members of the United Nations or its specialized agencies.

(b) Any other state which desired to become a party to the treaty could accede to the treaty with the approval of the conference on recommendation of the Control Council.

(c) The treaty would come into force when it had been ratified by states, including the United States of America, the Union of Soviet Socialist Republics, and an agreed number of the following states:

....

(d) In order to assure the achievement of the fundamental purpose of a permanent state of general and complete disarmament in a peaceful world, the treaty would specify that the accession of certain militarily significant states would be essential for the continued effectiveness of the treaty or for the coming into force of particular measures or stages.

(e) The parties to the treaty would undertake to exert every effort to induce other states or authorities to accede to the treaty.

(f) The treaty would be subject to ratification or acceptance in accordance with constitutional processes.

(g) A Depository Government would be agreed upon which would have all of the duties normally incumbent upon a Depository. Alternatively, the United Nations would be the Depository.

4. *Finance*

(a) In order to meet the financial obligations of the International Disarmament Organization, the parties to the treaty would bear the International Disarmament Organization's expenses as provided in the budget approved by the General Conference and in accordance with a scale of apportionment approved by the General Conference.

(b) The General Conference would exercise borrowing powers on behalf of the International Disarmament Organization.

5. *Authentic Tests*

The text of the treaty would consist of equally authentic versions in English, French, Russian, Chinese and Spanish.

United Kingdom Paper of 31st August 1962

THE TECHNICAL POSSIBILITY OF INTERNATIONAL CONTROL OF FISSILE MATERIAL PRODUCTION

The attached paper describes the technical aspects of the control of:
A. Current Production of Plutonium and U-235 (paragraphs 1–26);
B. Past Production of Plutonium and U-235 (paragraphs 27–53).
It also includes some observations on technical aspects of a Control Organization (paragraphs 54–62).

The argument in it, and the evidence presented, are related solely to the United Kingdom experience, and do not seek to anticipate the results of any fuller enquiry.

The paper assumes that an international agreement would have been reached that no country should manufacture or retain nuclear weapons, and that the Control Organization's duty would be to ensure that such an agreement was demonstrably being adhered to.

The paper assumes that there would be no politically imposed restrictions on the operation of the Control Organization, or on its constitution.

INTRODUCTION

1. As soon as the Control Organization was installed, it would have the duty of checking in the greatest possible detail the declarations which would be made by every Signatory about the total quantity of fissile material already made both for civil and military purposes. All existing stocks of fissile material would have to be produced for inspection by the Control Organization and compared with the declared inventories; checks would also need to be made as far as possible of the accuracy of declarations concerning the quantities of fissile material which had been used, destroyed, or lost in processing or in any other way.

2. The Control Organization would also need to institute controls on the current production of fissile materials; the continuous operation of these controls would be a major duty of the Control Organization.

3. Another duty which the Control Organization would fulfil is that of guarding against the possibility of there being clandestine plants whose purpose would be to make fissile materials intended for weapons.

4. In seeking to form our opinion about the accuracy with which

a Control Organization could guarantee past production of plutonium and U-235 and could detect clandestine plants in any country, we have largely restricted our considerations to technical matters. The declarations made by each country about its past production of fissile material would be supported by the production of technical records, materials, accountancy statements, and many other details upon which normal operations are based.

5.   If there were a false declaration some of the technical material produced would necessarily have to be forged. There might be no technical difficulty in making forgeries and any individual forged record might be indistinguishable from a genuine record. However, by using scientific analysis on a set of records, or by introducing some technical considerations pertaining to the nuclear complex as a whole, the forgery might be discovered.

6.   It is therefore desirable to make an objective study of what limits of accuracy could be achieved by technical control.

7.   Of course, a technical Control Organization might receive adventitious help which was not of a technical nature. For example, a person compelled by a violating country to participate in a forgery might reveal the forgery to the Control Organization. The estimation of the chance that a false declaration by a violator could be revealed by somebody who participated in the forgery is not a technical question and we would suppose that there was little possibility of international agreement based on an assessment of such chances. For this reason, we have concentrated on studying the possibilities of control using only technical methods, but in a few places we have noted the scale of effort which might be required to support false declarations by forgery.

CONTROL OF CURRENT PRODUCTION

1.   It is appropriate to deal first with the control of current production since the knowledge which the Control Organization would obtain about plants currently producing fissile material would be essential to it in checking the past production.

2.   A nuclear industry consists in the main of a complex series of operations for the production and use of fissile materials. A typical range of nuclear plants is shown diagrammatically in Figure 1.

3.   If merely the final output of fissile material from an overt programme were controlled, a Government wishing to evade the Control could take material from a point one step further back and invest in plant to cover that step (and all subsequent steps) in secret. But for each stage of the overt plan that was successfully controlled, the violating country would need to invest in a corresponding stage of secret plan to circumvent the Control. This would apply to all stages of the overt programme, including ore procurement.

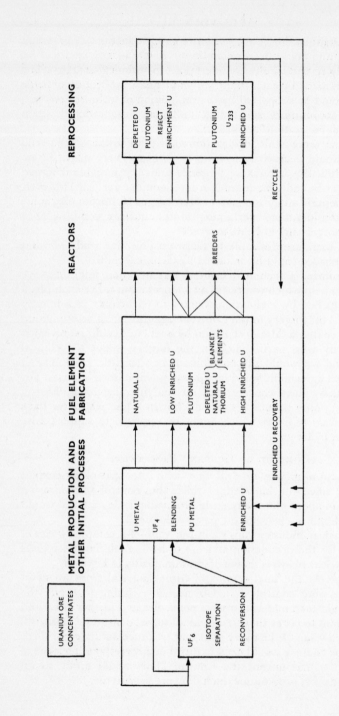

FIGURE I. A TYPICAL SCHEME OF NUCLEAR PLANTS

4. However, after such examination as we have been able to give to the possibility of a control on uranium ore and concentrates, we consider that this would only be feasible—if at all—with very great demands on men and money. Control at these stages would entail inspecting all possible mining areas, whether declared or not, and countering every possibility of Government-aided smuggling by land, sea and air.

5. The principle we have adopted, therefore, is to apply control to all processes in the overt programme following the ore procurement stage, but with particular attention to those stages at which material of most direct value to a weapons programme could be withdrawn. Such a control, by limiting diversion from overt plants of the feed material on which the secret programme depends and rendering it liable to detection, would compel the violator either to commit further investment in secret plant or to accept an increased risk of detection for his whole secret programme.

6. There are two basic methods of preventing diversion (a) physical security and (b) technical surveillance. In any particular operation, the Control would rely primarily on one of these two methods, using the other as a subsidiary check.

7. The special materials with which the Control would be concerned would have a continuous history from their separation from other materials, or their creation in a reactor, to the stage where they were either destroyed or rejected as waste material. During this history, their physical and chemical form would be changed from time to time. At some stages they would be in individual identifiable units such as fuel elements. At other stages their identity would necessarily be lost, e.g. when fuel elements are dissolved.

8. During the periods when the materials were in identifiable units, the main control proposed would be by physical security. The duty of the Control would then be to ensure that the count of units was correct and their identity was preserved. Sampling and measurement processes would only be involved as auxiliary checks if identity had been inadvertently lost, or illegal substitution was suspected. Thus while the material was in identifiable units no significant component of uncertainty would be introduced into the accounting process.

9. Physical control would be the principal technique applied to materials in stock during transportation and on-charge and discharge at reactors. Such control may be exercised by supervision, but in some cases it would be necessary for the personnel of the Control to undertake non-process operations themselves. For example, it would be possible to account for material in transit by a system of invoices and receipts supported by examination and analysis, but it might in general be cheaper and easier to make the Control itself responsible for all movements at the instruction of plant management.

10.   When the material could not be handled in identifiable units, control could be achieved by technical surveillance. This would include normal materials accountancy and technical inspection. The basic principles of materials accountancy would apply to all the plants involved, although their application would be dependent on the technological details. Technical inspection would ensure that no material flow escaped accountancy and that the measurement processes were not deliberately falsified.

11.   Technical surveillance would be the main method of control in chemical processing and reprocessing, in diffusion plants and in fuel manufacturing plants until the fuel element became an identifiable unit. The Control Authority would require access to the design drawings for such plants and would be assisted if plants which were inaccessible during operation could be inspected during construction. It would be important for the Control to be consulted by plant management on the system of materials accountancy, including instrumentation; operators would have to declare to the Control the methods of analysis which they were using. The Control would need to ensure that samples withdrawn for their own measurements, or measurements not requiring samples, were representative and that the frequency of sampling was at least as great as that applied by plant management for process control. Analytical and measurement methods would need to be standardized within the Control and results would only be released to plant management at the discretion of the Control. In cases where finished products such as fuel elements were sampled, the Control would need to have authority to undertake destructive measurements if inferential ones were inadequate.

12.   Reliance on technical surveillance, based on measurement, necessarily introduces uncertainties. These arise in part from the difficulty of measuring changes in the hold-up of material within the plant and in part from errors in measurement processes applied to material flows. The results obtained from measurement processes are subject to errors of two types:

(a)   random errors, the relative importance of which can be progressively reduced by increasing the number of measurements, and

(b)   errors of bias which are constant in magnitude and the effects of which cannot be reduced in this way.

13.   It is thus fundamental that the operation of the Control would not be perfect in the sense that it would not be able to give a complete account of the fate of all special material, but only an account which was correct to some specified degree of precision.

14.   In view of these uncertainties, it is important to attempt to forecast the precision with which the Control might be able to

operate. Our general assessment of the effectiveness of a Control Organization in preventing diversion is based on its application to a nuclear industry similar in characteristics and history to that of the U.K. We conclude that:

(a) during the first few months of operation of the control system, the Control would be able to detect diversions of plutonium equivalent to 5 per cent or more of total output; the corresponding figure for a diffusion plant would also be about 5 per cent.

(b) when the control system had been running for some time and was operating satisfactorily, the Control would be able to detect diversions of plutonium and of U-235 over a short period (3–6 months) of 3 per cent. Over long periods (one year or more) a continuous diversion of U-235 as small as 1 per cent would raise suspicions. In the case of plutonium, suspicions could probably be avoided with a clandestine diversion of 1 per cent, but a diversion of 2 per cent would almost certainly be detected.

15. The previous paragraph can be simplified to the statement that by the time that the Control Organization has been running for two or three years, it could thereafter control U-235 to within 1 per cent and plutonium to an accuracy of between 1 and 2 per cent of current output.

16. The foregoing assessment of the limits of possible diversion is derived, as stated, from our study which has been based on the present U.K. nuclear organization. In other organizations, however, there are likely to be variations of practice which could alter the limits within which diversion from an overt programme could be detected.

17. For example, a greater or a lesser skill in operating a chemical plant or a more complete or a less complete historical knowledge of its performance would change the data available to the Control and hence affect the limits of detection of possible diversion. Again, newly commissioned plant could not in the initial period be subjected to a control as close as that applied to established plant.

18. The growing use of enriched uranium and plutonium for reactors in future will entail recycling operations which must increase the throughput from which diversion would be possible, thereby increasing the work of the Control Organization.

19. However, some of these features are less unfavourable than they appear because they apply to future and to new industrial systems. The techniques of the Control would be expected to improve progressively as experience was gained. Furthermore, the quantities

of material produced and circulating in a newly established system or in new plants added to an existing system, would be smaller than in those industrial systems which have had time to grow. In some cases, more advanced operating techniques would be in use and these would tend to assist the Control.

Hidden Plant

20. There is no general feature that makes it easy to distinguish a nuclear installation from a similar installation associated with a non-nuclear activity. There are, however, some secondary features which would be of assistance to the Control Organization in the task of finding or identifying a clandestine plant engaged in producing fissile material.

21. Nuclear plants require special feed materials and unusual quantities of certain more ordinary materials. The special nature of the components used in the nuclear industry and the elaborate health and safety precautions needed in handling active materials would make it difficult to disguise from the workers the activities in which they were engaged.

22. The chemical processes in the nuclear industry result in comparatively small quantities of high-activity effluent and large quantities of very low activity effluent. The latter are difficult to hide because of their volume and are detectable in much lower concentrations than normal chemical effluent can be detected.

23. A country which wished to defeat the Control would need to go to considerable lengths to overcome such disadvantages in particular those of effluent disposal. For example, effluent could be concentrated by evaporation or ion exchange and ultimately stored underground; plant could be modified in commercially uneconomic ways to make it easier to conceal; remote siting in places and situations (e.g. underground), which would normally be considered uneconomic, would make the task of detection more difficult.

24. It is possible that a violator seeking to produce clandestine fissile material would attempt to build a secret centrifuge plant for separating U-235. The power consumption would be small and the generating plant could be hidden. If the violator were prepared to go to great expense to develop and fabricate the components and then to build a small centrifuge plant, the risk of being caught could be minimized; and it might be possible secretly to produce somewhat more fissile material by this means than by diversion from overt plant. To make weapons components from this clandestine fissile material would require equipment and machine tools but the provision of these items from normal industrial sources would not disclose the purpose for which they were required. The specialized design of a centrifuge

and the necessity of having criticality controls as well as some health precautions, both in the centrifuge plant and in the metal fabrication plant, would reveal to the operators the purpose of their work. A violator might also attempt to operate a small clandestine reactor but the dispersal of the heat generated and the processing of the fuel taken from the reactor would pose major problems of concealment, certainly more difficult than those of concealing a small centrifuge plant and its ancillary facilities.

25.   Disregarding the problem of controlling past production, the possibility of a violator successfully building and operating large secret plants for producing fissile materials is remote; the existence of the plants would be obvious and the violator would be caught by the Control Organization. However, the possibility of a violator operating small secret plants, particularly a centrifuge plant, cannot now be excluded. The detection by technical means of small clandestine centrifuge plants by the Control Organization is a formidable problem to which there seems to be no easy solution.

26.   As far as the major nuclear powers are concerned, the control problem of the secret plan would be small compared with the problem of clandestine retention of fissile material made before the Control began to operate.

CONTROL OF PAST PRODUCTION

27.   The percentage reliability with which a comprehensive control system could estimate the total production of fissile material prior to the date at which the Control Organization began to operate, would be much less than the percentage reliability of estimation of current annual production once the control system was operating. The reliability on past production could vary from country to country, and within any country, from plant to plant.

28.   In regard to the accuracy of declarations made about past production of fissile material, the uncertainty would mostly relate to the comprehensiveness, the availability and the variety of past records, and the extent to which the truth of records and accounts could be verified by a technical analysis using the established properties of the nuclear plants in the country concerned. It would be necessary to interrogate staff to explain what the records were, how they had been obtained, any special events which would need to be taken into account and other technical matters of this kind. (It is possible that only sample or master records would have been kept relating to a period several years past. If such were the case, the Control Organisation would be handicapped and some loss of accuracy of control would result.)

29.   A country which intended to make a false declaration about its total past production of plutonium and enriched uranium would,

D.V.–Q

of course, seek to declare production totals which were less than the real ones. The discrepancy between the actual past production of fissile material and the declared total production would not arise from one single item. The discrepancy would be built up from a large number of small items.

30. The amount of plutonium which had been made in any country could, in principle, be determined accurately from the quantities of fission productions still remaining; and the total quantity of U-235 separated could in principle be determined by measuring the depletion of U-235 below the natural content in the stockpile of depleted uranium in the country, allowing for the quantity of U-235 used. Neither method however is fully reliable, since a violator could take steps to falsify the situation.

31. The radioactivity of the fission products at any time, and the proportions of the individual fission species resulting from the operating life of a reactor can be estimated closely if the details of the reactor and the complete operating records are available. Thus, in principle, it would be possible for the Control Organization to measure the total radioactivity of the fission products in any one country, and the proportions of the individual radioactive species, and thus check that the quantities were closely consistent with the declarations made about the operating life of the reactors and the quantity of plutonium made. Small corrections would, of course, be made for the unavoidable small quantities of low level effluent which would have been dispersed by some suitable safe method. However, this type of check is not worth much. A violator would not have any great difficulty in extracting suitable quantities of highly concentrated waste from his highly active storage tanks in such a way that everything that the Control Organization measured would be found to be consistent with the false declarations made.

32. Somewhat similar considerations apply to the depleted uranium waste products of diffusion plants and reactors. The violator could remove some of the depleted uranium waste products of diffusion plants and reactors and hide it in some secret place. He would also have the possibility of removing some of the depleted uranium and then mixing natural uranium with some of the remaining depleted uranium, thus slightly falsifying the stripping ratio used during a certain period of operation of the diffusion plant, or the burn-up in the reactors. The U-235 ratio could be measured but would not be significant.

33. Many of the plants which would be subject to the control system would have been operating for several years and in some cases might have been operated for as long as fifteen years. The method of operation, the over-all efficiency and indeed some of the actual

components might have changed substantially during the period that the plant had been operating. Certain plants might have been used for a period and then shut down.

34. In general, falsification is easier for the early periods of operation of a plant when fissile material accountancy is less precise and the method of operation of the plant is being continually adjusted, than at a period when the plant operation and procedures have been established.

35. The Control Organization in seeking to perform its duties with regard to the total past production of fissile material in each country would work mainly by the following methods. From a technical study of the reactors, the chemical separation plants, the diffusion plants and supporting plants and laboratories and from a study of their records, an estimate would be made of what the total production had been. The Control Organization would prepare its inventory of all the existing fissile material in the country. This inventory would include the material resulting from the breakdown of weapons, all existing stocks of unfabricated fissile material (mostly in metal billet form), plutonium and enriched uranium in any stocks of new fuel elements, in fuel elements in reactors (including zero energy facilities) and in fissile materials in use by experimental establishments. Account would have to be taken of the declarations made about process losses and about the past consumption of enriched fuel in reactors which use such fuel, including both military and civil propulsion reactors. Separate account would have to be taken of fissile materials used in weapon trials or lost or destroyed by any other means. In verifying the declared quantities of fissile material produced as the result of breakdown of weapons, the fissile material would presumably be produced in billet form in order not to make the shapes and weights of weapon components common knowledge.

36. The Control Organization would be faced with a particularly difficult problem in regard to declarations made about the quantities of fissile material used in weapons trials. If the Control Organization brought in nuclear weapons experts and had access to all drawings of nuclear devices tested, all experimental records obtained in nuclear tests, and could inspect weapons establishments and interrogate staff, it might be able to guarantee that the quantities of fissile material declared as used in tests had not been over-declared by more than perhaps 50 per cent. It is unlikely that these possibilities could be realized. On the other hand if the Control Organization were only given a list of the fissile contents of each of the nuclear devices tested, it would have no technical grounds for challenging the statements made. No doubt some countries have reached technical conclusions about the contents of nuclear devices tested by other countries based

on long range records and, in some cases, on radiochemical evidence. However, the accuracy of such interpretations cannot be high. Low yield explosions, which were, or were falsely declared to be, fizzles, might have completely escaped detection. It would therefore be optimistic to expect that the Control Organization would be able to certify the accuracy of the quantity of fissile material used in weapons trials better than within a factor of two or three.

37. The Control Organization would thus prepare a balance sheet giving all the details of past production and showing what had happened to the fissile material.

38. It can be anticipated that the International Agreement which set up the Control Organization would require the Organization to make a statement about the reliability of this balance sheet. Included in this statement would be the accuracy within which the Organization considered that the figures were reliable. From the statement, it would be easy to make a technical deduction about the possible size of clandestine stockpiles of weapons.

39. The Control Organization could not, however, make much progress on forming its conclusions about past production until its staff had been installed and had had time to familiarize themselves with the nuclear plants in each country concerned, a process which might take a year. The verification of past production and the preparation of a reliable balance sheet would be a difficult but important task which would need to be carried out by a team of extremely experienced high grade staff of a calibre higher than that normally necessary for the routine work of the Control. Since the task of verifying past production would only have to be done once, such a specialized team could be attached to the Control Organization in each country for this specific purpose for a period of six months and starting a year after the Control Organization had begun to operate. It would therefore take at least eighteen months from the time when the Control started before the declarations of past production of fissile material could be verified.

40. We have attempted to assess the accuracy within which the figure in the balance sheet could be considered reliable, based on our experience with our nuclear plants in the United Kingdom.

41. Diffusion plants for the separation of U-235 have great flexibility. Sections can be cut out at will for maintenance or other reasons. A plant could be driven over a range of power levels, depending on whether it was desired to get material at the lowest unit cost, or to get more at a higher unit cost. The total output over a given period of several months is not a uniquely defined function of the total power consumption. Percentage variations are possible, depending on how the plant has been operated during this period of several months. The

efficiency of the plant, in terms of power consumption will have improved during the life of the plant as operating experience was gained and modifications introduced.

42. The maximum possible extent of falsification depends considerably on whether the records of the total electricity consumption are reliable or not. If the electricity consumption figures could for some reason be accepted as reliable, then we believe that the total past output of U-235 from the Capenhurst plant could be falsified by more than 5 per cent but less than 10 per cent; but if the electricity consumption could be falsified by 10 per cent, the past output of Capenhurst could be falsified by 15–20 per cent. There would be no technical difficulty in falsifying the electricity consumption to within 10 per cent but there are certain factors in the United Kingdom which may not apply in other countries. Electricity is supplied to Capenhurst on commercial terms by a complete separate organization from the one actually operating Capenhurst. The commercial accounts of this other organization have been audited by independent auditors. The task of falsifying the records of electricity supply would therefore be much greater than if the Capenhurst plant had been driven from a power station under Capenhurst management. There would be many less records, and the records would be in one place, instead of being possibly in three or four places.

43. Thus in the U.K. we would have good hopes that the Control Organization would be able to certify our past production of U-235 to within 5–10 per cent, but we can visualize that if the plants and responsibilities had been organized differently, the certification would not have been better than 15–20 per cent.

44. It would also be possible to make false statements slightly exaggerating the losses of U-235 in processing, and the quantities used in the civil programme, and to exaggerate substantially the quantities of U-235 used in weapon tests. Thus we conclude that in the special circumstances of the U.K., the total quantity of U-235 remaining from past production could certainly be falsified to 10 per cent. With a different organization of the electricity supplies, the falsification might have been estimated at 15–20 per cent.

45. Turning now to the possibilities of falsification of the quantities of plutonium already produced in the United Kingdom, we have to take into account a similar but less stringent constraint that substantial quantities of electricity have been sent from the reactors at Calder and Chapel Cross in the South of Scotland grid. However, considerable quantities of electricity generated from the reactors are used by the reactor and associated plant, and considerable quantities of heat have been dumped from these reactors and from the earlier Windscale reactors. However, there would be considerable scope for

falsifying the records of the total power levels of the reactors, without involving other organizations in the forgeries.

46. Taking account of all the possibilities of falsification, including weapons tests, it is the opinion in the U.K. that the plutonium declared could be 10–15 per cent less than the declared total of that still remaining from past production without detection by the Control Organization.

47. Even on our most optimistic assumption we do not expect the Control Organization would be able to certify that the U.K. did not have the technical possibility of secreting 10–15 per cent of the fissile material produced for inspection by the Control Organization as the result of the breakdown of weapons.

Scale of Effort Required for a False Declaration

48. A country intending to make false declarations about its past production of plutonium and enriched uranium would be compelled to falsify some of its records and documents in order to make everything consistent with the false declarations. The amount of falsification required and the number of people involved would depend considerably on whether the violator was content with a small percentage violation or whether he attempted the maximum violation which he thought would remain undetected by the Control Organization.

49. A violator could probably secrete 3–5 per cent of his total past production without involving more than a relatively small number of people in the technical organizations producing and supporting the production plants. Process losses could be exaggerated, the quantities used in weapons could be exaggerated, small distortions could be made about shut down, power levels and so on. Of course, certain other people would know that some weapons had been secretly hidden.

50. A violator seeking to secrete the maximum possible amount of plutonium and U-235 which we consider could escape detection by the Control Organization would have to undertake a large and complex series of falsifications and would have to involve several hundreds of people in technical organizations. Even though the risk of the violator being caught by technical considerations would be small, the violator must also be prepared to accept the risk that some of the staff involved in the forgeries would reveal their part in the forgeries to the Control Organization.

51. Given the resources that the violator could deploy, the technical job of falsifying records, accounts, minutes of committee meetings, documents and letters would be well within the capability of any of the nuclear powers. The forging of data sheets in the

analytical and technical records sections could present more difficulty. In the U.K., for example, many entries are in the handwriting of individuals, and it would be necessary to make a selection of people in the sections who could be relied on not to disclose that they had made false copies of their own work.

Uncertainty about the Possible Size of a Clandestine Weapons Stockpile

52. It may be assumed that the Control Organization would prepare a balance sheet which accounted for all past production of plutonium and U-235 in every country. An important question would be the size of a possible clandestine stockpile of weapons expressed as a percentage of the declared stockpile. The situation can be illustrated numerically by some simple arithmetic applied to a hypothetical case.

53. Suppose that a hypothetical violating country which had a stockpile of weapons declared that its total past production of plutonium and enriched uranium was 100, in certain units, and suppose that the real quantity in the same units was 115. Apart from the clandestine stockpile of 15 units, there would still be some opportunity of cheating within the total number of units (100) declared. Suppose for example, the country declared that 75 units were in the existing military stockpile and that 5 units had been used in weapons trials and 20 units used for civil purposes, whereas in fact only 3 units had been used in weapons trials and 19 for civil purposes. Then the amount of fissile material produced for inspection to the Control Organization would be 75: and the clandestine stockpile would be 18. In other words, about one-fifth of the total stockpile of nuclear weapons could be secretly hidden and retained.

TECHNICAL STAFFING AND MANAGEMENT OF THE CONTROL ORGANIZATION

General

54. The staffing policy of the Control Organization would be determined largely by:

(a) its international composition, and

(b) the requirements of exercising physical security and technical surveillance over the production, transportation and use of fissile materials;

(c) the requirements of having a central headquarters to co-ordinate results and of having one or more central laboratories.

55. The Control Organization would need the greatest possible degree of independence in recruitment in order to ensure the quality and integrity of its staff. Terms of service would need to be the subject of independent decision by the Control Organization. Most of the staff

would necessarily work in small international communities in countries of which they were not nationals, and much of their work would be routine. However, the conditions of service would be more attractive than those of a nuclear test control organization. There would be scientific work to be done at all times, and the staff would be working in a scientific or technical environment.

Duties of Senior Staff

56. Although a great deal of the work would demand adequate personal qualities rather than high scientific qualifications, there would be a need for men of high personal qualities and considerable general technical ability at the headquarters in each country and at the head of major sectors of the Control Organization's operations. The senior staff of the Control Organization, though small in number, would take the responsibility for its effective technical operation and integrity. They would plan the operation of the Control Organization and its extension to new areas at the appropriate times, and they would take personally the responsibility for enquiries that had to be made outside the Control Organization's standard activities—for example, in industries or establishments not ostensibly concerned with a nuclear programme.

Scientific Staff

57. The senior staff of the Control Organization would require supporting staff as follows:

(a) Scientists, who would direct the control teams or, in the central laboratories, develop new techniques and instruments and run training courses;

(b) Assistants, who would be adequate for most of the scientific work of the control teams.

Other Staff

58. The following types of staff would be needed in addition to the scientific staff:

(a) Technicians, who would be needed to support the scientific staff and their assistants in the ratio of about one technician to two scientists;

(b) Guards, whose duties would cover the several aspects of physical security—storekeeping, exits from and entry to controlled areas, transport of controlled materials;

(c) Administrative Officers, who would be responsible for services to the technical teams;

(d) Auxiliaries, for services such as transport, though some of these might in practice be provided by the host country.

Estimates of Numbers Required in the United Kingdom

59.   We have made estimates of the numbers of staff who would at present be required to man such a Control Organization in the United Kingdom. As the numbers of nuclear power stations in the United Kingdom increase, the numbers of staff required would increase steadily. Over the next ten years, the numbers of scientists and technicians required would increase by about 40 per cent and the number of guards by 100–150 per cent.

60.   Our estimates are based on controlling the Capenhurst diffusion plant, controlling all of the enriched metal processing and fuel fabrication plants, controlling all of the chemical processing facilities for irradiated fuel elements, controlling the research establishments using fissile materials for experimental purposes (including zero energy reactors), and staffing a central laboratory and headquarters in the United Kingdom. We estimate that the numbers required at present would be:

Scientists	....	....	....	160
Technicians	....	....	....	80
Guards	....	....	....	400
Administration		....	....	250
Auxiliary	....	....	....	200
Total		....	....	1,090

61.   We can only make very rough estimates of the total strength of the Control Organization which would be required to control nuclear work in all other countries; but we would expect the number would be approximately ten times the number required in the United Kingdom. On this assumption, a world-wide Control Organization would at the present time require about 1,500 scientists and a total strength of about 10,000.

62.   The Control Organization would also require the assistance of a team of extremely experienced, high grade staff about one year after the control had begun to operate for the purpose of verification of past production of fissile material. This team would be attached to the Control Organization for a period of about six months and its numbers would be quite small.

SUMMARY OF MAIN CONCLUSIONS

63.   The main conclusions emerging from our study, which has been based upon the present U.K. nuclear organization are summarized below.

64.   The accuracy with which the Control Organization would be

able to guarantee the control of current production in each country would not vary from country to country since the same techniques would be used everywhere. It should be possible for the Control Organization in due course to control the current production of plutonium to an accuracy within between 1 and 2 per cent, and of U-235 to within 1 per cent.

65.   The possibility of a violator successfully building and operating large scale clandestine plants is remote; they would be caught by the Control Organization. If, however, the violator were prepared to go to great expense to conceal a small plant, the risk of being caught would be minimized and it might then be possible secretly to produce somewhat more fissile material by this means than by diversion from overt plant.

66.   The percentage accuracy with which the Control Organization could guarantee past production would, however, be very much less than that possible with current production when the Control Organization is operating, and could vary considerably from country to country. Operating and accountancy procedures are likely to have been different in different countries, and until the facts are revealed and compared it is not possible to do more than indicate the order of accuracy which might be achievable by the Control Organization with regard to past production.

67.   In those countries which have never had a nuclear weapons programme, the work of the Control Organization in verifying past production and use against declared stocks would be comparatively simple compared with the work in countries which have had a nuclear weapons programme.

68.   Much of the fissile material so far made in the world has been intended for the manufacture of nuclear weapons; and the total quantity of fissile material made for such purposes is now enormous. The Control Organization would be attempting in several countries to estimate the total past production from a set of plants of various ages, all of which will have been improved substantially by a sequence of small modifications, and some of them (the diffusion plants) having great flexibility which will have been frequently exploited to meet varying needs. It is difficult to anticipate to fine limits what reliability the Control Organization would be able to attach to its estimates of the total production.

69.   Arguing from our experience with our plants in the United Kingdom, we have reached the conclusion that the Control Organization would not be able to guarantee with better than 10–15 per cent accuracy a correct declaration by us about our total past production of plutonium. The maximum degree of falsification of past production of U-235 would be between 5 and 10 per cent if the records of

electricity supplies to the diffusion plant could be proved not to have been falsified, or 15-20 per cent if these could also be falsified.

70. Allowing for falsifications which slightly exaggerated the processing losses and the uses of fissile material by the civil programme and which considerably exaggerated uses in weapons trials, the maximum degree of falsification in the U.K. without the falsification of electricity supplies would enable 10-15 per cent of the weapons stockpile to be retained secretly.

71. Without having the necessary knowledge of the nuclear energy plants and of the detailed organization in other countries, we cannot estimate what conclusion the Control Organization would be able to make about past fissile material production in these other countries. However, we consider that our materials control in the U.K. has been very tight and has been extensively instrumented, recorded and documented. We therefore think it unlikely that the Control Organization would conclude that in other countries the maximum possible violation would permit less than 10 per cent of the weapons stockpile to be hidden, and we would not be surprised if the maximum possible violation in some cases proved to be of the order of 20 per cent.

72. If the accuracy of the statements is accepted, it follows that the Control Organization would not be able to guarantee in those countries which have had nuclear weapons programmes that some 10-20 per cent of the weapons had not been hidden, the percentage figure perhaps varying somewhat from country to country.

73. The falsification of past records in any country would involve the suborning of a considerable number of staff in the violating country and would, as a consequence, put that country at risk of being caught due to the possibility of one or more of the suborned staff revealing to the Control Organization that cheating had occurred. However, the fact that nobody had revealed to the Control Organization that forgery had occurred would not prove that there had been no forgery.

74. The Control Organization could not make much progress on checking past production of fissile material until its staff had been installed and had had time to familiarize themselves with the nuclear plants in the country concerned, a process which would take about a year. Since the checking of past production would be a difficult rask, but one which had to be done only once, we consider that the Control Organization should be assisted in its work of checking past production in each country by the temporary attachment of a team of extremely experienced, high grade staff for a period of about six months. It would therefore be about eighteen months from the date of installation of the control system before declarations on past fissile material production could be certified.

75. We can only make a rough estimate of the total strength which we believe would be required for a world-wide Control Organization based on the number which we consider would be required in the U.K. On this assumption a world-wide Control Organization would, at the present time, require about 1,500 scientists and a total complement of about 10,000.

APPENDIX VII

TREATY BANNING NUCLEAR TESTS IN THE ATMOSPHERE, OUTER SPACE, AND UNDER WATER, 25TH JULY 1963

The Governments of the Union of Soviet Socialist Republics, the United Kingdom of Great Britain and Northern Ireland, and the United States of America, hereinafter referred to as the 'original parties'.

Proclaiming as their principle the speediest possible achievement of an agreement of general and complete disarmament under strict international control in accordance with the objectives of the United Nations which would put an end to the armaments race and eliminate the incentive to the production and testing of all kinds of weapons, including nuclear weapons.

Seeking to achieve the discontinuance of all test explosions of nuclear weapons for all time, determined to continue negotiations to this end, and desiring to put an end to the contamination of man's environment by radioactive substances, have agreed as follows:

ARTICLE 1

1. Each of the parties to this treaty undertakes to prohibit, to prevent, and not to carry out any nuclear weapon test, explosion, or any other nuclear explosion, at any place, under its jurisdiction or control:

(a) In the atmosphere: beyond its limits, including outer space; or under water, including territorial water or high seas; or

(b) In any other environment, if such explosion causes radio-active debris to be present outside the territorial limits of the state under whose jurisdiction or control such explosion is conducted. It is understood in this connection that the provisions of this sub-paragraph are without prejudice to the conclusion of a treaty resulting in the permanent banning of all nuclear test explosions, including all such explosions underground, the conclusion of which, as the parties have stated in the preamble to this treaty, they seek to achieve.

2. Each of the parties to this treaty undertakes furthermore to refrain from causing, encouraging, or in any way participating in, the carrying out of any nuclear weapon test explosion, or any other nuclear explosion anywhere, which would take place in any of the environments described, or have the effect referred to in paragraph 1 of this article.

ARTICLE 2

1. Any party may propose amendments to this treaty. The text of any proposed amendment shall be submitted to the depository Governments which shall circulate it to all parties to this treaty. Thereafter, if requested to do so by one third or more of the parties, the depository Governments shall convene a conference, to which they shall invite all the parties, to consider such amendment.

2. Any amendment to this treaty must be approved by a majority of the votes of all the parties to this treaty, including all of the original parties. The amendments shall enter into force for all parties upon the deposit of instruments of ratification by a majority of all the parties, including the instruments of ratification of all the original parties.

ARTICLE 3

1. This treaty shall be open to all states for signature. Any state which does not sign this treaty before its entry into force in accordance with paragraph 3 of this article may accede to it at any time.

2. This treaty shall be subject to ratification by signatory states. Instruments of ratification and instruments of accession shall be deposited with the Governments of the original parties—the Union of Soviet Socialist Republics, the United Kingdom of Great Britain and Northern Ireland, and the United States of America—which are hereby designated the depository Governments.

3. This treaty shall enter into force after its ratification by all the original parties and the deposit of their instruments of ratification.

4. For states whose instruments of ratification or accession are deposited subsequent to the entry into force of this treaty, it shall enter into force on the date of the deposit of their instruments of ratification or accession.

5. The depository Governments shall promptly inform all signatory and acceding states of the date of each signature, the date of deposit of each instrument of ratification of an accession to this treaty, the date of its entry into force, and the date of receipt of any requests for conferences or other notices.

6. This treaty shall be registered by the depository Governments pursuant to Article 102 of the Charter of the United Nations.

ARTICLE 4

This treaty shall be of unlimited duration. Each party shall, in exercising its national sovereignty, have the right to withdraw from the treaty if it decides that extraordinary events, related to the subject matter of this treaty, have jeopardized the supreme interests of its country.

It shall give notice of such withdrawal to all other parties to the treaty three months in advance.

ARTICLE 5

This treaty, of which the English and Russian texts are equally authentic, shall be deposited in the archives of the depository Governments. Duly certified copies of the treaty shall be transmitted by the depository Governments to the Governments of the signatory and acceding states.